## DATE DUE

| | | |
|---|---|---|
| MY 28 98 | | |
| NO2 00 | | |
| JE 02 | | |
| MY 1 3 '09 | | |
| | | |
| | | |
| | | |
| | | |
| | | |
| | | |
| | | |
| | | |
| | | |
| | | |
| | | |
| | | |

DEMCO 38-296

# INVESTIGATING COMPUTER CRIME

# CRC SERIES IN
# PRACTICAL ASPECTS OF CRIMINAL
# AND FORENSIC INVESTIGATIONS

VERNON J. GEBERTH, M.S., M.P.S., B.B.A., FBINA *Series Editor*

**Practical Homicide Investigation: Tactics, Procedures, and Forensic
  Techniques, Second Edition**
Vernon J. Geberth

**The Counter-Terrorism Handbook: Tactics, Procedures, and Techniques**
Frank Bolz, Jr., Kenneth J. Dudonis, and David P. Schulz

**Forensic Pathology**
Dominick J. Di Maio and Vincent J. M. Di Maio

**Interpretation of Bloodstain Evidence at Crime Scenes**
William G. Eckert and Stuart H. James

**Tire Imprint Evidence**
Peter McDonald

**Practical Drug Enforcement: Procedures and Administration**
Michael D. Lyman

**Practical Aspects of Rape Investigation: A Multidisciplinary Approach,
  Second Edition**
Robert R. Hazelwood and Ann Wolbert Burgess

**The Sexual Exploitation of Children: A Practical Guide to Assessment,
  Investigation, and Intervention**
Seth L. Goldstein

**Gunshot Wounds: Practical Aspects of Firearms, Ballistics, and
  Forensic Techniques**
Vincent J. M. Di Maio

**Friction Ridge Skin: Comparison and Identification of Fingerprints**
James F. Cowger

**Footwear Impression Evidence**
William J. Bodziak

**Practical Aspects of Kinesic Interview and Interrogation Techniques**
Stan Walters

**Practical Fire and Arson Investigation, Second Edition**
David R. Redsicker and John J. O'Connor

**The Practical Methodology of Forensic Photography**
David R. Redsicker

**Practical Gambling Investigation Techniques**
Kevin B. Kinnee

**Practical Aspects of Interview and Interrogation**
David E. Zulawski and Douglas E. Wicklander

**Practical Investigation Techniques**
Kevin B. Kinnee

**Investigating Computer Crime**
Franklin Clark and Ken Diliberto

# INVESTIGATING COMPUTER CRIME

**Franklin Clark**
**Ken Diliberto**

**CRC Press**
**Boca Raton   New York   London   Tokyo**

...d in this book are trademarks, registered trademarks,

**Library of Congress Cataloging-in-Publication Data**

Clark, Franklin.
    Investigating computer crime/Franklin Clark and Ken Diliberto.
      p.  cm. — (Practical aspects of criminal and forensic
investigation)
    Includes index.
    ISBN 0-8493-8158-4
    1. Computer crimes — Investigation.  I. Diliberto, Ken.
II. Title.  III. Series: CRC series in practical aspects of criminal
and forensic investigation.
HV8079.C65C58  1996
363.2′5;968 — dc20

                  95-52636
                  CIP

# Contents

Preface                                                        ix
The Authors                                                   xiii
Acknowledgments                                                xv
Resources for Law Enforcement                                 xvii
Introduction                                                    1

**1  Computer Search Warrant Team**                             9

Case Supervisor                                                 9
Interview Team                                                 10
Sketch and Photo Team                                         10
Physical Search Team                                          10
Security and Arrest Team                                      10
Technical Evidence Seizure and Logging Team                  10

**2  Computer-Related Evidence**                               13

Types of Computer-Related Evidence                            13
Where Computer-Related Evidence May Be Found                  19
Finding Computer Evidence                                     24
Examining the Evidence for Criminal Content                   26
Cautions and Considerations                                   30
Legal Requirements                                            33
Storage of Seized Evidence                                    37

**3  Investigative Tool Box**                                  43

Software                                                      43
Hardware                                                      46
Other Useful Stuff                                            48

**4    Crime Scene Investigation**                                      **51**

Evaluate the Scene in Advance                                            51
Set Up Search Teams                                                      52
Establish a Plan of Attack                                               52
Prepare the Search Warrant                                              53
Execute the Warrant                                                      54
Secure the Scene                                                         54
Teams Perform Their Functions                                          56
Completing the Search                                                   57

**5    Making a Boot Disk**                                             **59**

What is a Boot Disk?                                                    59
The POST Test                                                           59
The Boot Process                                                        60
What if There Is a CMOS Boot Password?                                61
So, How Do I Make One?                                                  61
What Problems Might I Encounter?                                        63

**6    Simple Overview of Seizing a Computer**                         **65**

**7    Evidence Evaluation and Analysis**                              **69**

Forms of Evidence                                                       69
Analysis Tools                                                          70
Analysis Procedures Using PROFILE.BAT                                  73
Other Analysis Procedures                                              77
Chronological Search Form                                               78

**8    Investigating Floppies**                                        **79**

**9    Common File Extensions**                                        **83**

**10   Passwords and Encryption**                                      **87**

What Is a Password?                                                      87
What Is Encryption?                                                      87
What Is the Difference Between Passwords and Encryption?               88
What Are Common Uses of Passwords?                                      88
Where Do You Get a Password?                                            89
How Do You Break or Bypass a Password or Encryption?                  90

How Do You Break or Bypass Encryption?                                   92
PGP                                                                                                 93
What Is a Common Use of Encryption?                                        96
Sources of Programs and Information                                          96

**11    Investigating Bulletin Boards                                              99**

Where Do I Start?                                                                       100
Initiating the Investigation                                                           105
Tips to Avoid Traps, Snares and Pitfalls                                          105

**12    "Elite" Acronyms                                                               115**

**13    Networks                                                                          119**

Network Ups and Downs                                                             120
Network Parts and Pieces                                                            121
Types of Networks                                                                     123
Physical Connections                                                                  124
Operating Systems                                                                     128
So What Does This All Mean?                                                        132
The Bottom Line                                                                       132

**14    Ideal Investigative Computer Systems                              133**

Desktop                                                                                   133
Portable                                                                                   136
Tools                                                                                        139
Computer Cart                                                                          141
Media                                                                                      141
Cables                                                                                     142
Bags                                                                                        142
Software                                                                                   143

**15    Court Procedures                                                             147**

Expert Witnesses                                                                      147
Pretrial Preparation                                                                   147
Speaking to the Judge and Jury                                                    148
Terminology to Use in Court                                                        148
Resumes                                                                                  149
Equipment                                                                               149

**16    Search Warrants                                    151**

   Case Law                                                151
   Writing a Warrant                                       152
   Hacker Case                                             153
   Search Warrant Samples                                  154
   Prodigy Services Warrant                                183
   Credit Card Warrant                                     188

**Conclusion                                            213**

**Glossary                                              215**

**Index                                                 221**

# Preface

Why do we need this book? There are tons of books on criminal investigation on the market, but the same is not true regarding the investigation of computer-related crimes. When we wrote this book, the latest one covering computer crime was 7 to 10 years old. Technology changes very fast. The software and hardware used by investigators may work one day and may not work the next, as the next generation of software and hardware comes into use. What is important are the *principles* of investigating computers and other electronic evidence.

Computer-related crime is defined as "any criminal activity that involves use of computer technology, directly or indirectly, as the instrumentality or object of the commission of a criminal act." Most of us think of "hacking" when we think of a computer crime, where some genius child plays war games with the Pentagon's computer system. The truth is that computers are used by ordinary people of average intelligence to commit virtually every traditional crime in the penal code.

Computers are rapidly becoming a part of everyday life, not just in business and education but for personal use. During the last few years they have become very affordable and attractive to individual users. Looking at television commercials is a good indication — companies such as IBM, Microsoft, Compaq, and Apple are buying prime-time commercial spots to show their latest technology in hardware and software.

Currently there is a low reporting rate for computer-related crimes. That is changing, as law enforcement becomes more computer literate, business becomes more comfortable with the ability of law enforcement to respond to the crime, and the media give more attention to high-tech crimes. The average reported computer crime by 1993 resulted in a loss of in excess of $475,000. Computer crimes account for an estimated loss to the U.S. economy of $5 to 10 billion each year.

The criminal justice system mirrors the society it serves, so it should come as no surprise that the proliferation of computers in our daily lives has resulted in a proliferation of computer-related criminal activities, a good example of which is the use of credit cards. Credit card fraud has increased steadily since the inception of the credit card to billions of dollars per year in losses to banks and consumers.

The variety of computer-related crimes that law enforcement is called upon to investigate is much broader than just the hacker problem; in fact, the variety is almost infinite. Some examples of previous cases include:

- Pedophiles who maintain bulletin board systems (BBS) or pose online as children on other BBS and online services to lure children for sexual acts.
- Skin heads and devil worshipers who manage a murder-for-hire bulletin board.
- Extremist and terrorist groups that use bulletin boards to spread their messages of hate and terrorist techniques, including instructions for building explosive devices.
- Extortionists who demand ransom in return for not destroying computer systems and data.
- The illicit trade in stolen telephone access numbers that results in tens of thousands of dollars in fraudulent long-distance charges each month.
- A 14-year-old boy who accessed the computers at TRW, downloaded hundreds of inactive credit files, and placed those credit card numbers on numerous pirate bulletin boards. Criminals in another state worked with the boy, picked up the numbers and manufactured an untold number of fraudulent MasterCard™ and VISA® cards. They gave two gold cards with fraudulent names to the boy for his efforts. The result of such schemes is a loss in the millions of dollars.
- A disgruntled employee who erased the company computers' hard disks, resulting in the loss of $250,000 per month in revenue.
- The programmers who create and introduce a computer "virus" into a computer as an act of vengeance or vandalism, causing large losses of data, programs, time, and money.
- A doctor who altered treatment billing records to bill at the next higher insurance billing rate, totaling over $1,000,000.
- The insurance company data processing manager who altered client records from a computer in California to a computer in Florida to send himself claim checks.
- Burglars who set up stolen property computer bulletin boards and burglarize business offices to fill the orders for computers, software, and hardware placed by customers.
- The boiler-room operations that use computer equipment to call up thousands of customers to make bogus sales pitches for goods that will never be delivered or to fraudulently obtain credit card numbers with which to make purchases.
- A 15-year-old boy who hacked long-distance calling card numbers and made hundreds of long-distance calls playing Dungeons and Dragons, running up thousands of dollars in long-distance bills for the customers' phone card numbers he had hacked.

- A 19-year-old blind man who obtained stolen long-distance calling card numbers and called a 976 phone sex number 976 times in one month.
- A gang that used a computer to obtain and store information about credit card numbers they acquired, then, using a computer and fax, set up fraudulent business credit for co-conspirators with numerous businesses, resulting in losses of tens of thousands of dollars.
- A man who scanned business, cashier's, and traveler's checks into a computer, altered them with different names and amounts, then created fraudulent identification for co-conspirators to pass the counterfeit checks.
- Suspect who scanned currency into a computer and printed money on a color printer, thus counterfeiting large amounts of U.S. currency.
- The computer hard disk that contained 12-step motive evidence in a homicide case.

If we, as investigators, are not to become dinosaurs in this age of technology, we must educate ourselves and develop the procedures and standards to assure that we have the means to investigate and prosecute violations when they occur. To keep up, investigators must learn the fundamentals of computer operations and procedures. That is not to say that we all must become "techies"; far from it. Just as we do not have to become MD's to investigate a homicide, we do not have to become computer specialists to investigate computer-related crime, but we had better know a little bit about the subject at hand (HEX does not refer to a magic spell). With a good foundation of computer basics, an investigator can at least manage the available experts who have the skills to process a crime scene computer. For all types of computer-related cases, investigators and support staff must be trained in the special precautions necessary for handling and storing magnetic media and other computer-related evidence.

# The Authors

**Detective Frank Clark** retired from the Fresno Police Department in January of 1996 after serving for more than 27 years. He was assigned to the Economic/Computer Crimes Unit for over 10 years. He has an extensive background in "white collar" fraud (including checks, real estate, and insurance), arson, narcotics, surveillance, and computer hardware and software. Currently his responsibilities include computer-related crimes, credit fraud, real estate fraud, insurance fraud, technical support, seizure, and forensic evaluation of computer-related evidence for all units in the police department and other local, state, and federal agencies involving computers and computerized research. Frank has taught classes for local, state, and federal agencies in various areas of computer crime investigation, including the Federal Bureau of Investigation, Secret Service, Internal Revenue Service, Bureau of Alcohol, Tobacco and Firearms, and the Royal Canadian Mounted Police. He has taught at the Federal Law Enforcement Training Center in Glynco, GA and the Canadian Police College in Ottawa, Canada. He is currently working as a criminal investigator for the Pierce County Prosecutor's Office in Tacoma, Washington.

**Ken Diliberto** is employed as a Network Systems Specialist for the City of Fresno Information Systems Division. His responsibilities include the installation, maintenance, and operation of local and wide area networks within the city of Fresno that involve several hundred users. He also is responsible for communications between local area networks and the minicomputers and mainframes of the city. He provides support to users for application programs on each network. He designed and implemented a county-wide MUG photo system and the Fresno Police Department Information Network, which allows personal computers on the network to access MUG photos, the RMS system, criminal history, and online police reports. Ken has more than 15 years experience in the installation and use of computers, computer networks, and data telecommunications, including minicomputers, mainframe, and micro-computers. Ken is also a licensed HAM radio operator.

Together, the authors comprised the high-tech crime investigation unit for the Fresno Police Department and have been involved in the seizure and examination of computers and evidence in many types of criminal cases, including pornography-oriented BBS, hacking; phreaking; anarchy; virus; credit fraud and terrorism boards; pedophile BBS; homicides and general computer crime; grand theft; child molestations; credit fraud; counterfeiting and forgery of checks, negotiables, and currency; burglary; corporate computer system intrusion; auto theft/chop shops; cellular communications fraud; and organized crime.

The authors have written dozens of search warrants for computers involved in criminal cases in the Fresno area and have assisted federal, state, and local agencies with cases involving computers in their jurisdictions. The authors developed this book out of a 1-week computer search training class they designed around real criminal investigations. The purpose of the classes and this book are the same: to prepare the investigator to deal with the investigation, seizure, and analysis of computer-related equipment in a manner consistent with rules of law. The class and this book are designed to assist the investigator in working step by step through an investigation, including the seizure of computer-related evidence and evaluation of that evidence. The authors have made lots of mistakes and have learned a great deal from each and every little transgression and are still learning. The authors tell folks that after years of doing this type of work they now realisze how little they really know. Computer-related investigations require constant study and upgrades of equipment, software, and investigative skills.

The authors can be reached at the following addresses:

**Frank Clark**
    Criminal Investigator
    Pierce County Prosecutor's Office
    930 Tacoma Avenue South, Room 946
    Tacoma, WA 98402-2171
    (206) 596-6753 (voice)
    (206) 596-6636 (FAX)
    fclark1@co.pierce.wa.us

**Ken Diliberto**
    City of Fresno Information Systems
    2600 Fresno Street.
    Fresno, CA 93721
    (209) 498-4230 (voice)
    (209) 488-1021 (FAX)
    kend@CSUfresno.edu

# Acknowledgments

It is appropriate in this section of the book to identify and thank those who were instrumental in the development and production of this work. The material presented here did not self generate in a vacuum. Without the open sharing of information and techniques and the selfless attitudes of the following people, this book would not have been possible. They are in fact our mentors and our friends.

We owe a great debt of gratitude to some very special people who are pioneers in the field of investigation and forensic evaluation of computer-related evidence. Some of these people have been involved with investigations and computers since "batch file" really meant a batch of computer punch cards.

We owe much to the members of the Federal Computer Investigations Committee (FCIC). This organization is made up of some of the finest minds and greatest investigators from local, state, and federal law enforcement agencies all over the U.S. It has ever been my pleasure to meet and work with these people. Foremost among them is Jerry Carlson, an inspector with IRS. Internal Security at the IRS. service center in Fresno, CA, who was and continues to be my mentor and strongest supporter since day one. Jerry introduced me to FCIC members Joe Connolly and Carlton Fitzpatrick at the Federal Law Enforcement Training Center, Financial Fraud Institute, in Glynco, GA. These men put together and administer the finest computer crime investigations classes in this country; they have contributed greatly to the high level of professionalism in this field. Dozens of members of the FCIC from many federal, state, and local agencies also have contributed greatly to their field of endeavor and to our own successes. I hesitate to list them for fear of missing some; they know who they are and that they have our appreciation and respect.

Through the FCIC, we met Andrew Fried and Danny Mares of IRS Internal Security. Both of these brilliant men write low-level utility programs for investigators. They have taught and given unselfishly of their time to us and hundreds of other investigators across this country and abroad. We owe them a great deal. The utilities they write are indispensable to investigators and have solved many of my problems even before I knew enough to ask questions. Their programs are available to law enforcement only (see below for addresses).

Jerry also introduced me to Gail Thackery and James Graham, prosecuting attorneys for Maricopa County, AZ, and the state attorney's office in Florida, respectively. Both of them have given thousands of hours for many years in the pursuit of excellence in the investigation and prosecution of high tech crimes and training of law enforcement. Jim Graham spent many hours of his own time assisting the authors in developing plans for the investigation of online predators years before online crimes became a major focus of the media. FCIC members Chief Alfred Olsen in Warwick Township, PA, and John Lucich, investigator with the New Jersey state attorney general's office, Bureau of Organized Crime, are both pioneers in covert online investigations. Al Olsen is a sex crimes expert who investigates pedophiles who prey on kids in cyberspace, and John Lucich is an incredible hacker/phreaker investigator. Both of these men have been and continue to be rich sources of information and expertise. They are always available to help in their areas of expertise. John runs a law enforcement bulletin board that every computer crime investigator should be aware of; the number is listed below.

I would be remiss if I did not mention Staff Sgt. Terry Hampel of the Royal Canadian Mounted Police, Computer Investigative Support Unit, in Ottawa. Terry spent hours patiently showing us the methods of analysis and types of investigative software and hardware used by their agency. He and the staff at the Computer Investigative Support Unit do an incredible job of forensic analysis.

Many other folks, from instructors at the FBI Academy in Quantico, VA, the High Tech Crime Investigators Association, to the Canadian Police College in Ottawa have given encouragement, training, and assistance over the years.

These people, though few in number and largely unappreciated by those who do not know their abilities, are pioneers in high-tech law. They have laid the foundation and brought the seizure and examination of computer evidence from a hodge-podge art to the point of being an actual forensic science. Their work in a field with very little or no case law has resulted in many arrests and convictions and saved many people and businesses from being the victims of high tech crimes.

The people and organizations listed below are some of the best contacts high-tech investigators can have. These folks write investigative-specific software or otherwise provide training and resources needed by every high-tech investigator. They also provide some of the finest instruction available in the areas of investigations in an automated environment, investigative utilities, forensic evaluation of evidence, legal aspects of high-tech crime, hacking/phreaking, and much more.

We would be in big trouble if we forgot to thank the two most important people involved in writing this book: our wives Corinne and Margaret. Without their support, this book would have never found its way into print.

# Resources for Law Enforcement

Note: Law enforcement investigative utilities are available to students at the Federal Law Enforcement Training Center and Canadian Police College Computer Crimes training classes.

**Maresware Investigative Software (pronounced Maresware)**
Contact: Danny Mares
Internal Revenue Service Internal Security
P.O. Box 450168
Atlanta, Ga. 30345
dmares@nocs.insp.irs.gov

**Andy Fried (pronounced "freed") Investigative Software**
Contact: Andy Fried
Internal Revenue Service
1111 Constitution Ave, NW
Mail Code I:ISI, Room 6017
Washington, D.C. 20224
afried@nocs.insp.irs.gov

**Sydex Software** (disk analysis and backup tools)
Shareware and law enforcement versions of Viewdisk and AnaDisk available.
P.O. Box 5700
Eugene, OR 97405
(503) 683-6033
BBS 503.683.1385

**High Tech Crime Network BBS** (This BBS is the finest online resource available for high tech investigators. It is closely monitored by John Lucich, and every user will be a verified member of law enforcement.)
BBS 201.729.8276
Contact: Investigator John Lucich, New Jersey State Attorney General's Office
Organized Crime Bureau Office: 609.984.6500
john@htcn.org

**Federal Law Enforcement Training Center** (Write for current curriculum)
Financial Fraud Institute
Building 210
Glynco, GA 31524

**HTCIA National Headquarters**
P.O. Box 90597
San Jose, CA 95109
http://www.sna.com/htcia/index.html.

**Canadian Police College**
Computer Training Unit
Box 8900
Ottawa, Ont. Canada K1G3J12

**RCMP Investigative Utilities**
Gord Hamma, P. Eng.
Information Technology Security Branch
Technical Security Services
2121 Thurston Drive
Ottawa, Ont. Canada K1A-OR2

# Introduction

Computers are not new. Crime is not new. Computers involved in crime are not new. Investigating computers involved in crime *is* new. The proliferation of computers in homes and businesses, combined with high-speed data communications, has caused a virtual explosion of criminal activity involving computers. Although computer crime has been going on for many years, most law enforcement management either does not realize or refuses to accept that computers are becoming one of the criminal's preferred tools. Most law enforcement agencies lack experienced investigators with technical computer experience. Many investigators are considered to be experts by their departments because they can use a word processor and get around in Windows™. This type of experience (expertise) is of more help to the criminal than to the public and gives the criminal a tremendous advantage over law enforcement.

Computers represent technology that, for the most part, came into the criminal justice system from the bottom up. Younger officers learn to use computers in school, while most older officers suffer from "cyberphobia" which, although frightening, is not fatal and can be treated by training and hands-on experience. Law enforcement resources are stretched to the limit almost everywhere, and management does not want to deal with any crime that requires still more resources. One problem we have in selling the need for training and equipment is that most of these crimes go unreported. Studies show that about a quarter of all businesses that use computers have a significant loss due to computer crime. Most are not reported because of the lack of confidence in the ability of law enforcement to investigate and reluctance by the company to admit the loss and take the heat from its shareholders. We have found that publicity about successful investigations resulting in arrests prompts calls from businesses that have been victimized by computer theft, damage, or fraud. The word soon gets out in the community, and calls for help from the business community and the public in general start coming in quickly.

Due primarily to media coverage and the growing population of computers in business and the home, the world is becoming aware of computers as a tool for progress and crime. The time is past when the criminal justice system could afford to ignore the problem. Training for law enforcement and prosecutors, from basic DOS to programming, is available at local training facilities, colleges, and adult schools. Specific investigative training is available through SEARCH, the Federal Law Enforcement Training Center, and the FBI. The Canadian Police College offers excellent courses in computer crime investigation at its facility in Ottawa. We highly recommend that law enforcement and/or prosecutors interested in high-tech crimes attend such classes. The police officer who is not computer literate is already falling behind in their field. It is our hope that this book will help to prepare investigators to enter the 21st century with the tools necessary to be effective. We wrote this book to provide investigators, attorneys, and criminology students who have some computer experience with a basic idea of how to investigate computers to obtain evidence from them. This book will also give computer professionals who may work with investigators an idea of how an investigator needs to get information from a computer to be used for evidence.

There is a need in computer-related investigations for both technical and investigative skills. No one knows all there is to know about computer hardware, software, criminal investigations, and the law. In these investigations, even when seizing and evaluating a single computer, the job is much faster and effectively completed when two or more trained persons are involved. We have found that good working teams of experienced, computer-literate investigators working with computer professionals who understand the techniques and purposes of preservation of evidence and are qualified in the forensic evaluation of the evidence make the most successful seizure and forensic examination teams.

No matter how great your experience and expertise, you will run into computer hardware and software that you are not comfortable in evaluating. When — not if — this happens, you will need to find computer professionals familiar with the programming language, hardware, and software you are dealing with. You will find many "computer professionals" who are more than willing to help you in your investigations. You must carefully evaluate each expert before allowing them near a crime scene or evidence. They should work under the direction of trained investigators. Remember, computer experts can be computer salesmen, programmers, or information systems people and they are computer oriented, not evidence oriented.

Computer professionals may have excellent technical training and backgrounds. Their weakness is in understanding the procedures and reasons for the preservation of evidence. Investigators may have vast investigative experience but lack the technical training needed for these types of investigations, and at times they have turned the responsibility for seizure of the computers over to computer professionals who were not prepared to seize and evaluate the evidence for court. The blending of the technical and investigative experiences and training is necessary to properly investigate, seize, and preserve evidence and to conduct forensic evaluation of computer cases.

We have seen hacking cases developed by investigators with little computer experience who have turned the seizure and evaluation of the computer over to computer experts from their computer services division. The experts invited the suspects to sit down at the computer to show them where the incriminating files were to be found. It should come as no surprise that the suspect did not find incriminating files. Rule number one in these investigations is *do not alter original evidence*. Rule number two is *do not allow the suspect to sit and work at his own computer*. In one incident, the suspect was running a bulletin board and was suspected of selling child pornography. Computer professionals were called by the district attorney's investigators to seize and evaluate the computer evidence. They did not have specific training in the seizure and analysis of computer evidence, nor did they have the proper equipment to make system backups. They searched the original disk and then restored the backup tapes to the suspect computer. They completely skipped checking for hidden or erased files and directories erased on the original hard disk on the suspect's computer. The result was altered and destroyed original evidence. There was one ray of sunshine in this case. We were called a few weeks later to see if there was any usable evidence which had not been found. We were given a blank tape to back up the suspect computer. This tape was assumed to be blank because it had no label on it. We found that this tape was in fact a PCTOOLS® backup tape containing incremental backups of the suspect's system. This tape was the only piece of original evidence which was not altered or destroyed. We "social engineered" (see the section on Passwords) a bypass for the passwords, protecting each of the incremental segments of tape, and restored them to the disk. These restored files contained the child pornography the investigators were seeking.

In another problematic case, Department of Justice medical fraud investigators served 14 search warrants on medical services offices and seized a mainframe, a mini-, a portable, and several personal computers. The investigation centered on medical fraud whereby the computer was using a translation program to inflate the billing for medical procedures. The investigators used the services of computer professionals from the Department of Justice laboratory to actually shut down the network and seize the computers. Several of the investigators were computer literate, but neither they or the computer professionals had received training in the investigation of computers.

Whether the computers should have been seized in the first place was not the only problem in this case. The network cables on the DEC mainframe, mini, and all the PCs were simply pulled loose and dropped into a hole in the floor of the buildings involved. None were marked for identification. Can you imagine dozens of cables all looking the same lying in a hole under the floor, then trying to locate every computer and printer in the system in order to get the system up and running again? (See Figure 1.)

**Figure 1**
Most types of network cable are a different color: silver, orange, gray, or black. The authors have actually had a case where the initial investigators disconnected dozens of serial cables from the back of the computer and dropped them to the floor without tagging or marking them in any way.

We became involved in the case the next day when we were asked by the attorney general's office to testify as to why they should keep this system and to do their analysis on it in the state office. The mainframe needed clean power and an air-conditioned room to function, and there were many other problems, not the least of which was that the computers contained the medical records for all the clinic's patients which, of course, were now unavailable to the patients or the treating physicians. Instead of testifying regarding their keeping the computers, we were able to make arrangements to move the computers back to their original environment, back up the entire system, and reconnect the cables. It took several days to do this and involved getting a computer moving company to return the computers; hiring a mainframe expert, a Mumps programmer, and some systems people; and then tracing the network cables with a "fox and hound" (cable locator). We backed up the system and gave the physicians copies of the records and kept one for evidence. We then ran an analysis at night when the clinics were closed. We were lucky none of the patients suffered for the lack of records being available.

All of the above problems could have been avoided if the investigators and others involved had been properly trained and had the equipment and resources available to complete their tasks. This book, then, is our effort to help others avoid mistakes already made by ourselves and others as we forge our way in this comparatively new field of investigation. It is clear even from the previous examples that computer crime investigations can be costly and time consuming and require the use of a lot of tools and techniques. It can be an overwhelming task. The answer to how to complete the task is a relatively simple one. Just like you eat an elephant — *one bite at a time!* What we mean is this: this book is broken up into small sections, each dealing with a skill or function that, when combined with the other parts, makes a complete documented investigation, seizure, and analysis of a computer. It is our goal that you take from this book a basic understanding of the principles of computer-related investigations. Those persons who will get the most out of this book are investigators and computer professionals working directly with law enforcement.

We have come a long way in computer technology in a very few years. The first PCs had small hard disks, perhaps 10 Mb, and floppy disks. Backing them up consisted of a DOS backup and a few floppy disks. Since there were very few programs (and most of them ran on floppy disks) and no viruses, evaluation of computer evidence was relatively simple. Now we have networks, off-site storage, and connections via modem or LAN or WAN, gigabyte disks, disk arrays, optical disks, CD-ROMs… well, you get the idea. Things have grown more complex, and an organized system is needed to allow for preservation and evaluation of all this information. (See Figures 2 and 3.)

The basic principles of seizure and evaluation of computer-related evidence as outlined in this book are standard principles in general use by computer crime investigators around the world. They are set down here in an organized manner to give the new investigator a standard approach to the investigation. The software, operating systems, and hardware will change continuously, but the principles of seizure, preservation, and evaluation of evidence will remain constant.

**Figure 2**
One communications server (right) and two file servers (center and left) and a keyboard/monitor switch box. The file server on the left has (four) 4 mm internal tape backup drives that can store four to eight gigabytes each. The file server on the left also has a Micropolis 15 gigabyte hard disk array.

This book grew out of a series of week-long training seminars given by the authors to state, local, and federal computer crime investigators during the last four years. The seminars were developed with the idea of a "hands-on" approach. We would present practical problems, software, and solutions one at a time in an organized approach to a real-life crime scenario. Then, when all the pieces of the seizure and evaluation of the evidence had been covered, we had the class put the pieces all together and conduct an actual investigation from search warrant service to presentation in court.

Many computer-related cases and civil suits are being lost due to poor investigative techniques. These are due primarily to the lack of training and experience of the investigators involved. It is our sincere hope that, after reading this book, investigators will be encouraged to approach computer crime investigations in an organized manner and to carefully document the process, thus preserving the evidence for court.

First we will build a basic understanding of the types of computer evidence, the investigative tools needed to conduct an investigation, and the concept of a team approach. Then we will cover search warrants, the crime scene investigation, seizure and backing up the computer and/or computer

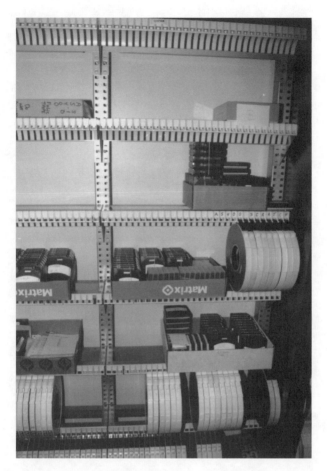

**Figure 3**
On-site storage vault containing reel-to-reel and tape cartridges.

system, and we will then work our way through actual forensic evaluation of the evidence contained in the computer and its related media. We have dedicated a chapter to the means and techniques of conducting covert BBS investigations. This is an art in itself, requiring time and preparation to successfully infiltrate illegal online operations. Each chapter title is self explanatory, and for a basic overall understanding, the book should be read from front to back. It will also serve as a reference if you consult specific chapters as you encounter related events during an investigation.

# Computer Search Warrant Team

Even when just one stand-alone computer is seized, there is too much for just one person to handle. All the work can be accomplished by two people when necessary, but time on the scene is reduced with an increased number of additional trained personnel available. The search warrant team is a best-case scenario. In the real world, you may not have the necessary number of people available to form a complete team, and one person may have to perform several functions to compensate. Know the skills and abilities of your team and use each member for the function they are best qualified to perform. Do not be afraid to call for outside expert assistance. Generally speaking, the time required is directly related to the number of people on hand to take care of the crime scene and the quality of the equipment used to back up the systems. We strongly recommend that computer crime investigators have a powerful portable or laptop computer with networking cards installed so they can back up the crime scene computers via LapLink® or peer-to-peer network software via the parallel, serial, or network ports.

## Case Supervisor

The case supervisor should have extensive investigative experience in complex cases. The case supervisor handles all media relations, manages and schedules manpower and equipment needs, and oversees the case. He may not have to stay at the scene beyond the initial entry and securing of the scene.

## Interview Team

This team consists of one or more people, depending on the number of persons to be interviewed. Their responsibility is to interview each witness and suspect. These team members should have excellent interrogation skills.

## Sketch and Photo Team

This team is comprised of one or more persons who immediately sketch the search scene and assign room letters. They photograph the entire scene inside and out and all evidence. Any, or a combination of, Polaroid, 35-mm, and/or video cameras can be used. We strongly suggest the use of video cameras. We have had a case actually hinge on a picture of a door lock we were not even concerned about when serving the warrant, but the issue of whether or not a lock was on the door became critical during the trial.

> *Note:* When using a video camera, the entire team should be very aware of what they are saying as it will be recorded for posterity and words lightly spoken could prove to be embarrassing when replayed in court.

## Physical Search Team

This team is comprised of one or more persons assigned to search each room. They locate and mark evidence with colored stick-on dots for easy location by the Seizure Team. They do not need to be computer experts but should be thoroughly briefed on the items to search for, and they should be thorough.

## Security and Arrest Team

This team provides physical security of building entrances, persons, and evidence, as needed. They also handle arrests and transportation of suspects. The size of this team can almost never be too large considering the available manpower. This team is often comprised of uniform patrol officers.

## Technical Evidence Seizure and Logging Team

This team is comprised of two or three people who seize evidence, enter evidence data into the computer, label and place the evidence in bags or boxes, and label the boxes after the evidence is photographed. This team is responsible for taking down a computer after the area is secure and the computer has been photographed. This team should include at least two people, one of whom is a computer investigator and the other (ideally) a computer professional who has been specially trained in the handling and evaluation of evidence. In most instances, this technical team will also conduct forensic analysis of the evidence. When a regional, state, or agency lab is available for such duties, some agencies simply box up the computer and send the evidence to the lab for analysis.

> *Note:* Consider skills in recognition and handling of evidence when picking these team members. They should be local officers, as they will be needed in court for chain-of-custody issues, and they should know how to handle electronic and magnetic evidence.

The Technical Evidence Seizure and Logging Team decides on appropriate action after discussing special circumstances with the case manager. They back up the computer to removable media, run investigative software, and shut down the system. They then mark all cables and safely pack the computer, cables, and attachments in preparation for transport. They then ensure that all evidence is logged and marked by the Technical Evidence Seizure and Logging Team.

For investigations involving a large number of computers, the Case Manager may appoint either an investigator or computer expert proficient in both roles to be in charge of all computer seizure teams and to handle all technical questions and problems.

# Computer-Related Evidence

*2*

## Types of Computer-Related Evidence

### Paper

Paper? Aren't we talking about computers? Many crimes, including property and person crimes, leave paper evidence. The presence of a computer normally does not change this. All of the hype about the paperless office is just that: hype. With a computer present, you may find less paper, but you are more likely to find more.

Finding a computer, or even evidence of a computer, may be a blessing. Keeping multiple sets of books in a computer is easier than on paper. Keeping copies of correspondence on a computer is easy after printing out the originals. There are many other examples of how a computer can keep the information you need for an investigation. To come up with more, just think of what you might put on paper and how a computer might be used to create that paper. Of the many tasks a computer can do, creating paper reports, notes, letters, spreadsheets, and graphics are the most common. Computers can produce a large quantity of paper reports very quickly; it seems that printer technology is always being improved in regard to speed, resolution, and even the use of color. Home computer users often are not satisfied with printers specifically designed for home users and their perceived needs. The home user wants the same or better equipment than they use at work. The only limitation is their budget.

### Computer Paraphernalia

Evidence of the presence of a computer comes in many sizes, shapes, and colors. People with little computer experience can recognize most computer pieces. Much of it looks like electronic junk. Some of this equipment requires special handling to maintain the preservation-of-evidence rule.

### Computers, Keyboards, and Monitors

Almost everyone can recognize a personal computer, a keyboard, and a monitor. Keyboards all look the same. Monitors all look like television sets, and the computer just looks like a computer. Of these three pieces, the personal computer itself requires the most care when handling. If you are dealing with larger computers, different rules apply. (See Figures 4, 5, 6, and 7.)

**Figure 4**
Typical "home computer" with a joystick, speakers, power director, and a removable Bernoulli drive.

### Disks and Diskettes

The labels on diskettes may or may not have important information on them. Some diskettes may not even have a label. You must look at each individual diskette to determine its contents. Occasionally you may suspect that a group of diskettes contain related material. If you are dealing with a large number of diskettes, you can check a random sample to insure the labeling of the diskettes is consistent with the contents. (See Figure 8.)

### Magnetic Tape Storage Units and Media

Magnetic tapes are used mostly as backup devices. They are an inexpensive way to store large amounts of data for off-site storage. For personal computers,

**Figure 5**
Hacker's systems are often identifiable by open cases and nonstandard wiring and hardware. Here you can see the exposed hard drive and all the installed hardware. It is also not unusual to find food wrappers and empty beverage containers laying around.

**Figure 6**
Four-line BBS with external modems and 150mb Bernoulli back up.

**Figure 7**
Computer monitor with passwords and other potentially confidential information stuck to
it with post its. This is typical of many programmers and hackers.

**Figure 8**
Expect to encounter large numbers of diskettes even in investigations of a single home
computer system. There are over 1000 diskettes, both 5.25" and 3.5" in this picture.

**Figure 9**
Tapes come in many sizes. The size of the tape is not an indicator of its capacity. These tapes hold from 40mb to 8 gigabytes and the smallest has the greatest capacity.

the following tapes may appear: DC20x0, 4-mm DAT, 8-mm video, DC600, and a few others. The number refers to the type or model number of the tape. Most can fit into a pocket. (See Figure 9.)

### Circuit Boards and Components
Your average computer user will not have circuit boards lying around; they have no interest in dealing with the insides of a computer. They may have an old board in a box in a closet. The exception to this is the computer hobbyist who is frequently tinkering inside their computer. This type of person may have several circuit boards laying around their office or home. (See Figure 10.) Handle any circuit board or electronic component with extreme care. Small amounts of static electricity from your body can damage delicate components. Do not leave anything behind that is specified as seizable in your warrant. If you use the example warrant in this book as a template, you should have almost all computer components specified for seizure. (See Figure 11.)

### Modems
"Modem" stands for modulator/demodulator. Modems originally were designed to allow computers to talk to each other over the phone lines.

**Figure 10**
Loose circuit boards and even partially assembled computers are often located at the search site.

Modem technology has advanced to the point where modems can send and receive faxes and even act as voice answering machines. Modems are key to using the information superhighway. Most on-line service providers only allow access to their service by dial-up modem. These devices can be very important as evidence. When you encounter a modem, note its connections, such as the computer cable and the phone cable. If possible, note the phone number if the modem is connected to a phone line.

### Printers and Other Hard-Copy Hardware

There are dozens of types of hard copy devices including laser, ink jet, dot matrix, daisy wheel, and thermal printers. (See Figures 12, 13, 14, and 15.)

### PCMCIA Cards

Small and portable, PCMCIA cards are designed for use in notebook and laptop computers. A small PCMCIA card is the size of a thick credit card. There are PCMCIA hard drives, network interfaces, flash memory cards, modems, SCSI, CD-ROM, and audio devices. Adapters are available for using PCMCIA cards in desktop computers.

**Figure 11**
Modem rack with dozens of dedicated and dial-up modems connected to a mainframe —
always a security concern.

### Software and Manuals

Seeing manuals on a shelf or on a desk next to a computer can give a good
idea of the types of software that might be encountered on a computer. (See
Figure 16).

## Where Computer-Related Evidence May be Found

You will find computer-related evidence in much the same way as evidence
in a regular investigation. Keep in mind that some computer-related evidence
is small and almost insignificant and can easily be missed. (See Figure 17.)

**Figure 12**
Two large color plotters attached to a network.

**Figure 13**
What appears to be a standard Canon color copier may also act as a color printer when attached to a computer. Canon color scanner/printers are often used for counterfeiting.

**Figure 14**
Counterfeit money scanned and copied on a Canon color copier: looks very good at 200dpi. Fake funds only have to fool the clerk at the grocery store, which these can easily do.

**Figure 15**
A warning about fake checks and money orders sent to merchants: created in Corel Draw® counterfeit checks have become all too common. Scanned signatures look as good as or better than the originals when printed with a decent printer.

**Figure 16**
Software and hardware documentation is often needed by investigators to aid in analysis of evidence. Some scenes might have hundreds of pounds of documentation for all the software and hardware owned by the suspect.

## Desktops

The desktop can contain a large variety of paperwork including notes, ledgers, bills, statements, messages, memos, computer media, manuals, computer equipment and cables, plates and glasses, small containers, radios, televisions, tapes, and regular office supplies. If examined properly, some of this material may be useful as evidence.

## Monitors

Computer monitors are popular places to stick notes which can be especially useful for locating user and system passwords. Many computer professionals

**Figure 17**
Documents are important sources of information. Phone numbers, access codes, and passwords are commonly found near the computer, sometimes taped or pasted to the monitor.

as well as computer criminals use multiple passwords for the networks and systems they log onto regularly. Since passwords must be changed regularly on many of these systems, they can be difficult to keep in one's head. (See Figure 18.)

## Next to Telephones

Evidence found around phones might include telephone numbers, passwords, user names, messages, or other conversational notes of evidentiary value.

## In Wallets

Identification cards, credit cards, phone cards, notes, hacker names, numbers and passwords, schedules, and even diskettes can all be found in wallets. Also, electronic pocket organizers are gaining in popularity and may contain similar types of evidence.

## In Suspect's Pocket

For many who work with computers, a common place to carry diskettes is in a shirt pocket. These diskettes can contain massive amounts of information.

**Figure 18**
This picture is for real! It is also a security nightmare. Passwords are on notes on this
programmer's monitor.

With the new magneto-optical technology, a 128-MB diskette can fit in a
shirt pocket.

All of the above evidence can be carried in vehicles. The advent of
powerful laptops, cell phones, and cellular modem capability with a readily
available 12-V power supply makes the car a second office for many people.

## Finding Computer Evidence

Most locations that have computers will have definite signs of the computers being used. Cars leave tire marks and oil spots. The perforated edges
from computer paper in the trash are a good sign of the presence of a
computer. Printed reports, multiple copies of correspondence or spreadsheets, and printed graphics are good signs of a computer. Do not neglect
the trash! In many cases the suspects have disposed of key paper and disk
evidence by throwing it in the trash, where it was then recovered by alert
investigators. We have found that passwords, hacking notes, and other such
valuable pieces of evidence are often routinely discarded by suspects. (See
Figures 19 and 20.)

**Figure 19**
Computer evidence can be found in the strangest places — even taped to the bottom of a keyboard.

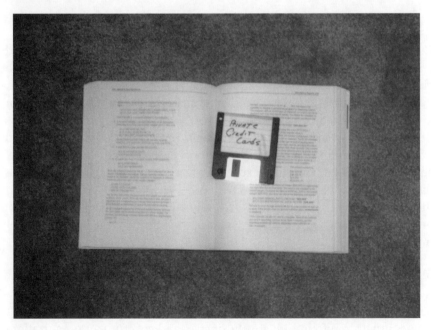

**Figure 20**
Diskettes of evidentiary value often are hidden in less than obvious places.

## Examine the Evidence for Criminal Content

Computers can maintain an extremely large amount of information in a small amount of space. A floppy diskette is small enough to fit inside a pocket, can easily be hidden in books, taped to the bottom of the keyboard, etc. The floppy can hold more than enough information to make your case by providing direct evidence or direction to evidence.

If there is printer activity, this information can consume a great deal of time to sort through. Do not blindly push this potential evidence aside; to do so may well cost you your case. Buried deep inside that mountain of paper may be the secret bank account number where the suspects have hidden their assets or their list of past, present, and future victims for rape and murder.

### Evidence Preservation

Determine if the evidence can be collected and preserved for future analysis; this is not as easy as it sounds. You must constantly check your warrant for what you can and cannot take. If you find something you need that is not covered, amend your warrant before proceeding. If you make a mistake, you could lose everything for which you have been working.

*Note:* Always back up the suspect's computer before moving it.

### Collecting the Evidence

Computer-related evidence is like any other evidence you might find with one exception: *It tends to be very volatile and can easily be damaged or destroyed.* Handle all computer equipment with extra care and follow documented procedures for preserving computer and electronic evidence. Following documented procedures gives you some ammunition in court if a defense attorney wants to get your evidence thrown out of court because of potential mishandling. It is advisable that only officers with sufficient knowledge and hands-on computer experience deal with computers, peripherals, diskettes, programs, etc., as well as with other technical or specialized equipment, during the execution of a search warrant and subsequent examination of the seized property. However, it is paramount in the following four instances.

#### Mainframes

A mainframe is a very large computer that usually requires a specially prepared computer room with reliable power and good air conditioning. Mainframes usually are found in large businesses and government organizations.

**Figure 21**
IBM ES-9000 series mainframe computer.

When serving a warrant on a mainframe, it is necessary to obtain the assistance of someone familiar with the operation of the mainframe and with software, such as a systems programmer. Most organizations with a mainframe will have a systems programmer on their staff. If you do not trust the one on site, contact the computer manufacturer. They normally have such technical people on hand for customer support. (See Figure 21.)

**Minicomputers**
A minicomputer is similar to the mainframe in that it requires a specially trained staff to maintain. Often the vendor will provide the support needed for these smaller systems. As with mainframes, contact the hardware vendor for technical support when investigating this type of system. (See Figure 22.)

**Specialty Computers**
When any specialized computer system, not necessarily a mainframe or mini-computer, is encountered for which software is specially written, enlisting the assistance of someone familiar with the operation of the computer and software is essential. The system vendor well may be your best source for technical assistance. (See Figure 23.)

**Figure 22**
IBM AS/400, a powerful minicomputer.

### UNIX Workstations

UNIX workstations (another term for computer, as far as we are concerned) are gaining in popularity for both business and the home. UNIX is the father of the Internet and provides one of the simplest ways to merge onto the information superhighway. UNIX presents us with some interesting challenges. Extra care must be taken to properly shut down a UNIX machine to prevent any damage to the file systems. You should always have help when dealing with any flavor of UNIX (there are many varieties of UNIX, including AIX by IBM) due to the complexity almost inherent to the operating system.

## Hacker Systems

We can give you a different definition of the term "hacker" for each hacker we encounter. If an electronics, computer, gadget, or software freak (often a teenager) runs a system, or if bizarre images are floating across the screen or strange looking connections are made with jumpers and covers are missing from equipment, then it probably is some sort of hacker system. (See Figure 24.) Before you depress the wrong key and wipe out the system, call an investigator who has some knowledge and experience with hacker systems.

**Figure 23**
IBM RS/6000 model 560 minicomputer (UNIX machine) with multi-gigabyte disk cabinet.

*Note:* When you have a case involving a computer as the object or means of committing a crime, do not turn the computer off if it is on until you are sure the data in temporary memory has been saved. *Do not let the suspect touch or handle the computer system.* Information can be wiped out permanently with just one keystroke. Depending on the circumstances, you might consider isolating your suspects from telephone contact with the outside world to further protect your evidence.

Generally speaking, you do not have to be an expert on a computer to safely collect computer-related evidence. Simply follow these general guidelines and procedures that can be applied easily to over 90% of the computers you will encounter.

**Figure 24**
Hackers' computer rooms often are cluttered with computers, modems, disks, food, and soft-drink bottles.

## Cautions and Considerations

All evidence requires some form of special treatment to prevent contamination and destruction. Computers and computer media are no different. A little protection and caution will go a long way toward preventing a defense attorney from having your evidence thrown out of court because of improper handling procedures. Using a little common sense and the basic knowledge of some of the possible dangers, you should have no problems preserving the evidence you seize.

## Heat

Heat is one of the greatest enemies of computers and computer media. Do not place the items near excessive heat or in direct sunlight in your car. Most computer media will melt or warp if kept inside a car during the day. This will render the media useless. Using damaged media may lead to damaged equipment. Heat is not as much a problem to the computer hardware, but it is a good idea to keep equipment out of the heat for extended periods of time.

## Magnetic Fields

Information is stored on the media using a precise magnetic field similar to that of a tape recorder. Sometimes the slightest exposure to a magnetic field can erase information from the magnetic media. Magnetic fields generated by your car radio (in the trunk next to the transmitter), electric motors, speakers, magnetic clips, and refrigerator magnets can really ruin your day if you do not take the proper precautions.

## Exposed and Unprotected Magnetic Media

Oils from your skin can damage computer media if it is handled carelessly. Using damaged media in a disk drive can destroy the disk heads and ruin other media inserted after the damage occurs. If you do contaminate a piece of media, it can be carefully cleaned by an expert to make it usable again.

## Exposed Wires or Circuit Boards

Electronic components are very susceptible to damage from static electricity. The static electricity that you can carry on your body is enough to destroy electronic components. The damage is not apparent and is only evident when the equipment does not work. Exposed wires and electronic components also may carry very high voltages that can severely injure or even kill you.

## Plastic Evidence Bags

Plastic bags produce a tremendous amount of static electricity and can cause permanent damage to computer equipment, very similar to damage caused by touch.

## Treat the Items Gently and with Care

Do not drop or throw any computer equipment. Do not pile heavy objects on top of them. Look around and ask the suspect if he has the original packing material. Often the suspects care more about protecting their equipment than anything else. Paper products do not generate static electricity that can damage electronic equipment.

## Do Not Photocopy Magnetic Media

Photograph them instead. The heat and electrical fields generated by photocopy machines will likely degauss (magnetically erase) the media.

## Tag All Cable and Connectors

Tag each wire, cable, or other connector before it is removed and tag the port from which it is removed to facilitate accurate replacement. (See Figures 25, 26, 27, and 28.)

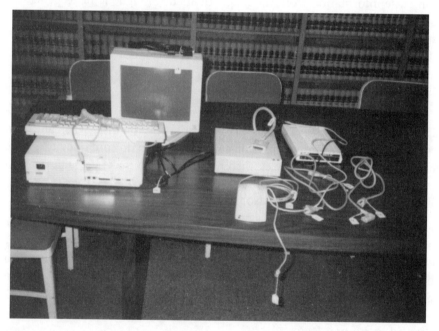

**Figure 25**
Reassembly and evaluation of seized systems are facilitated by keeping the tagged and numbered components and cables together.

## Follow Normal Evidence Collection Procedures

Follow the normal evidence collection procedure that you would with any other type of evidence. Take pictures and mark and tag the items with the locations from which they were seized. Tags and photographs can be crucial when reassembling the equipment for examination and when having to account for actions in court. When equipment is seized, take all manuals,

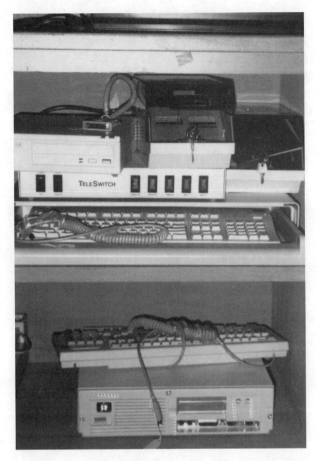

**Figure 26**
Electrician's stick-on number tape is used to identify ports on hardware which correspond
to the tags on related cables as shown on the CPU here. The number tape is available from
electronics supply stores. You can see the tape on the computer at the bottom of the picture.

cables, and components that relate to the seized items, as these may be
required for the analysis. (See Figure 29.) Before transporting a seized computer, make a complete backup. No matter how careful you are when moving
a system, there is a substantial risk of losing whatever information may be
contained on the system; much of which could be irreplaceable. Spend the
extra time to verify the backup. The sanity you save may be your own.

## Legal Requirements

Follow the same rules that you would for any other type of evidence; however,
take extra care so that the seized equipment is not damaged. If you are ever
in doubt, contact someone you know with the expertise you require. In your

**Figure 27**
Network cables are often routed under the floor in a computer room. We have seen cases where dozens of network cables were disconnected from the servers and dropped back in the floor without identifying tags.

reports, make sure you detail how you protected the evidence, where it was placed for transportation, and who transported the items. This could become crucial if the defense attempts to challenge the validity and condition of the information later retrieved from the system or media.

The Electronic Communications Privacy act gives some special protection to certain types of information on computer systems, particularly e-mail and "published" material on bulletin board systems, where multiple persons other than the system operator use the system and store information with an expectation of privacy. (See Figure 30.)

There also may be some consideration needed as to whether or not just data is needed or the computer itself is needed. For instance, a bulletin board provides confidential e-mail exchanges between members. Evidence shows that information which constitutes a crime is being sent between several

**Figure 28**
Terminal wiring board for a VAX minicomputer. Just the presence of complex wiring schemes should alert the investigator to the need for expert assistance. Keep in mind the extra time required to tag the cables.

members but no information exists showing that the system operator is involved in criminal activity. The search warrant would have to be limited by the facts and to mail between the parties involved in criminal activity. Taking and/or searching the entire computer including the e-mail of parties not involved in crimes is a violation of the Electronic Communications Privacy Act.

In another instance, the computer was used in a medical practice for patient records and insurance billing. The program was designed to overcharge the insurance company. Taking the computer could have put the patients' health in jeopardy, and only the data and program are needed for evidence.

The world we live in and the laws in regard to seizure of computer evidence are becoming more complex. Case law instances in regard to the evaluation of computer-related crimes and seizure of evidence are rare, and

**Figure 29**
Take everything when so empowered by the search warrant. Some cables are very customized and hardware specific. Printer ribbons and bottles of ink also might be useful.

**Figure 30**
Even small home hobbyist BBS can have protected published material and e-mail.

many of the questions change daily as new laws are enacted. In general, follow the same rules that you would for the seizure of any other type of evidence.

## Storage of Seized Evidence

Golden Rule for Storage of Electronic/Computer Equipment:

"If you are comfortable there, the computer and components will be com fortable there."

### In General:

1.  Store in temperatures between 60 and 90°F (see Figures 31, 32, and 33).
2.  Store in dust-free environments.
3.  Store away from strong magnetic fields (do not place a box of disks next to a stereo speaker).
4.  Storage of electronic/computer equipment and components often will be for extended periods of time due to the nature and complexity of the case. Nearly all current computer-related crimes in our experience are going up on appeal due to the lack of case law. Often we are holding evidence for several years in these cases.
5.  Many evidence storage rooms are also used by arson units used for the storage of cans of fire debris which often contains caustic or potentially destructive materials such as gasoline. Special care should be taken to separate computer-related evidence from such potentially destructive materials.
6.  If possible, have a location separate from "normal" evidence to store electronic/computer-related evidence. It will be there a long time, and investigators and attorneys will want to check and evaluate parts of the evidence often. (See Figure 34.)
7.  Keep all the evidence for each case together. It is often necessary to reassemble the computer for tests, backups, and demonstrations. Even one missing piece of equipment or cable can cause great difficulty in accomplishing this. (See Figure 35.)
8.  Use wood shelves and cabinets for storage whenever possible (see Figure 36).
9.  Ensure that each item is properly tagged and identified as electronic equipment. Computer evidence has a language all its own for naming items. When called on to locate evidence and check it out or return it, you need to know what to look for when the tag says "multi I/O board with 16550a UART". (See Figure 37.)
10. Small and similar items, i.e., computer disks, should be placed in individual envelopes and small boxes and stored together in one large box. Each small envelope should identify its contents, and labels on the outside of the large box should identify the small envelopes and boxes contained inside. (See Figure 38.)
11. When packed in envelopes and boxes, evidence is further protected from magnetic fields and dust (see Figure 39).

**Figure 31**
Typical police property storage. Sensitive computer equipment is stored in locations where temperature extremes and dust can damage or destroy computer evidence.

**Figure 32**
Dust-covered computer cabinet in a hot dusty storage area. This is not a good choice for storing computer equipment.

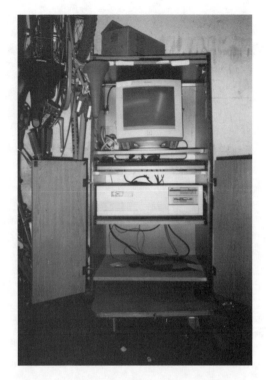

**Figure 33**
How not to store computer evidence — in an open area susceptible to extremes of temperature and humidity. Depending on the climate, you might not be able to start a computer stored like this.

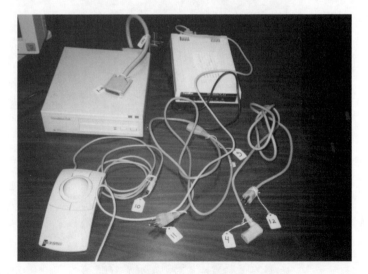

**Figure 34**
Mark and tag each cable with a unique number which corresponds with a number on the hardware port. Keep components and cables together.

**Figure 35**
Computers and diskettes should be stored in a cool, dust-free environment with no magnetic sources nearby.

**Figure 36**
Simple wooden cabinets inside an air-conditioned building make excellent storage facilities.

**Figure 37**
Diskettes and cables and all computer evidence should be placed in boxes and clearly labeled.

**Figure 38**
Package diskettes together for each room after marking them appropriately. This will save time during later evaluation.

**Figure 39**
Stick-on, hand-written labels can be used to mark evidence. We prefer computer generated labels, as many investigators write as if they were physicians (read, not legible).

# Investigative Tool Box

Getting together the tools to do the assigned task is a basic function of any job; computer crime investigation is no different. If you have the right tools, the job proceeds smoothly. Based on our experience, the following items either have been needed or proven useful during an investigation. We have found that we can assemble all of the equipment listed below in a couple of carrying cases and easily transport them across town or across the country.

> *Note:* All software should be available in both 3.5" and 5.25" formats. You should have extra copies of the search warrant and LapLink® programs, as you may have additional search warrants to serve and you will need LapLink® for both your machine and the suspect's machine at the same time.

## Software

See Figure 40.

### Computer Search Warrant Program®

You should have this program available on 3.5" and 5.25" diskettes or on the hard drive of your investigative computer. This is a database program which allows entry of all the important information needed for labels on your evidence. It also creates receipts and search warrant return itemized lists of seized evidence. You can design your own program if you are knowledgeable in database programming.

### Bootable Diskettes

Having bootable diskettes in 3.5" and 5.25" low-density media for each DOS version is still a necessity. Usually, MS-DOS™ version 6.0 will do everything

**Figure 40**
Soft disk packs containing device drivers and investigative utilities. All should be clean,
write-protected copies in 3.5" and 5.25" versions.

you need for IBM-compatible PCs, but some older machines might require
version 3.0 or below. Take care to find out if the suspect's computer uses a
storage-enhancement program such as Super Store®, Double Space®, or
Stacker® to manage the hard drive. If so, you will need to make a bootable
disk with the drivers installed. Check the suspect computer's CONFIG.SYS
and AUTOEXEC.BAT for programs.

## XTreePro Gold

XTreePro Gold™ is an excellent file management program that can find files
almost anywhere on a network or hard drive. We use XTree™ as a primary
investigative tool to evaluate the suspect's hard disk as well as floppies. XTree
allows you to read most programs in their native form, read them in HEX
as well as ASCII, copy, search for words and file names, and much more. An
example would be sorting files by date to see when the suspect was working
on the computer and when he was not. One of our cases involved a child
molester who ran a witchcraft BBS and was usually playing games from the
evening to early morning on the BBS. He was suspected of molesting baby girls
in their cribs on several dates at 3 to 4 a.m. The computer showed that the
suspect normally was at home playing games at that hour but was not on the
computer on the dates of the molests which occurred in his neighborhood. This

is not conclusive evidence, but it played a part in the overall investigation. The entire XTree Pro Gold package is too large to fit on a single diskette. In the documentation included with XTree™ is information on configuring XTree™ to fit on a single floppy. Unfortunately, XTree is no longer available for DOS, so you may have to search for it.

## LapLink

We have a rule that all seized computers must be backed up before being moved just in case the suspect computer is damaged in transit and all the evidence lost. We also do our analysis on a copy of the suspect's disk so as not to alter the original evidence. LapLink® is a program run from a floppy that allows for copying data from the suspect computer to a backup disk by serial or parallel cable. Version 5.0 has some very useful features, but there have been instances where version 5.0 has not functioned; in these cases, version 3.0 should work. LapLink works best on fast computers with disks under 500 MB. If you run into stacked or compressed disks and larger hard disks, LapLink can take several hours to complete a backup, as it is limited by the speed of the computer and the speed of the interface. In those cases where larger hard disks or systems need to be backed up, we recommend using Lantastic® peer-to-peer software with Ethernet cards. Backing up computers via Ethernet is many times faster than LapLink. We have used both token ring and Ethernet at speeds of from 10 to 16 MB.

## McAfee Virus Scanner and Removal Software

Running SCAN on each computer may reveal the presence of virus-infected programs and let you protect your computer. You can obtain the latest versions of these programs from the McAfee BBS at (408)-988-5190. If you use the programs, do not forget to register your copy and pay the nominal fee for this excellent shareware product.

## AnaDisk/Viewdisk

AnaDisk™ and Viewdisk™ are available from Sydex Software in both civilian and law enforcement versions (see Acknowledgments for the address and BBS number). These packages will keep an audit trail of the evaluation of the floppy disks being interrogated. This software will allow you to examine floppy diskettes formatted with unusual formats. See the section on investigating floppy diskettes for additional information on this subject.

## Generic Disk Drivers

These are third-party formatting utilities that are needed to boot disks formatted with these programs. Typical of these are the Disk Manager Utilities.

## Fried and Mares Utilities

This collection of utilities, written for law enforcement, performs a number of specialized functions. They are used to make what we call a profile disk to examine the suspect's computer remotely. That is, we create a compressed diskette using PKZIP which makes a RAM disk on which it unzips the programs we are using to examine the suspect's computer one program at a time, executes the program, and saves the data to a floppy disk. This gives us a profile of the information on the suspect's disk. We normally run a series of programs, starting with hard disk sentry to prevent destructive disk writes to the suspect's disk, then we save the boot sector, CMOS, and a copy of the AUTOEXEC.BAT and CONFIG.SYS; list all directories and files; list all the hidden, system, and erased files; and list those files which have not been backed up. This gives us a good picture of the suspect disk to use in court, if necessary.

## PC-Tools

PC-Tools is a set of utilities that helps users better care for their computer. One utility included is Central Point Backup, probably the most common PC-DOS backup program around. Be aware that different versions of this program are *not* always compatible with one another. We make it a habit to keep all older versions of our utilities and DOS just in case they are needed. This is particularly true of PC Tools, as the older and newer versions of the backup utilities are not cross compatible.

## Lantastic

This peer-to-peer networking software can be run from a floppy, and, thus, no writing to the suspect hard disk is necessary to use Ethernet cards and cable and backup the suspect computer quickly.

> *Note:* Other computer operating systems have their own investigative software. For instance, for Macintosh investigations, you might want to have the Norton Utilities® and Operating system diskettes along with Iomega Drivers and the Public Utilities for the MAC. Bernoulli drives use a standard SCSI interface and work well with MAC's as well; all that is needed is a Mac SCSI cable.

# Hardware

See Figures 41 and 42.

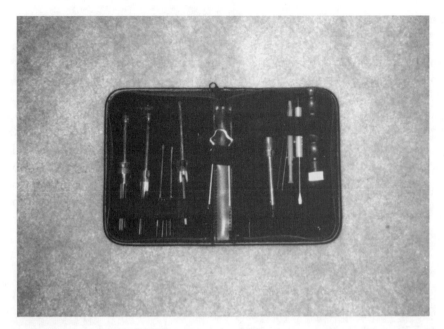

**Figure 41**
A simple tool kit is sufficient for the vast majority of cases.

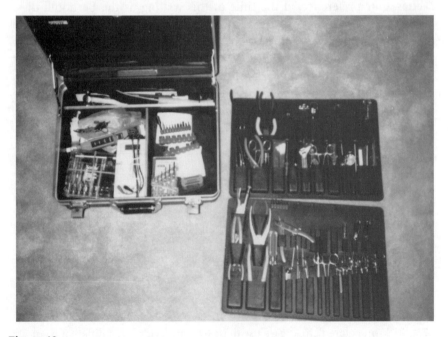

**Figure 42**
Tool kits can be simple or extensive depending on the tasks to be performed and the investigator's expertise.

## Full Set of Screw Drivers and Hex Wrenches

Heavy duty tools are recommended. Do not use magnetic tools. Include a knife in your tools; there are times when a suspect's computer needs to be opened to access or add cards. An electric screwdriver can be very useful. Power tools can be great time and wrist savers during an investigation, particularly when there are many computers or hard disks to analyze. We have seized large numbers of computers and loose hard disks in burglary cases where we backed up several computers at one time to the LAN and swapped the loose hard disks in the computers in order to back them up also; this saved days of work. If you use any power tools, be careful not to damage the hardware with the high torque of the tools and be careful not to erase any of the evidence with the magnetic fields produced by the electric motors used to drive these tools.

## Backup Hardware

This can be a Bernoulli drive, optical disk, or tape backup. With the increased capacity of the average computer, backing up all data to floppies can be impractical, requiring hundreds of high density diskettes and many hours of time. These devices can store the equivalent of several hundred high-density diskettes. Our preference, at the time of this writing, is the Bernoulli disk. With 230-MB disks, most systems can be backed up with 2 or 6 disks. We use a rewritable gigabyte optical for the larger disks. Tape can be used to back up suspect computers. Some new tape drives provide a great amount of storage capacity for the price of both the drive and media. If you decide to use tape, make sure you have access to a computer with enough available disk space to restore the tape to analyze the evidence.

# Other Useful Stuff

1. Printer cables
2. Serial port connectors
3. Gender changers, breakout box, and null modem cable for serial communications
4. Tractor-fed computer paper (this type of paper can be used for reports, receipts, search warrants, and other documents)
5. Computer labels for evidence boxes
6. 3 × 5" cards
7. Stick-on colored circles (we use these to mark evidence, a different color for each room searched with the finding officer's initials on each to preclude any problems with the chain of evidence in court)

8. Graph paper and ruler for sketch of scene
9. Portable printer and computer
10. Surge protector, extra power cables, and extension cords
11. Blank police reports
12. Evidence booking forms
13. List of contacts (usually a list of investigators and hardware and software manufacturers such as the FCIC, HTCIA, and other computer and investigative organizations who can provide on-site and over-the-phone consultation)
14. Adhesive numbers for marking cards and cables (when you unplug any computer equipment, it is important to uniquely label both ends of the connection to ensure proper reconnection)
15. Folding boxes
16. Packing tape
17. Rubber gloves, bleach, and disposable wipes (some places are not exactly sanitary)
18. Flashlight and extra batteries
19. Polaroid camera and extra film
20. 35-mm camera, film, and batteries
21. Search warrant template on diskette or search warrant documents for additional search warrants, as needed
22. Boxes to store all seized evidence
23. Cart to carry boxes and other equipment
24. Felt tip pens or indelible markers
25. Small UPS (uninterrupted power supply) for your equipment (we have experienced many problems with power at search sites, so bring a 3-prong 110-volt to 2-prong plug adapter with the UPS) See Figure 43.

*Note:* Based on our experience, you will need an open purchase order or quickly available funds for the purchase of software, hardware, tools, and disks and for the hiring of experts and technicians during investigations, or you may find yourself in the middle of a search warrant without the ability to complete service of the warrant for lack of equipment or technical assistance. This may also be a problem when evaluating the evidence.

This seems like a lot of stuff to carry to a crime scene, but we have found that it meets most of our needs. Keep in mind Murphy's Law of Computer Investigations:

"The equipment you do not have is the equipment you need the most."

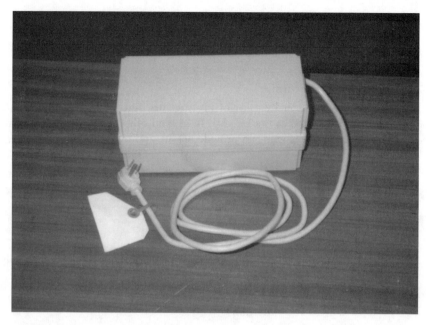

**Figure 43**
A small UPS (uninterrupted power supply) is an indispensable tool to protect your computer
from spikes, surges, and brownouts.

# Crime Scene Investigation

The information in this section is designed for a best-case scenario. You will not be able to follow all of these steps all the time. There is no set guide for investigating a crime scene. You must use your best judgment for every case and may sometimes need to change the steps depending on the situation. Some of these steps are only applicable for search warrants.

## Evaluate the Scene in Advance

When planning a raid, it helps to have some advance information. Knowing the location, type, and quantity of the equipment to be seized can reduce the amount of frustration and delays during the raid.

### Map the Area

Draw out the site or get a copy of the floor plan if available. This information may be obtained from the contractor who put up the building, informants, customers, or just an undercover recon of the place to be searched. On your map, identify all known computer equipment including computers and printers. If a safe or vault exists, include it on the map and identify what might be contained in it.

### Determine the Type and Number of Computers and Media Involved

Plan what equipment you will need for the raid and the storage media you will use to back up the suspect's equipment. Always try to overestimate your media needs; this will save you having to send someone back to the office for additional media.

### Obtain Necessary Hardware/Software

If you anticipate needing any special hardware or software, this is the time to get it. Knowing how difficult it is to get money for emergencies, the more time you allow for this step, the less stress you will heap on yourself.

### Make Sure You Have all the Items for Your Tool Box in Advance

Preparing for a raid is much easier if you have a checklist of all the tools and equipment you may need. Your master checklist can include everything you would ever need; you can then omit items you will not need for each raid.

### Have Necessary Media for Backups and Copies

## Set Up Search Teams

Setting up the teams sounds easy; in reality, there is enough involved to need a written plan for putting your teams together so that nothing is forgotten. You may have ideas to add to this section that will help you function more efficiently.

### Assemble the Required People

Give team members as much notice as possible to prepare for the raid. This ensures that all will have the opportunity to be prepared with a plan and equipment to do the job.

### Assign Team Member Responsibilities

Make sure all team members knows their jobs. Write a plan of what is expected of each member as far in advance as possible and distribute it to your team.

## Establish a Plan of Attack

A plan everyone can understand is essential to make your search successful. Write out your plan with diagrams and a checklist; a written plan will increase the efficiency of your team. The checklist helps ensure that you (or members of your team) do not forget anything. Before leaving for the scene, review the plan with all team members at the same time. An easy acronym is SMEAC (situation, mission, execution, avenues of approach and escape, and communications), which is the five-paragraph military order well suited to law enforcement planning.

## Situation

What are we facing? It would be foolish to take on any investigation without an idea of who or what you are up against. You need to define everything you are up against. Included in this definition are the number of people, type of equipment, and geographical location.

## Mission

What do you want to accomplish? Do you want to catch your suspect at the computer, or do you want the computers unattended? Determining your suspects' patterns might take a few days of surveillance during the same times as you have selected for serving your warrant.

## Execution

How will we accomplish our mission? What time of the day is best? If the target is a business and you do not intend to seize the equipment, you may want to consider entering before the business opens to avoid any contact with customers. Your surveillance will help you determine traffic patterns.

## Avenues of Approach and Escape

How will you get there and handle the scene? Depending on the type of raid, your methods will vary. If you are taking a SWAT team, you will proceed differently than if you are going with an auditor. Keep in mind how you will get your civilian help in and out of the crime scene. A good map should identify where you want all the vehicles to park, where potential obstacles are, where you will allow any media coverage, and where you might load seized property.

## Communications

How will you talk to each other? This sounds fairly simple. Radios and cellular phones are common methods as long as everyone is on the same frequency and everyone knows all the cell phone numbers.

## Prepare the Search Warrant

With search warrants involving new technology (or technology that is new to the attorneys and the judge), you should take as much time as necessary to compose your warrant. Have your warrant reviewed by experienced investigators and your prosecutor to make sure you have everything covered. Do not use terminology you are not familiar with or do not understand. When having a judge sign your warrant, spend time explaining the terminology so the judge understands the entire warrant. These steps prevent your warrant from being thrown out because it did not include some important piece of evidence and ensures that the judge understands what he or she is signing.

## Execute the Warrant

The basics of executing a search warrant do not change when computers are involved. Try not to give any advance notice of your raid even when at the site. Since computers can run on battery power, do not cut off building power and then casually approach the suspects. The data you are seeking can disappear within seconds of tipping off the suspect.

### Knock and Notice

Stick with your plan to announce yourself and why you are there: "Police officers, we have a search warrant." This will minimize any confusion on your team.

### Document the Notice Verbatim

If you have a video recorder, use it. The videotape will be very useful during the trial as well as to resolve complaints and claims which may arise out of the service of the warrant.

## Secure the Scene

See Figures 44, 45, and 46.

### Immediately Locate all Computers in the Building

With the declining price of computers, there could be tens or even hundreds of computers, depending on the size of the business. There have been cases where several computers have been found in a home or apartment. This is where a little advance intelligence pays off. If a network is involved, immediately locate the file server(s) in order to disable logins or to disable the current connections.

### Each Computer Must Be Physically Protected by an Officer

If left unattended, a suspect can completely erase evidence from a computer in seconds. With the ever-decreasing cost of networking computers, it is possible for one person at a remote computer to destroy the information on all computers on a network.

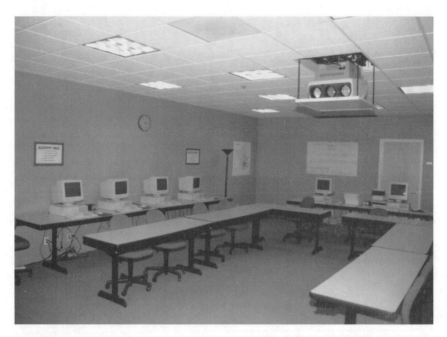

**Figure 44**
There may be several computers in a single room and they may be connected to a network. They will not always be as conveniently located, though.

**Figure 45**
Several network servers in a common computer room. The pictured equipment consists of three computers, a disk array (bottom right), a tape array (center), and monitors for each machine. The disk and tape capacity are over 10 gigabytes each.

**Figure 46**
Even a simple home computer system can be challenging and time consuming to seize.

## Have a Location to Interview Suspects and Witnesses

Try to keep this location away from the computers.

## Teams Perform their Functions

The Case Agent makes assignments and is available for direction and questions. It is best if he is free of other responsibilities so as to properly evaluate and direct the overall scene. Sketching, interviews, photography, and searches can be done simultaneously. Reports are written by one member of each team. All reports, sketches, and photographs then go to the Case Agent. An interview report, photograph and sketch report, arrest and interrogation report, evidence search and seizure report, and a computer search and evaluation report are usually necessary.

> *Note:* Maintain the chronological worksheet during the entire investigation. Stress this to all non-law enforcement personnel. Documenting even the smallest step could prove to be important during the investigation and prosecution of a case. Most computer professionals do not understand the need for documentation and its purpose later during the trial.

Use only clean, write-protected disks in the suspect's computer. Do not use the suspect's computer commands or software, as you may alter evidence. Some programs alter data and dates when executed and there may be ANSI bombs or other schemes which damage, erase, or format the computer.

## Completing the Search

### Team Debriefing

Before leaving the scene, debrief the team and try to eliminate any unresolved questions.

### New Problem Documentation

If you encounter any new problems, write them down in your procedures book for future investigation. This section has dealt with rules and concepts, not laws. You need to decide each time what will and what will not work for your particular circumstance. The most important consideration is the current law regarding search and seizure of computer evidence.

# Making a Boot Disk

# 5

## "I would really like to give this computer the boot!"

There may be times you really do want to give a computer the boot; this section does not cover that topic. Making a boot disk is a very important part of interrogating a computer. The boot disk is your first level of protection from any tricks and traps your suspect might have waiting for the unsuspecting, unauthorized user. A second benefit is that you can control everything that takes place during the computer startup.

## What Is a Boot Disk?

Now that you have an idea of what a boot disk can do for you, we will tell you what a boot disk is. First, a disk (really, a floppy diskette) is a removable storage medium used in almost every computer. You should already know this. What you might not know or understand is the boot part. Boot comes from bootstrap, which is the process of loading an operating system on a computer. So when we say "booting a computer" you know it means loading the operating system.

## The POST Test

A computer is not usable by most people before it is booted. The operating system allows the computer to interact with people and application software. When you first turn on a computer, a program called the Power On Self Test (or POST) is run. This program is found in the read only memory (ROM) of the computer and can take anywhere from a few seconds to several minutes.

This usually includes checking the memory, video hardware, floppy and hard drives, and the keyboard. After the POST is complete, the POST software loads the program from ROM that tells the computer how to start the operating system. For many computers, this software checks the floppy diskette drive for the operating system software before checking the hard disk drive. Some computers have a configuration option in the system setup that changes the boot sequence from floppy diskette first to hard disk first. To avoid this potential problem, you need to have an expert familiar with checking and changing the CMOS setup that controls this option.

## The Boot Process

During the boot process, the base operating system is loaded. After the base operating system is loaded, other programs might be loaded also. These programs might include some of the following:

- Device drivers used to run or manage devices such as CD-ROM drives, tape drives, sound boards, network interface cards, removable hard drives, bi-directional printer interfaces, bulletin board modems, scanners, and optical disk drives.
- Supplementary file systems such as HPFS, FAT, NTFS, or NFS
- Network access software
- Keyboard enhancements such as those that let you recall commands you typed earlier
- Drivers that allow application software to send FAXs
- Security software to prevent unauthorized access
- Graphical user interfaces such as Windows™

Some of the software loaded during this stage may be required for the smooth operation of the computer for each particular user. Some might be required to utilize all the components of the computer. This all depends on the intended use of a particular computer. Chances are you do not want every little piece of software loaded while you are evaluating the system; this may impede your progress by interfering with the operation of your investigative software. This is also when many viruses are loaded.

When you boot a computer with your customized boot disk, you skip loading all the special device drivers and other software found in the CONFIG.SYS and AUTOEXEC.BAT on the hard drive and only load the programs you want. This lets you evaluate the computer without unwanted software interfering with your investigative software. This may not seem like a big deal, but when you experience problems running some of the investigative software available, you begin to appreciate this extra step.

## What If There Is a CMOS Boot Password?

If you turn the computer on and are prompted for a password, do not give up all hope. You can still attempt to "social engineer" the password (as we discuss in Chapter 10) or you can have a computer expert bypass the password. Unless you are familiar with how to bypass the password and are confident you will not be shot down in court for not having the expertise for this operation, resist the temptation to tinker with the insides of the computer. Leave this to the experts.

## So, How Do I Make One?

The process of making a bootable diskette is very simple with the DOS operating system. The process becomes more complicated when other operating systems and other file systems enter the picture. The process also depends on the file system you want as your destination from which to conduct your investigation. If you want to store all the recovered data on an HPFS disk, you need to use software that allows you to run HPFS on your investigative disks, such as the OS/2 operating system. To accomplish this right now you need to use OS/2. If you do not understand what this means, you probably need to get an expert to handle this for you.

We will create a plain DOS boot disk on both 3.5" and 5.25" diskettes. This boot disk will use MS-DOS™ version 6.0. For this example, we will have MS-DOS™ 6.0 loaded on our desktop computer. The 3.5" diskette drive is A:, and the 5.25" diskette drive is B:. The diskettes are brand new and unformatted. The finished diskettes will let us boot a computer to a DOS prompt and prevent us from writing to the hard drive with a program called HDSENTRY (Hard Disk Sentry) and a good prompt. (Note: HDSENTRY is a utility available from Andy Fried; see Acknowledgments for his addresses.)

In this example, we will create a 3.5" bootable diskette. To make a 5.25" bootable diskette, change all references from A: to B:. Keep in mind that C: is almost always the hard drive; there are very few occasions where the hard drive is other than C:.

**Step 1:**
Format the diskette with the following command:

FORMAT A:/S

This will format the diskette for the FAT file system and install the MS-DOS™ 6.0 boot files. These boot files include IO.SYS and MSDOS.SYS, which are flagged System, Hidden, and Read-Only, and the command processor COM-MAND.COM.

### Step 2:

Create the CONFIG.SYS file. This file contains information for the operating system on how to configure itself. To create this file, use the DOS EDIT program on your hard disk. The command used to create this file is

EDIT A:\CONFIG.SYS

This will prompt the system editor to creat the CONFIG.SYS file. When the main edit screen appears, you should not see anything in the file. With the blank edit screen, enter the following:

DEVICE = A:\SETVER.EXE<br>
FILES = 50<br>
BUFFERS = 10

Save the file and exit. The first line in the CONFIG.SYS file loads a driver that allows older versions of some software to run on a newer operating system. The second line configures the operating system to allow up to 50 files to be opened at one time. The third line limits the file buffers to 10 to preserve memory.

### Step 3:

Create the AUTOEXEC.BAT file. This file contains information for configuring the operating environment and running special utility and configuration software. Terminate-and-stay-resident (TSR) programs usually are run from this file because it is always executed when the system is booted. The command used to create this file is

EDIT A:\AUTOEXEC.BAT

This will start the system editor creating the AUTOEXEC.BAT file. When the main edit screen appears, you should have another blank file. With the blank edit screen, enter the following:

PATH A:\<br>
HDSENTRY<br>
PROMPT Safe $P$G<br>
SET DIRCMD = /A/OGNE

Save the file and exit. The first line of the AUTOEXEC.BAT file sets the search path to look at the A: drive. The second line runs the HDSENTRY program. This program protects the suspect hard drive from being written to during the course of your investigation. Many available programs that fill the functional position of a hard disk lock. If a disk write is attempted, the software lock intercepts the write and notifies you that a write was attempted. The third line changes the displayed path to display the word "Safe" before the name of the current path. This will remind you that you are using a cleanly booted version of DOS. The fourth line sets the DIR command to display all files in the directory including System and Hidden files. The resulting list is also sorted by name and with the directories displayed before the files.

**Step 4:**

Copy the SETVER.EXE program from the hard drive to the floppy diskette with the following command:

COPY C:\DOS\SETVER.EXE A:\

The only thing to keep your eye on is the location of your DOS files on the hard drive. Some installations store DOS files in another subdirectory such as DOS62 or DOS6.

**Step 5:**

Copy the HDSENTRY program from your hard drive to the floppy diskette. You should have this program readily available on your hard drive. Copy the file from the investigative software directory on your hard drive to the floppy diskette using the same command format as that used to copy SETVER.EXE but change the path and file name to reflect the proper program.

**Step 6:**

Scan the disk for viruses; then write-protect it.

## What Problems Might I Encounter?

Even though creating a boot disk is fairly simple (especially after you've done it many times), problems can still creep in. The few problems you might encounter and a possible solution follow:

### Cannot Read a Diskette in the Suspect's Computer

This may be caused by using a high-density diskette in a low-density drive. There rarely is a way to tell what type of drive is in a computer just by looking at it. You might need to look at the CMOS setup to tell for sure. If this is the case, format the proper diskettes with the low-density parameter for the FORMAT command. The information on how to accomplish this is available in the online help. Do not try to format high-density diskettes as low density. This can cause problems, and sometimes the format does not work.

## I Am Getting Errors with my Low-Density Diskettes

This may be caused by formatting a low-density diskette on a high-density drive. This problem almost always shows itself on 5.25" diskettes. The 3.5" diskettes are fairly immune to this problem. To get around this problem, try formatting your diskette again. Make sure you do not do a quick format, as this will not actually reformat the diskette. If you are unable to get your newly formatted diskettes to work, you might have to find a computer with a low-density diskette drive to format your diskette. Keep in mind that you might have to use that low-density drive to copy your data files as well. Low-density diskettes work fine in high-density drives.

## The Operating System Will Not Boot

There may be several reasons for this problem.

1. *You are attempting to boot a non-PC with a PC operating system.* With some of the new computers available, it may be difficult to tell what type of processor is used. You might mistake a new Macintosh or Power PC system for a conventional PC. Many computers share case styles that look the same to the untrained eye (well, at least the eye that is not looking) but have little markings that tell you who the manufacturer is.
2. *There is a hardware problem.* Hardware problems include dirty or broken diskette drives, damaged hard drive partitions, incorrect CMOS settings, bad memory, bad motherboard, bad processor, and bad power supplies.
3. *My all time favorite: operator error.* You are doing something wrong, such as forgetting to use the/S parameter for the FORMAT command which formats the diskette but does not install the operating system files. You might be trying to boot from the B: drive. For 5.25" disk drives, you might have the diskette in sideways or upside down.

# Simple Overview of Seizing a Computer

I. Start chronological case work sheet.
   A. List the date, time, and description of the computer.
   B. List the names of those assisting you and witnesses to your activity.
   C. List the date, time, and action taken as you perform your search.
   D. Record your investigative clues and leads which you might follow up on later.
   E. List the date, time, and programs or utilities used to evaluate the computer.
II. Evaluate the condition of the computer.
   A. Is the computer on or off?
   B. If the computer is on, what is it doing? If a computer is on, there is a good chance it is doing something, depending on where it is (for example, running Windows™, accounting software, BBS, word processor, etc.).
   C. Assess the potential for loss of data due to outside threats such as weather, electrical, and magnetic conditions.
   D. Determine if the computer is connected to other computers by network or modem. Networks are gaining in popularity as their prices come down. Simple network prices are at the point where they are affordable for average home users.
   E. Consider the previous conditions to determine if the computer should be turned off or left running for a period of time and photograph the screen with a video camera. *Thought:* If the computer has a large RAM disk and all your evidence is on the RAM disk and you turn the computer off without saving it, what happens to your evidence?

III. Photograph the computer.
   A. Photograph the screen using a 35-mm, Polaroid, and/or video camera.
   B. Photograph the front and back of the computer.
   C. Photograph the cables.
   D. Photograph attached hardware.
   E. Take pictures of anything that may be of value or used for evidence. This could be the hidden location of floppies, printed material, hard drives and other hardware.
IV. Boot the computer from the floppy drive.
   A. Decide whether to go to A:\> from a running computer or to reboot from floppy; 999 times out of 1000 this is all right, but there are systems that have been modified to cause problems for anyone not knowledgeable in their use. Also, if a virus is active, you could infect your diskettes and hard drive.
   B. If computer is off, *always* boot from a clean write-protected floppy system disk. MS-DOS 6.0 should be able to handle the majority of all computers encountered. Refer to Chapter 5 for making a boot disk.
   C. Determine if special drivers (Stacker, Super Store, Disk Manager) are present; if so, you will need them in your boot disk CONFIG.SYS.
   D. First start a computer hard disk-lock program so destructive disk writes are not made to the suspect's computer, run a virus scan, then save the CMOS, Boot Sector, AUTOEXEC.BAT, CONFIG.SYS, and device drivers to a floppy disk. Save a directory of the suspect computer files to a floppy disk. We run software utilities by Andy Fried and Danny Mares of IRS Internal Security on a disk using a PROFILE.BAT to accomplish the above automatically against each disk drive and partition on the suspect computer. These specific computer interrogation utilities are available to law enforcement from Danny Mares and Andy Fried. Their numbers are listed in the Acknowledgments in the front of this book.
   E. Back up the computer with LapLink®, Safeback, or network software to removable media. Refer to Chapter 3 for information on what you will need to backup the suspect computer.
V. Mark and tag all cables and hardware.
   A. Use wire tags and stick-on labels to ensure you can return the computer to its original configuration.
   B. If you are seizing more than one computer system, first number the computers and then tag the cables and hardware using the computer number so that when you get the whole mess back to the shop they can be put back together properly.

VI. Prepare the computer for transport.
  A. Park the hard drive.
  B. Shut down the computer.
  C. Package the computer, cables, and other hardware in boxes after entering the evidence description in the search warrant program.
  D. Keep boxes for each computer together during transport and storage.
  E. Place the first label on the item or its bag.
  F. Place the second label on the box identifying each item in the box.
VII. Seizing floppies and other removable media:
  A. Run floppies through Diskcat® or similar diskette cataloging program and number them appropriately. Use an indelible colored marker or labels. Do not use pencils or ballpoint pens as they may damage the diskette media.
  B. Keep magnetic media separate from other seized items. This will help later in inspection of the disks so you do not have to look through dozens of boxes and envelopes for diskettes.
  C. Place seized diskettes in separate boxes for each room; it will save you a lot of time and trouble when sorting through them later.
VIII. Search the area carefully. Diskettes hide themselves in the strangest places. We often find them inside books, taped to the bottom of keyboards, in chests of drawers, in shirt pockets, and in other surprising places.
IX. Pack the property van with care.
  A. Place the CPU and other computer-related hardware and software in a safe place in for transport.
  B. Items fall out of pickups and bounce around in large trucks. Magnets in radios in the trunks of vehicles and excessive heat can damage media or hardware.
X. Magnets and degaussing equipment: Be aware of the possible presence of degaussing (magnets) equipment placed at the crime scene by the suspect. The Secret Service was the victim of just such a dastardly plan during Operation Sundevil. A simple compass will detect any strong electromagnetic currents.

*Notes:* If you are seizing computer equipment, take *everything*. If you leave any computer equipment, you may need it further on in your investigation. Also, after you leave, the equipment may disappear altogether.

# CHRONOLOGICAL SEARCH FORM

Case # _____

|    | Date | Time | Action Taken/Investigative Leads |
|----|------|------|----------------------------------|
| 1  |      |      |                                  |
| 2  |      |      |                                  |
| 3  |      |      |                                  |
| 4  |      |      |                                  |
| 5  |      |      |                                  |
| 6  |      |      |                                  |
| 7  |      |      |                                  |
| 8  |      |      |                                  |
| 9  |      |      |                                  |
| 10 |      |      |                                  |
| 11 |      |      |                                  |
| 12 |      |      |                                  |
| 13 |      |      |                                  |
| 14 |      |      |                                  |
| 15 |      |      |                                  |
| 16 |      |      |                                  |
| 17 |      |      |                                  |
| 18 |      |      |                                  |
| 19 |      |      |                                  |

# Evidence Evaluation and Analysis

7

## Forms of Evidence

Computerized evidence takes many forms. These can be readable by an investigator using standard operating system commands or may require a special program to format the information.

### Word Processing

Modern word processors save their documents in a format requiring a special program to be viewed clearly. Word processing documents can include correspondence, stories, diaries, minutes of meetings, schedules, plans, and financial information.

### Spreadsheets

Spreadsheets are used to handle numbers, although in rare instances spreadsheets may be used for word processing. Spreadsheets are a good source of financial status and planning information.

### Databases

Database management programs are capable of managing files containing millions of records. Databases are used to organize large quantities of information. Database management systems (DBMS) can produce many types of reports depending on the type of data being managed. Simple uses are mailing lists and birthday lists. More sophisticated uses are for financial information and business transactions.

## Graphics

Many forms of graphics are used on computers. These include business charts and graphs, publishing clip art, scanned images and color pictures ranging from scenery to pornography. Graphics can be created by hand (drawing), scanned into a computer using a hand scanner or flatbed scanner, or captured from still and video cameras.

## Windows™

Microsoft Windows is a graphical user interface (GUI) that runs on top of DOS on PC computers. Windows™ provides a multitasking operating system that can run Windows programs and DOS programs. Windows includes many tools and utilities with their operating system that provide all the basic software features needed in a computer. One of the advantages of Windows is that it creates a swap file and a large number of temporary files. These can provide investigators with a wealth of information that might not normally be available if the suspects save all their work to floppy diskettes.

## Other Operating Systems

The trend is to include "applets" (mini-applications) with a PC operating system. You must keep your eyes open for the possible use of these little applications.

## Analysis Tools

The following are some of the best tools available for analyzing information found on a computer. This list is by no means complete. Some of these tools are shareware. A shareware product is one which the author lets you try for free. If you like it, you are supposed to send them the requested registration fee. With few exceptions, this software is all under $100 and much is under $50. Shareware authors will sometimes make special changes for their registered users when asked.

### WordPerfect™

1. Concordance and index: With the Index feature, WordPerfect provides a strong tool for locating specific information in a large text file.
   a. Import the text information into WordPerfect, creating a new document. Include the codes to print page numbers on each page.
   b. Create a second document containing the key words and phrases you expect to find in the text.
   c. At the end of the main document, add the index codes and specify the file containing the key words and phrases as the concordance document.

d. Generate the index. WordPerfect will locate all occurrences of the key words and phrases in the document and associate page numbers at the end of the document. When you print the document, the index will allow you to quickly locate the information required for investigation of a case.

2. *Reporting:* Virtually any type of report can be produced in WordPerfect. These reports can contain graphics, lines, and equations. WordPerfect has printer drivers for almost any printer you care to use. WordPerfect also can provide all of the features you need to produce your regular police reports.

## XTreePro Gold™

XTreePro Gold by Executive Systems markets one of the greatest disk and file management packages available for PC/MS-DOS computers. This program can show you every file on a single or multiple hard and floppy disks, including hidden and system files. All of the features discussed here are available in version 2.5. Older versions may support some or none of these.

1. *File name search:* When starting XtreePro Gold on a hard drive, you will be presented with a tree structure of the directory. A small window at the bottom of the screen will show the files in the current directory. You can expand this view to include every file on the disk. It is even possible to show all files on every logged disk on the system.
2. *Text search:* You can tag all or a group of files and perform a text search. The files containing the information being sought will remain tagged for copying to another disk or for viewing.
3. *Attribute search:* Files can be tagged by their attributes.
4. *Formatted file view:* XtreePro Gold™ can produce a fully formatted view of a large variety of file formats. Viewing a Lotus® or Quattro Pro file will provide a read-only spreadsheet view.
5. *Raw and formatted HEX/ASCII view:* There are many cases where looking at the raw display of the contents of a file can provide more clues than using other formatted views.

## Norton Utilities 7.0™

The Norton Utilities provide great flexibility for viewing information on a hard or floppy disk. One of its most useful features is UNERASE. The UNERASE program is very simple to use and has online help and a friendly user interface.

1. UNERASE to other disk: If you find erased files that may be of use, you can UNERASE the file to another disk or diskette. This allows you to maintain the integrity of your evidence while still being able to see erased information.
2. View erased files on entire disk: UNERASE allows you to view the contents of an erased file before unerasing it. The view is a formatted dump of all the characters in the file.

## Sydex™

AnaDisk® and Viewdisk® from Sydex Software can be used to analyze floppies with unusual disk formats. These problems are encountered most often with hacker systems. AnaDisk also can be used to make exact duplicates of a diskette, format diskettes with different sized sectors, read strangely formatted diskettes, and often to read non-DOS diskettes. AnaDisk can identify incorrectly labeled COM and EXE files.

## Andy Fried Utilities, Danny Mares Utilities (Maresware), and Gord Hamma (RCMP Investigative Utilities)

Andy Fried and Danny Mares of the U.S. Treasury Department, IRS Internal Security, and Gord Hamma of RCMP Technical Security Services write utilities specifically for investigators. All are excellent programmers who produce utilities for law enforcement. See Acknowledgments for their addresses.

## CSHOW™ (Compushow, Shareware)

CSHOW provides a great deal of power for viewing graphic image files. You should capture any of these images on videotape for presentation in court if a computer is not available.

## QUICKFLI™ (.FLI, Shareware)

FLI files are animations. They can be simple cartoons, business multimedia presentations, computer-aided design/computer-aided manufacturing processes, and pornography. QUICKFLI allows you to play these animations on the screen. You should capture any of these animations on videotape.

## DL-VIEW™ (.DL, Shareware)

DL files are similar to FLI files in that they are animations. They are not as popular as the FLI files or the GL files. You should capture any of these animations on videotape.

## GRASPRT™ (.GL, Shareware)

GL files are fairly common because the program used to create them has been available on BBS for several years. Like FLI and DL files, they are animations. You should capture any of these animations on videotape for presentation to a jury.

## ALCHEMY™ (Graphics File Converter, Shareware)

This program allows you to manipulate assorted graphics files to be used in desktop publishing programs and to print them. ALCHEMY also allows you to convert graphics files to different formats.

## Analysis Procedures Using PROFILE.BAT

*Number one rule: Do not alter the original data.* Analysis of data on a single computer can take from hours to months. This figure varies with the amount and the type of data on the computer being searched.

The original PROFILE.BAT was created by Andy Fried, a programmer/inspector with IRS Internal Security. The Fried utilities include this batch file, designed to create an image of a computer system for informational and archival purposes. The new and improved version has been significantly modified to run with a single floppy diskette. The PROFILE diskette is bootable. The PROFILE boot process creates a RAM drive, copies the required files to the RAM disk, then exits to the DOS prompt. At this point, you run PROFILE for each fixed disk logical drive on the system. For partitions under 100 MB, you should need only one high-density data diskette. For larger partitions, you may need two high density diskettes. If the data created by the PROFILE utilities will not fit on two diskettes, you will need to resort to using a network drive with a program such as Lantastic or Personal NetWare.

Using PROFILE will save a lot of time interrogating computers, particularly when there are many computers to be evaluated. We use a number of utilities and programs in our PROFILE diskette which are part of DOS or are readily available as freeware or shareware.

The actual interrogation diskette uses CONFIG.SYS, AUTOEXEC.BAT, AUTO2.BAT, PROFILE.BAT, and PROFILE.EXE, which is a self-extracting compressed file created with PKZIP, and contains the computer interrogation programs. The text and contents of each file are listed below. These may not meet all your needs, but they do work with nearly all DOS-based computers we have encountered. This diskette is often altered by us in the field, depending on the suspect computer configuration.

### PROFILE CONFIG.SYS

```
device = a:\ramdrive.sys 330 512 64
FILES = 30
buffers = 20
lastdrive = z
```

### PROFILE AUTOEXEC.BAT

```
echo off
PATH = a:;
prompt $P$G
if exist auto2.bat call auto2.bat
@echo off
echo your drives in the system are:
ram_driv -q
```

## PROFILE AUTO2.BAT

```
if errorlevel 5 goto E_DR
if errorlevel 4 goto D_DR
if errorlevel 3 goto C_DR

:E_DR
echo copying files to drive e:
copy PROFILE.BAT e:
copy prof.exe e:
copy COMMAND.COM e:
set comspec = e:\COMMAND.COM
e:
goto DONE

:D_DR
echo copying files to drive d:
copy PROFILE.BAT d:
copy prof.exe d:
copy COMMAND.COM d:
set comspec = d:\COMMAND.COM
d:
goto DONE

:C_DR

echo copying files to drive c:
copy PROFILE.BAT c:
copy prof.exe c:

c:
goto DONE

:DONE
```

## PROFILE.BAT

```
@echo off
Echo Suspect Computer Information Gathering Process
Echo -----------------------------------------------
Echo This batch file brought to you courtesy of the Hackers
@ Fresno P.D. (Ken and Frank)
Echo This process will save information from the suspect
computer to a
Echo floppy diskette. The parameters for the process is:
Echo PROFILE d1: d2: d3:
```

```
Echo Where:
Echo d1: is the drive you want to check.
Echo d2: is the drive you want to save the information to.
Echo d3: is the drive you are running PROFILE from.
Echo Do Not include the : for the drive letters.
Echo.
Echo Running with the following parameters:
Echo PROFILE %1 %2 %3

if "%1"=="" goto noparms

Echo d1: parameter present.

if "%2"=="" goto noparms

Echo d2: parameter present.

if "%3"=="" goto noparms

Echo d3: parameter present.

Echo Processing commencing.

REM-Load HDSENTRY to prevent destructive calls to hard
disk
prof -o hdsentry.com
HDSENTRY
del hdsentry.com

echo Please insert a clean formatted diskette in %2:
echo If hard disk is over 100MB. use high density disk
pause

REM - Record the date of the ROM BIOS
prof -o romdate.exe
ROMDATE > %2:\ROMDATE.DAT
del romdate.exe

REM -Save CMOS memory to file
prof -o cmos.exe
CMOS %2:\CMOS.DAT > %2:\CMOS2.DAT
del cmos.exe

REM -Capture the master boot record and save to file
prof -o getboot.exe
```

```
GETBOOT %1 %2:\BOOTSEC.DAT
del getboot.exe

REM -Examine fixed disk partition table
prof -o dospart.exe
DOSPART %1 > %2:\DOSPART.DAT
del dospart.exe

ECHO Please wait as PROFILE:
ECHO Obtains list of all directories and files
ECHO Obtains list of all files not backed up
ECHO Obtains list of all system files
ECHO Obtains list of all hidden files
ECHO and writes the data to files on your data disk
ECHO Please wait as PROFILE writes data to a file
Echo off

REM -Determine list of all directories and files
dir %1:\ /s/a > %2:\allfiles.dat

REM -Determine list of all files not backed up
dir %1:\ /s/a:a > %2:\riskfile.dat

REM -Determine list of all system files
dir %1:\ /s/a:s > %2:\sysfile.dat

REM -Determine list of all hidden files
dir %1:\ /s/a:h > %2:\hidden.dat

REM -Determine if there are any erased files anywhere on
disk
prof -o ferase.exe
FERASE %1 > %2:\FERASE.DAT
del ferase.exe

prof -o beep.com
REM -Beep to indicte processing finished
BEEP
goto done

:noparms
Echo .

:done
```

## Other Analysis Procedures

### UNERASE

Using UNERASE, evaluate any erased files found on the computer. This process may include unerasing files to another disk. This is where the Norton UNERASE utility fits: it lets you run UNERASE from a floppy disk and save recoverable erased files to a floppy diskette. In this manner the original disk is not altered. Remember to never UNERASE a file to the original disk.

When using erased files as evidence, fully document the file dates and directory location and why an erased file is important. If you went to extra effort to recover a file, you should document each step you took during the process.

### XTreePro Gold™

Use XTreePro Gold to locate and view data files and programs anywhere on the hard drive and on floppies.

### Other Programs

The remainder of the computer investigation depends on the findings of the previous steps. This might include viewing graphics, reading and printing documents, viewing spreadsheets and databases, and reading communications log files. Processing some files might require assistance from a computer expert to properly process the data for court. An observation from previous experiences has provided this little bit of insight into investigating computers involved in crime:

*Never allow pride to interfere with your investigation.*
*Seek outside help if you are in doubt.*

Attempting an investigation without proper knowledge and experience can result in losing the computer as evidence, losing the case, and possibly facing criminal charges.

# Investigating Floppies

On occasion, the only evidence you have to investigate is floppy diskettes. Other times, you may have a quantity of floppies and a hard drive. In either case, there are techniques you can use to greatly speed up the investigation of floppy data. (See Figure 47.) Use the following steps:

1. *Start an investigative notebook for floppies.* Document each step of the process for report writing, investigative leads, and court testimony. List any problems, including bad sectors and damaged media.

2. *Write-protect each diskette.* For 5.25" diskettes, a small piece of cellophane or masking tape works well and is usually handy.

3. *Label each diskette.* Use a numbering scheme consistent with all the diskettes you process. If you find diskettes in several rooms, consider using a room code on the label. An example of a labeling scheme is **A0001, A0002, B0001, B0002,** where **A** and **B** are the room codes used in the search warrant and **0001** and **0002** are the diskette numbers.

4. *Catalog the diskettes.* Use a disk cataloguer program to list each diskette, that is, a listing of all the files on each diskette in a single database that can be searched for specific files, dates, and sizes and can produce good-looking reports for use in court.

   a. *Disk Catalog System version 7.01.* This program allows investigative notes to be added to the file name. The program is shareware and has a few drawbacks; the major one is that it will use an existing diskette label if one is present. It will also ask if you want to write a label to the diskette. Always answer **NO** to this question.

   b. *DISKCAT from Maresware.*

5. *Virus check.* To protect your computer from a virus attack during the investigation, you should consider using a virus scanner that can be loaded as a TSR. A good example of this type of program is VSHIELD from McAfee which can be obtained from the McAfee BBS (listed in the back of this manual). **Do not erase a virus from an original diskette.** Be sure to mark the diskette as being infected so you do not inadvertently use the programs

**Figure 47**
Seizing and analyzing diskettes can be a formidable and time consuming task. There often are hundreds or thousands of diskettes found when seizing even home computers.

found on it in your computer. If you do find a virus, chances are you will find others on other diskettes.

6. *Copy the contents of each diskette to your hard drive.* Be sure your hard drive has enough space to hold the contents of all floppies you need to investigate. There are two ways to look at floppies, depending on the quantity.

   a. Just a few floppies:

      1) Make a directory called DISKETTE on drive C:\> — MD C:\DIS-KETTE.

      2) Using XTreePro Gold or LapLink, copy each diskette to a subdirectory under the DISKETTE directory, using the diskette label as the new directory name. Both XTreePro Gold™ and LapLink® copy hidden and system files. They will also create the new directory and copy selected files to it.

   b. More floppies than you wish to deal with (*Lots!*): Look at the catalog listing. If you find that the contents of the directory listing are consistent with the original diskette labels, you may want to consider not looking at the diskettes that appear to be simply program files and instead deal with the diskettes that interest you in the same manner as you would with just a few diskettes.

7. *UNERASE deleted files.* Use the Norton UNERASE utility to unerase files from each floppy to another subdirectory on the hard drive under the DISKETTE directory using the floppy diskette label. When asked for the first character of the file name, use the letter **X** to be consistent.

8. *Print a directory of each diskette.* You can use this listing for investigative notes and leads and to highlight suspicious files for further investigation. *Note:* If you use Disk Catalog, version 7.01, you can add investigative notes in the file listing database and print the directory with the notes later.

9. *Search with XTreePro Gold.* Search all the files found in the DISKETTE subdirectory for key words, file creation dates, and file extensions. You can also view graphics, spreadsheets, word processing, and databases files in their native formats.

10. *Print.* Print all suspicious or evidence files, identifying them by diskette label and file name, date, size, and time.

11. *Examine diskettes with AnaDisk.* When investigating hackers, programmers, and suspicious diskettes, use AnaDisk to evaluate the original. AnaDisk reveals misnamed EXE and COM files as well as strange formatting, unusual sector sizes, and data in gap bytes. AnaDisk can also be used to copy diskettes that have an unusual format. You must format the destination diskette before you can copy to avoid a bug in AnaDisk which can cause the program to lock up. AnaDisk will accurately duplicate diskettes that are copy protected.

# Common File Extensions

The following is a list of extensions and the programs that can be used to view them. This list is by no means complete and changes almost every day.

ALL    Lotus Allways

ARC    Archive file, PKARC

BAS    Basic source file (program)

BAT    DOS batch file

BK!    WordPerfect® backup file

C    C programming source file

CDR    Corel Draw/Mosaic, graphics file

CFG    Configuration file for an application

CGM    Computer graphics meta file (graphics file), Corel Draw

CHT    Harvard Graphics chart file

COM    Executable DOS program

D##    Peachtree Accounting Company data file (## is the company number)

DAT    Data file

DBF    dBASE format database file, dBASE II/III/IV, Foxplus/FoxPro

DBT    dBASE format memo file, dBASE III/IV, Foxplus/FoxPro

DIF    Visicalc spreadsheet file

DLL    Dynamic link library (Windows and OS/2)

DRV    Device driver

DXF    AutoCAD graphics file

ENV    WordPerfect, environment settings

EPS    PostScript graphics file, Corel Draw/Mosaic, PageMaker

EXE    DOS, Windows, and OS/2 executable file

GIF    Bitmapped graphics file: CSHOW, VPIC, Corel Photo Paint/Mosaic, Zsoft Publishers Paint, XTreePro Gold

| | |
|---|---|
| PCX | Bitmapped graphics file: Corel Photo Paint/Mosaic, Zsoft Publishers Paint, Windows Paint, CSHOW, VPIC, XTreePro Gold |
| PM3 | PageMaker publication, version 3.0 |
| PM4 | PageMaker publication, version 4.0 |
| SET | WordPerfect, program settings |
| TIF | Bitmapped graphics file: Corel Photo Paint/Mosaic, Zsoft Publishers Paint, CSHOW, XTreePro Gold |
| WPG | WordPerfect, graphics file |
| WPK | WordPerfect, keyboard definition file |
| WPM | WordPerfect macro file |
| FMT | dBASE screen and printer format file |
| FON | Telephone number file: Procomm, Telix, Qmodem font file |
| FRM | dBASE report format file |
| FTN | Fortran source code file |
| GIF | Graphics interchange file (picture), VPIC |
| HLP | Help file for an application |
| ICO | Icon file: Windows™, OS/2, Qmodem Pro, version 1.5 |
| IDX | dBASE index file |
| NTX | Foxbase/FoxPro index file |
| NDX | Clipper index file |
| IMG | Image file, Ventura Publisher |
| LBL | dBASE label file format |
| LBR | Library file |
| LZH | Compressed file: LHARC, LH |
| LIB | Language compiler library file |
| MAC | Macintosh graphics file: VPIC, CSHOW |
| MEM | xBase memory image file |
| OBJ | Object file from a language compiler |
| OVL | Program overlay file |
| OVR | Program overlay file |
| OVY | Program overlay file |
| PAL | Personal appointment locator |
| PAK | Compressed file format, PAK |
| PAS | Pascal source code file |
| PCB | PrintShop color banner |
| PCC | PrintShop color calendar, PC-Paint image file |
| PCG | PrintShop color card |
| PCX | Zsoft graphics file: VPIC, CSHOW |
| PDM | Deskmate program file for Tandy™ computers |
| PIC | Graphics image |
| PIF | Program information file: Windows, DESQview Program instruction file, DisplayWrite |

PNM    PrintShop name
PRG    xBase program file name
PSC    PrintShop calendar
PSF    PrintShop system file
PSG    PrintShop saved greeting card
PSL    PrintShop letterhead
PSS    PrintShop sign
PUB    First Publisher publication
QDT    Quicken data file
QRY    dBASE query file
RBF    RBASE database file
SDR    PMTools print master
SDX    PMTools print master
SHP    PMTools print master
SP1    Sylvia Porter Personal Finance program
SYL    Multiplan spreadsheet file
SYM    Harvard Graphics symbol file, language compiler debugging symbol
       file
SYS    System configuration file, system device driver
SWP    System swap file: Windows, OS/2
TIF    Tagged image file format graphics file: VPIC, CSHOW
TRX    Prodigy program file
TTX    Prodigy program file
TXT    ASCII text file
VUE    dBASE view file

# Passwords and Encryption 10

"Please enter your password:"

## What Is a Password?

"What's the password?" is a phrase often heard when children are playing in a clubhouse. It is also frequently heard by people dealing with computers. A password (or pass phrase) is a secret word or phrase used to limit access to locations, computer systems, programs, and data. When you first sign onto a BBS, network, or mainframe, the system asks you for a user name (identifying yourself) and then a secret password to prove you are who you say you are. With the proper combination, the system grants access. Passwords are supposed to be secret but rarely remain that way. Passwords might be found written on notes stuck to monitors or scribbled on notepads. So much for keeping them secret.

## What is Encryption?

Encryption is the coding of data so it is unreadable without decrypting it. Encrypting messages before transmission is a safe way to send confidential or secret information over the airwaves or over a public computer network. Sometimes a password is used as the key to an encryption algorithm. Programs such as PKZIP from PKWare use a password to encrypt the data stored by PKZIP. Encryption algorithms can be simple. Here are some examples:

- *Incrementing each character by one.* In this example, "A" becomes "B", "B" becomes "C", "C" becomes "D", and so on. Using this technique, the word "computer" would translate into "dpnqvufs". The protection offered by this type of algorithm is almost nil but is sometimes enough to prevent the discovery of protected information by the average looker.

- *Alternating between incrementing then decrementing each character by one.* This is a variation of the first example. It is a little better at hiding the information, but is still decipherable fairly easily. With this technique, the word "computer" would translate into "dnnovsfq". Both techniques can be more confusing when other than alphabetic characters are figured into the equation.
- *Using a password as the key.* This method is similar to the first example. The difference is the number added to each character. We have simplified the example for this technique to make it easier to understand. The nature of the ASCII character set makes it work a little differently. With this technique, the word "computer" encrypted with the key "24" might look like this: "esotwxgv".

As you can see, the chances of deciphering an encrypted file without some serious work decrease significantly as you add different methods of encryption. Some encryption programs use complex mathematical equations with a password and a random number, providing military-grade encryption to protect top-secret love notes or classified dinner dates. We do not intend this to discourage you from attempting to break any possible encryption technique you wish to tackle. Realize that there may be some things you are completely unable to break.

## What Is the Difference Between Passwords and Encryption?

Passwords are like a padlock on a wooden door. They prevent people from seeing what is on the other side of the door. Encryption is like a lock on a solid steel door with the combination in a foreign language. You need to decode the language before you can unlock it. With password-protected information, almost anyone can read the protected data. With encryption, you need the algorithm used to encrypt the data and the key used with the algorithm to decrypt the data to read it.

## What Are Common Uses of Passwords?

Passwords are commonly found on networks, mainframes, minicomputers, bulletin board systems, portable computers, operating systems, screen savers, burglar alarms, combination locks, and parental lockout controls. Yes, the combination to a padlock is a form of password. So is the code to activate and deactivate a burglar alarm. Without the code or combination for these locks, you cannot get access to whatever is protected by these locks.

## Where Do You Get a Password?

Passwords come from the strangest places. Since a password protects important information, you would think the password would be something hard to guess. Think of the PIN code you use for your ATM card. Is it something easy to remember? If so, it is probably a number that is simple for someone to deduce with a little effort. Here are some common password sources:

- A person's own name (or modified spelling, including backwards and initials, alias or nickname)
- Social security number
- Birthdays (one's own, spouse's, children's, parents', or combinations)
- Anniversaries
- Names of children (first name, middle name, combinations, nicknames)
- Name of spouse (first name, middle name, nickname)
- Name of pet
- Name of victim
- Name of favorite teacher
- Address (including number, street, city, and zip code)
- Car license plate number or driver's license number
- Favorite sports figure
- Favorite fictional character
- Favorite television show
- Favorite computer manufacturer
- Other identification information

This list can go on forever. What we have listed is some common information you can look to for sources of password information if you find yourself having to "social engineer" the password. As you come up with other sources of passwords, you should write them down for future reference. Such a list is also useful when creating a dictionary for brute-force, password-cracking programs.

There are some suspects who make it easy to isolate possible passwords. Take, for example, "Trekkies". Star Trek fans will almost always use some bit or bits of information from any of the Star Trek episodes. Common passwords might be things such as "NCC-1701", "1701", "Enterprise", "enterprise", "ENTERPRISE", "Kirk", "Spock", "Phaser", and "Bones". Notice the difference between all the passwords. Each password is unique. For some programs, the case (upper or lower) is significant. This means that "ENTERPRISE" is different from "enterprise" if the program is case sensitive. If your suspect is a combination hardcore "Trekkie" and hacker, the password might be "EnTeRpRiSe" (see Chapter 11 for more on this topic) or a similar variation.

## How Do You Break or Bypass a Password or Encryption?

There are many ways to circumvent any password. Since a password only acts like a combination lock on a door, sometimes all you need is to find the combination to the lock. Other times you need to make another door to gain entry. Depending on the type of password and the program using the password, one method may be better than others. Included here are some programs we have encountered that use passwords and the way we bypassed, broke, or recovered their passwords.

### Oracom Bulletin Board System

This case involved a suspected pedophile BBS "SYSOP" (system operator). After seizing the computer running the bulletin board, we tried to locate the password for our suspect, the sysop. We backed up the BBS computer and set up a system to run the backup. After looking at the user file for awhile, we were not able to isolate the password even though we could easily identify the user names and IDs. To come up with the location of the password, we created two new users with different names but the same password. This gave us the location of the password. We isolated the password in the user file then overwrote the sysop password with the password we used for our new users. This method gave us instant access to the sysop login for the BBS. The modification was accomplished using a HEX editor (one of the nice features of XTreePro Gold). The password is encrypted so you cannot easily recognize its location in the user database. The encryption technique is simple to understand once identified. The technique involves adding two times the position number for each position in the password. This means adding two to the first character, four to the second, six to the third, eight to the fourth, and so on. Using "AAAA" as an example would give us "CEGI" in the user file. When dealing with lower case characters higher up in the alphabet, a HEX representation is essential to successfully deciphering the encrypted password.

### Quicken® for DOS

A laptop computer that had been stolen by an employee of another law enforcement agency was recovered. To make a case against the offending officer, we needed to show the computer had been used for a long period of time and there was no intention of returning it. The agency brought the data taken from the recovered computer for us to evaluate. Starting Quicken® revealed that a password was used to protect the data from unauthorized access. Previous attempts to identify the location of the password in the data files had proved unfruitful. Using a debugger, we traced through the program to isolate the location where the password was checked for validity. After a few hours of tracing through the Quicken® executable, we located the password check routine and changed the program to accept any password except the real password.

## NetWare® 3.11

Novell NetWare uses a nonreversible encryption technique to store the passwords in the Bindery. When a user tries to log on to the network, the password is encrypted at the workstation, sent to the server, and compared to the stored encrypted password. This rules out using a HEX editor or network analyzer to find the password. Direct access to the Bindery is not an option since supervisor or equivalent access is required to manipulate the contents. There are two ways to gain access to the supervisor user when you do not have the password. The first is to use a program loaded on the server (NLM) that changes the password to something known. The second method is to patch the SETVER.EXE program to change the name of the Bindery database. This forces the server to create a fresh bindery database with only guest and supervisor and no passwords. After you log on as the supervisor, you then run the BINDREST program to restore the original Bindery files. Since you are logged on as the supervisor, you still have full access to the system. Make sure you either change the supervisor password or create a supervisor equivalent user to conduct your investigation. It is recommended that only an expert with specific NetWare experience do such a procedure, since it is easy to wipe out an entire file server if the person working the keyboard does not know what he or she is doing.

## WordPerfect®

A city employee password-protected the emergency response documentation for the fire department before leaving and refused to divulge the password. At the request of the fire chief, we recovered the password. To reveal the password, we located a program called WPCRACK on a BBS. The program took at least one and a half seconds to tell us the password. Of course, we did not tell anyone it took that long.

## PC-tools®

A suspected pedophile who ran a Star Trek-oriented bulletin board was suspected of having child pornography for distribution on his BBS. The disks were examined without locating any files of criminal content. The final piece of evidence was a password-protected PC-Tools backup tape. In fact, several passwords were needed to restore this incremental backup. We performed the investigator's standard procedure of "social engineering" and checked for the suspect's name, family names, dog's name, and the names and key words he used when playing games on the computer. The end result was we located all the passwords and recovered child porn from the backup tape.

There are many programs on the market designed to provide the password for protected data. One source is Access Data (telephone 801-224-6970, 560 S. State Street, Suite J-1, Orem, Utah 84058). They have programs that provide the passwords used to protect Quattro Pro, Lotus 123, WordPerfect, Quicken, PKZIP (using brute force), and a few others.

If you intend to break a password, here are a few steps that might be of help:

1. Identify the program or encryption technique.
2. Look for the location of the password.
3. Compare the encrypted version of a known password (unless you can readily identify the password).
4. If you have good information or a reasonable suspicion that the suspect may have password-protected files before service of a search warrant, include in the warrant an order of the court for the suspect to provide said passwords to law enforcement.

## How Do You Break or Bypass Encryption?

A good hacker or computer expert might be able to break some of the simpler encryption techniques. The more secure techniques, however, may require an experienced encryption expert to determine the technique used. If these methods do not work for you, you can always resort to traditional police techniques to get your suspect to tell you everything you need to know to unlock all their data. If that fails, there is always "social engineering" (a fancy term for attempting to guess the password or passwords) to unlock the data. Be warned, this method can take days or weeks, if ever, to show results, and requires a tremendous amount of patience.

Some programs use a brute-force technique to deduce the password. Programs using the brute-force method work by trying sequential passwords or passwords found in a dictionary until they get a good result. When you sit down at the keyboard and try to guess the password, you are using the brute-force method. The brute-force programs run best on fast computers, since they may try up to millions or billions of passwords before getting the right one. You may be chuckling about the billions, but when you start at "A", then go to "B", then "C", "D", "E", "F", and on to "Z", then come back to "AA", "AB", "AC", and so on, the combinations appear endless. This example illustrates using only the upper-case letters in the ASCII character set. There are also lower-case letters, numbers, and symbols. If the suspect is into the computer underground culture, they may be using characters in the upper and lower sections of the ASCII character set.

To help you understand the scope of possibilities for a password, each character position can have one of 256 possible ASCII characters. Of these, 26 characters are "A" through "Z", 26 of these characters are "a" through "z", and 10 of these characters are "0" through "9". The remaining characters include the characters used for punctuation, control characters, and the high order ASCII characters.

## PGP

When talking about encryption, the most common program people will talk about is Pretty Good Privacy. This is a public key encryption program that is in the public domain, freely available for private use, and can be found also on the Internet and most public and private bulletin board systems. Getting around the security in PGP without the secret key is easy: you can't. PGP is regarded as the most secure encryption program available. It is so secure that the complete source code is available for anyone who wants to study the encryption engine and attempt to crack it. There are two different versions of each release: the U.S. version and the version for the rest of the world. PGP includes features such as:

1. *Adding a digital signature to a text message to verify the sender:* A unique digital signature is generated by running the encryption algorithm against the text in the message. The result is a string of bytes which can be used to verify that the message is authentic and who it came from, using the sender's public key. The message can be read by anyone in this form. There is no protection applied except for guaranteeing the message is unaltered.

```
-----BEGIN PGP SIGNED MESSAGE-----

This is a sample message meant to illustrate the various methods of
encryption available in PGP. As you can see, unless this text is
clearly visible (with only a digital signature) you will not be able
to read this message.

PGP is designed to provide an easy way to encrypt and verify messages,
encode binary files and provide a lighter encryption technique for
archiving data.

-----BEGIN PGP SIGNATURE-----
Version: 2.6.2

iQBVAwUBL/ldVj/NbiHdqWwRAQHtMwIA2u8dK6LY9ad8PfjGeSpSs6F5TS/QYq/j
LgrG1B8EWX+oGigtK6yK1XKRakYbkjOsKn3ciCA3KM/HqwbZWgS7cQ==
=UoU2
-----END PGP SIGNATURE-----
```

2. *Encrypting a message:* The message to be encrypted is run through the encryption algorithm, producing an encrypted file that in no way resembles the original. The resulting file can be either ASCII or binary, depending on the options selected during encryption and the way the message is to be sent.

```
-----BEGIN PGP MESSAGE-----
Version: 2.6.2

hEwDCkuhroeoAcEBAf4wo0EUfyV0aFJ2tAuxSi9t7ph+zSNW0LMISnXAPFnExY6Q
YRulDq9J2IfFm/Yr6kBD8o2qhqPxWB2taRU0OYhEpgAAAaHXaeN5gT1cp6brDrvO
f5yVOWKXdk0gL1bYit0ke01pKUrCUbuxHB1cikQ7NstxVBHfDLaCTSp58n9yqsp2
EoNeVLgebbrQEOYOiAhZA+gp3Iz2heCdqZa7wle+m7LJpEgFUbwtxav3mLTNrPqV
4DdTEv6BGxNf055Ye1O+BHMsxjTxhg74oAmGHcaCnjmGqwvNIkF6MeOgotRNoRji
4WDnX1x4F9qCk7XGU/xEQDyMnQTzG5LM5DbSVVovJf3H3SXhg9wL4SRt+vqD07ws
BI3X7n5AfQzMhmv0WrBvSfQlNojS0VFOtz9WehknWKBVt+bNPiEShEOj32Ao7UVg
eTvc2+npc3LX6K7X83QtgnRIky3uPl4eqmEHNAOtPMJ6hbPLBNAwTO5M5n4ZTHSp
ryG7CBu8WGS8kuv4lTjudOwfatBGPyQu/ZGznQZNu05icxjAzET1xHajB0Sh3N+X
TCvY+MPARDtJUD/ExXgz0NO1XrGHnFOBf68RK2M2zPPlESmsNxU4oN9mre4vJPAd
z7jYiOKOL1T6vo31QWE/8zFIKXs=
=8WKC
-----END PGP MESSAGE-----
```

3. *Encrypting a binary file such as a ZIP file:* PGP can encrypt a binary file the same way as it does ASCII messages. The resulting file can be either ASCII or binary, depending on the options selected during the encryption process.

```
-----BEGIN PGP MESSAGE-----
Version: 2.6.2

hEwDCkuhroeoAcEBAf9kklsnGKuDWo8llSH2unMOm0tzS68ArN8JsXrG1djf4/6Y
AVCXg3WRHu8q+4o2gflgvhUKTbY4AOaUwiXZXDSSpgAACWufVovF/c3AnK9uONn3
HACWUmQ8kxvus/QoJY0jOm3i5lynHwEC50z+Nt8e/yrb3B1xC4bFeJwv3vlGgOI+
Am0JjCMVTmxvaL2qHa/B4fJrnK5ZyBr2Bvl0kJAbd+0e8diUU4ZTM2UCxSw61APu
RECxt+exwxKkrkuqVJTCBPQUMgEB3ty3s9zkCWl/mep1GjflTwAjHh8nVtmp7EZC
rTIES0d8WGyKmcfrsT1SS6XBs9ZBDBCmV14J/qtbJA4CtxSW8PNGZZvpyITSoEOY
VqeE3725XBenejEGhlmmqK0fIZ6D52ie52QQWGFIViieAujlEKmMFNv1OpVvJwmK
gbvWPuTHFlvNSbmftvGsV/2kR6xXDtR4JSX6F/jW4ebNFE85Ae6ZstXp58fKrGJe
o/P7HjMoWAd7MK632mff9N5nfcegCGdFlRZZ6P8H/VE0xwSip72nISvNP+wOfD/M
zuTadI54sWwONe0BcMPJrqgKnwYJTMVmlpsrzCkxNfHkOH+hkMNUH4eNrBDMTK+y
MJ/0QmFZ3nyXBADblUrDf6Af3yU6sxq/3VcKWoJ7gBEIssw8jVkWqlkZdSyksTFy
WSpumMr0VfCygZo0R0+ClD529tTmkptBphpva1Xr2DWSAxH+wPoVei7ze5tAaDy2
Qj1ZXaTpjFYNCpT3tZmqaKmhxHm92M5qHYRm/4VGuxiYEqjzLC/4mA2eASZnAV4c
e84sp4s5Ic9wmqAZGpARthTyfGrYvCD2+Nc7kVK/j4SlXvjvWqUUiNZnXaX9Zdij
HXmD99qH3bvSQTe+tJCScWFtvsiMgarMUO7SGzUpwdOBKtW8fxIVRzlOJWN134Xt
S3Pwf/6eI1QA8OxNth9F4fyUg4WnFe1w2oV7/d9N23kcn9ThIoCzzeAVsfA32fGG
xB1QiVSNGGgpstJsAPEBDL3jU65C6gp79qvn8I1mTNyOuBdPOsaSKByq1H53TS/E
qTTayb21QD+Z676GPrnJfPNEcSqS0bv68XA0ddlhPlNpiRDZizWLS42jr6yUj8CS
nAygGA8ncpVoHPCVeJwiRdFKVI+Ktr/gtBu5IwL9IKYdhM1+/77HDyDxQ972vGXF
V9quHifQCA6Y0isS+ZNiTnYUauwhGa7+xSYkVGKYCAh6ofDZGd9dIOjPLQZQNT04
T71eta+nJU6pb8rcKOTP9RcCsb9iKG5N0/blhXH90Kgcjpl/eupMH6jmMLCpDMAS
DvMhnbwIp4EXZelbocIpeNMXtdlp1ZCYW+/YC+dM2u5W65Q5jJKAJsCvNnTEx21h
R0Ps9MjPwimqqg9S9ee4W3lOEucouQZxEk4k0Xl/DBGYuVmO63oiP8YW3PFgRMh4
+rSxH0g6zsmtZPUKAazqvlLdYGt4mzecbuymTzaWdm8o8GqC//UQrG82dF1Nm0E7
IESgR9Md2iWgpX+mtdtZS6LNLRsIIMFwWpRXsNV4zh6PD9K3rmwDnxZvuy2a2PA0
gCOjy/jiFaezDhsH0hC5ozhDH70+sHf6rXB+P+Jsi+zcgKYKhEOt/bSROOnRafi/
cQ2BR8Ht6j0vCRc+qA3eswVEPylCQgJQ1huT130mCR0VXOwJ0SURjS6VzoT6nxHM
```

ve/t4f0RWoPi8B5XsWYq09mdvVG98EwiqVJVzxwBOyvlCQ9Tn6j83f3xgXBSdtA+
/PX96r3jTjpAOJn6pmbyldEQM3LoX5eOE8wPrROMIA+hgfv9AUI9URStLpLDDXeI
1y8ZL0MGNufr1ffyZr6ev2m3jP1eTtiYp69UEURXyGa6b35gJxVuM9+y2LXq8bb9
jETkWANIGMiv66cQ1i56flJKXZXmKKKiIbdAvGADk07ZXYEFBdudrFdArhVQq0Wp
s5g0qCnp8wF/f7buRT+iMobzrEDO+7YbP/KYTdq39lhtIVYdAc7sv2QM7i41ficv
6E8x2HuyeAil0lD7+QmfJDsnERookXJOHNsfsK9CLMt3zFvzVYc9bkUuTkrvs9E3
ol1xqbeHRKVo6azYKNy8mZH0nYDFJKWvwfhDGZErppa6HsXtu8QVBuUDZt3XqKsi
7kQVT2VyX1WMfKuGzH4gf8sxOx02mp0to1Y47HrvXpQtWKZkjv3jcujjvS1G2O6r
ig//rQ7RbxDR5eJEBVB6a+PovNOYlEszbb/qRBqPymZHxM4N6krtFJaJCGCHu+wC
hdMtBslLmiLo9panc0ZZSd6yXE6Plz4VQU4WqyPCkd061cp8+EyUPm7o72zQB3Ni
fAl4I1+aZLd8Yo50snCyVn8WCo3Arp4Af7hRZ1dRsJ00Jz40kN30qZUGBXPoj+Ik
nIzgxYYQUErP2c50lCuNfv5tuFahnc32jZPUD184BlzKUXkRPni8/fmzPcdkj3HP
9wB8bJESBhCCJTh11jmyhc8o9VJfvVm3i0aJOEPocQsTTl8AdXRFkCj9xNtSWH4n
px/ysRLj79fBfdHWYIqV8zZxQFxA5by9YpKJTasdVWWtnwZCDKYhNgsc0M4UBQD8
ZI58ecHEzT4h3idDpYW4AkBhaUlyaZd8E5dhABKFtARMyYTiRJZmj/eMSG9xs6WT
VQJnlBNA4KEPQjsPpAEbvFwP9gr7WhNx0KdLkgjtl4spYw2ps1IHdfMJtPMiJKUW
LoQm2pFOzBuXrjTm6/duSJHBkybc6ngYhJfL4b/A4WA/xpzuiJ3n0qkoVtB3/72k
Y8StXNvufeAj3b8TmQUWb1JDIwoJAMz+N1L7eIn5uuDjKZLyTRcrPVvXmVM4Pzh2
mmyLYjIMfAa9vTvXMYXF7UDzYj2Zk62wM7ihTqLqu5mGJx8nFbihmTGGAhiCJiUl
8xlqhOeGoWcNm46Tesk2QGE6tc+VblaZF8FgrXwHXq8Zf3clg0FifYlfXdN9krXg
m+ub9u58nGUFFFzoPqQ2NB5mYVtx8swKw19e6wC0aCeMG/2uUyFeh4Iky/nlQmyZ
mO6vtDi9gYdUAuv4p55A7ySLMWzUyeaWvnaim3etvdb0PF00AdclNkoeScknIHLN
t8KNId2ntjg57srxrZOwn67RE0BWwcc9j7/Iw/EfR93Wok/cJOrDmPYldjUTuGaO
usyXjvNB1TjdwqafqIHyMUaQ+hB0TKU4HbD+mfwGXdAmAYu2P8O8LmSYI0eIeFd6
SpsvGqa/KhXvC1h8LnJYM43QD900/NnY1nDsSQupLtKdUCRp959H/BbpLuX4tA==
=MbiL
-----END PGP MESSAGE-----

4.  *ASCII Armor a binary file:* ASCII Armor is similar to UUENCODING a file.
    This allows an 8-bit binary file to be sent through a 7-bit mail system. This
    is a common way to send binary files. Encryption is not necessary when using
    the ASCII Armor feature and no keys are necessary to remove the armor as
    long as no encryption is used.

-----BEGIN PGP MESSAGE-----
Version: 2.6.2

rQkFYgtzYW1wbGVzLnppcAAAAABQSwMEFAAGAAgAJUPkHkEXZBGvAQAAfQIAAAsA
AABTQU1QTEUxLkFTQ1VSzW/aMBS/R8r/8I6b1oFKNcYmcQhrFhCFAeGj7PYSP5JH
XRtsJ1n++81ZW3W+WPKzf5/+7NckTmZZLWCUrSGfJMr6HRZymURJ3wzAIg23JFtgC
gsXniyR4Jmux8DsqB04DS11ZZ9ARuJKgRsO6svBMrtTCgj6FAanctBfHWgHWyBIz
ScDK8/YAIgutriBHBZboBiolyVpwntnRHwdswyCXhEa2ULNl//pDw64ErWQLCIIL
dijBcqHQVYY+dogNSwlKO8gIPGUYOA2GUPzDfnHS8zZ9AmxBkIcg4X1djK5ZEKAC
QttCg60/fvECqATUZPjUvkZibzqnWhBkrNC0cGJJtrv5BgaSi9KRgXeZOMpLxdeK
4KRNGKDJS65ZFSDQYSevq+P/rqLtbvNa056MZa2+w6A37A28H15P91Gzmzz0pdif
+8uMp+J6aDbReuoWzSwaVCMxHz4cv6EYrU7nhNJLaoc/v2zT/vp47Z/D4KEwye1k
FB8eP+mECzcftvPbx/kGn47Z0/mXnau7nH9Ed/NFf3ptst+HIv2ar8fjMBjv9G4Q
Bp3meHn/9rveK/4LUESsDBBQABgAIALRLA5B6Upqze9gAAAIUBAAALAAAAU0FNUExF
MS5UWFRNkDFuKzEMRHsBe4FUU+YDge+Qyu0WuQC94q4IOJS/yF1Htw/kOEEqAgT5
Bm8+ijjEQXCC63pRxZXfaxiQLRIWo7h6NghGFcVCTujuuHKVmR12nxLa0fgupBjpI
1C7KEMN8nk/Au6PXHQsZnPkNuym7I0Zy8GdAfEqLMjXtOMR1fL/eJOqqaQchyyZB
CpfNKPbG/x7Eu6jCauDCGJFTiorGlL/ZT5PT1KY0n+dhmXkgOA+vW6uHZAYZmLzj
Tn2sny4gyzi4ydp/KvG3h2nNjIsYtY5VlP1x+QuDylaCG/50ErwUk/87Y61tStSW
IofYhkxBpym9fAFQSwMEFAAGAAgA+ETkHmEfywZjAgAAAwMAAAAsAAABTQU1QTEUy
LkFTQ1VR23SubKaUACA4Z4Z3uH2TCKym5lbHOAAKhxAdjtQdlllk6fP5Nb5y7/+fvlL
hOoZfVmq9WVAxwEq/Lk45qfju+zaP1/Ub+43hWM4VsBVluq5GLu0Aw8ogoxZOxJ6
2ccnY+VCTWDenPI08X1B7A4KSN04O20ILKWFW8TZOBbd5pc8nC7UOVOaQzRytSgL
HTUUg7UFIjXFN480owL2OQAg1sI4RWzuHh8914zyuJg41rEfnwyu4bMmc/2YROVE

```
lin56q/eKHnJvGni8VHWNo/e0+aLWibrseQ6PSuOp8/w7ikcgx1KfT1Pk2SOoRmZ
JSjugMh7+rxTRSo9h3vMr6+UaHj90sNc8ZJ12uKFbnQXjdbg4xgjP124cKK6oYxk
2Sg9moSoGe+tcrci55kONKr2iKW2atRhXdC5VjgjNfNuuqHuVpU4xgRyGx43RjkN
Us2HqnfYoC1/jNZ2d5XVDVZOHN/vlktGa7QTFvlp1RnnNhHLIJP8+sYx8UyHfMuC
zN6NolnIYBQXJ7NfqKsc01fMaT8FaVG3wVX0JyJBVgmdApoVTYGO9/wcx1J3eVBE
2z9oPeSufCjQ9pS3t3P9oWfrxaRDAzUEzMkyLlyRWLqIwOqarMG2zN3VnB7Hxo/K
S+IsBKoj1PPCvNxqfpprFk+ian3s+XBX99a+o51ky8dWgR26x02LK5FOChoRIY65
OhIRhgVu8nTx5APcwnwnkXkMR1VrFVPMOOF2pQxqt6wXdJo32jymQ6dmTJnlYoEn
ju18FZXmldRfLrd09NEO4EHY1fM1fH/j2LcQXCUc+xENkfwf5X8BUEsDBBQABgAI
ALRA5B6Upqze9gAAAIUBAAALAAAAU0FNUExxFMi5UWFRNkDFuKzEMRHsBe4FUU+YD
ge+Qyu0WuQC94q4I0JS/yFlHtw/kOEEqAgT5Bm8+ijjEQXC63pRxZXfaxiQLRIWo
7h6NghGFcVCTujuuHKVmR12nxLa0fgupBjpIlC7KEMN8nk/Au6PXHQsZnPkNuym7
I0Zy8GdAfEqLMjXtOMR1fL/eJQQqaQchyyZBCpfNKPbG/x7Eu6jCauDCGJFTiorG
1L/ZT5PT1KY0n+dhmXkgOA+vW6uHZAYZmLzjTn2sny4gyzi4ydp/KvG3h2nNjIsY
tY5V1P1x+QuDylaCG/50ErwUk/87Y61tStSWIofYhkxBpym9fAFQSwMEFAAGAAgA
tEDkHpSmrN72AAAAhQEAAAsAAABTQU1QTEUzLlRYVE2QMW4rMQxEewF7gVRT5gOB
75DK7Ra5AL3irgjQ1L/IXUe3D+Q4QSoCBPkGbz6KOMRBcLrelHFld9rGJAtEhaju
Ho2CEYVxUJO6O64cpWZHXafEtrR+C6kGOkiULsoQw3yeT8T8C7o9cdCxmc+Q27Kbsj
RnLwZ0B8SosyNe04xGV8v941CqppByHLJkEK18009sb/HsS7qMJq4MIYkVOKisaU
v91Pk9OUpjSf52GZeSA4D69bq4dkBhmYvONOfayfLiDLOLjJ2n8q8beHac2Mixil
jlWU/XH5C4PKVoIb/nQSvBST/ztjrW1K1JYih9iGTEGnKb18AVBLAQIUABQABgAI
ACVD5B5BF2QRrwEAAH0CAAALAAAAAAAAAAEAIAAAAAAAAABTQU1QTEUxLkFTQ1BL
AQIUABQABgAIALRA5B6Upqze9gAAAIUBAAALAAAAAAAAAAEAIAAANgBAABTQU1Q
TEUxL1RYVFBLAQIUABQABgAIAPhE5B5H8sGYwIAAAMDAAAALAAAAAAAAAAEAIAAA
APcCAABTQU1QTEUyLkFTQ1BLAQIUABQABgAIALRA5B6Upqze9gAAAIUBAAALAAAA
AAAAAAEAIAAAAIMFAABTQU1QTEUyL1RYVFBLAQIUABQABgAIALRA5B6Upqze9gAA
AIUBAAALAAAAAAAAAAEAIAAAAAKIGAABTQU1QTEUzL1RYVFBLBQYAAAAABQAFAB0B
AADBBwAAAAA=
=Skvp
-----END PGP MESSAGE-----
```

## What Is a Common Use of Encryption?

Encryption has found a place on the information superhighway. With millions of users accessing the Internet every day, and people snooping at other's data and mail, PGP fills the need for a secure way to communicate with others without fear of snooping.

## Sources of Programs and Information

Internet newsgroups are one of the best sources of information on breaking passwords and bypassing security. One of the best sources of cracking information is alt.cracks. Another source is alt.2600. Following these groups can lead you to a wealth of software for cracking most protection schemes. If you are desperate, you can ask for information in these groups. Word your message carefully, because the participants in these groups do not look kindly on law enforcement. Make sure you do not leave any traces of your identity in your post.

Other sources are the newsgroups dedicated to the application whose protection you want to crack. These newsgroups are not quite as touchy about dealing with members of law enforcement. Finally, monitoring comp.security and comp.security.misc should be worth your time.

# Investigating Bulletin Boards

So you have decided to investigate underground bulletin board systems. With the recent proliferation of bulletin board systems, you should not have very far to look. Many bulletin board systems cater to the underground community and include hacking, phreaking, virus, anarchy, carding, and terrorism (H/P/V/A/C/T) boards. You should have no problem recognizing a board offering illegal products, services, and information. They often identify themselves in various ways by advertising "warez" (copyrighted commercial software made available via download or FTP to members) or H/P/V/A/C/T boards somewhere in their advertising.

These underground boards were very elite several years ago, requiring tremendous effort to locate. Obtaining access was very difficult and usually required a reference from another member of that particular bulletin board. With the explosive growth of the Internet and personal computers with online software, gaining access to locations catering to the underground community is fairly easy. There is a growing openness in cyberspace resulting in the distinction between bulletin boards, online services, and the Internet becoming blurred with everything focusing on the Internet. The very ease of sharing of information between the various systems makes them a large playground for criminals. You can find virtually every crime that can be committed being committed online. We have investigated pedophiles stalking children and distributing child pornography, credit-card fraud, and anarchy on the Internet, online services, and private bulletin boards. For example, look at the chat rooms on some online services and IRC (Internet relay chat) on the Internet.

This is not meant as a condemnation of cyberspace as a place inhabited solely by criminals. Some areas of cyberspace are more like the bad area of town. We tend to equate the so-called information highway with a frontier where civilization and order are not yet present. It has become a frontier civilization due to the sudden influx of a population which has changed its makeup from the intellectual forum to a more accurate reflection of our population, which means there will be a certain percentage who are criminals. If there are criminals of all types in the average city, of say, 500,000 individuals, how many criminals are there in cyberspace where there are perhaps as many as 30,000,000 (yes, millions, and still growing) people? The really strange thing about this cyber city is that it is worldwide, with virtually no rules. Legal jurisdictions do not exist, not even national boundaries. No one person, company, or government is in charge. No cops patrol the streets of this cyber city. At times it looks like total anarchy, a perfect environment for criminal predators. *Note:* For the purpose of this discussion, bulletin board systems and online services are synonymous.

## Where Do I Start?

First you need to locate online sites where illegal activity might be occurring. This is assuming you are starting your investigation cold. If you have a tip from a citizen, this step is much easier. You will find that after making a few publicized cases you will no longer have to go looking for illegal activity. Concerned citizens will begin alerting you of online crimes in your area, and your phone will not stop ringing. When this starts happening, forward your calls to a secretary.

### Download BBS Lists from Local Bulletin Boards and the Internet

On the Internet, check the USENET news groups in the alt.bbs hierarchy. Pay special attention to bulletin boards on the list which advertise maintaining bulletin board databases. Each of these bulletin boards often will have other lists of bulletin boards which have lists, and, well, you get the idea. You can usually find from 15,000 to 30,000 bulletin boards in just an hour or so of such research, and some of them will almost always lead you to illegal activity.

The following Internet news groups were found on our news server that pertain to BBS lists: alt.bbs, alt.bbs.ads, alt.bbs.allsysop, alt.bbs.doors, alt.bbs.first-class, alt.bbs.gigo-gateway, alt.bbs.internet, alt.bbs.lists, alt.bbs.lists.d, alt.bbs.majorbbs, alt.bbs.metal, alt.bbs.pcboard, alt.bbs.pcbuucp, alt.bbs.public-address, alt.bbs.searchlight, alt.bbs.unixbbs, alt.bbs.uupcb, alt.bbs.watergate, alt.bbs.wildcat, alt.bbs.wwiv.

As you can see, there are many sources of bulletin board lists and numbers. (See following samples.)

Path: zimmer!nic-nac.CSU.net!usc!howland.reston.ans.net!news.moneng.mei.com!news.ecn.bgu.edu!ixc.ixc.net!news
From: hoopla@inx.net (NiteLife Adult BBS)
Newsgroups: alt.bbs
Subject: Revolutionary New Adult BBS
Date: 13 Jul 1995 13:26:40 GMT
Organization: Intermac Corporation
Lines: 59
Sender: -Not-Authenticated-[7803]
Message-ID: <3u36ug$l82@ixc.ixc.net>
NNTP-Posting-Host: pm1-67.inx.net
X-Posted-From: InterNews 1.0.8@pm1-67.inx.net
Xdisclaimer: No attempt was made to authenticate the sender's name.

Welcome to NiteLife
A FirstClass-based Adult BBS
The No-Skanks BBS
Only $19/yr, COMPLETE access, no other charges!
Modem: (212) 740-8235

NiteLife BBS is a revolutionary new online adult service. First of all, we cost only $19 a year for FULL ACCESS, no hidden charges. Compare us to other adult services and you'll find that we have absolutely no peers. Most adult services cost in the neighborhood of around $100-200 a year; that's a far cry from our $19.

Second of all, we're committed to quality. We custom make all of our files. They're ALL in JPEG format for truer color and sharper images as well as significantly smaller file sizes for faster downloads. We also have a significant library of Quicktime video clips. These are all mostly HARDCORE adult images and clips. Our files do not have BBS labels and are freely distributable. All of our files are carefully archived with full descriptions and immediate online PREVIEWS. In all your search through the adult BBS market, you'll never find a better library than ours.

The fully multimedia and multitasking nature of the FirstClass software makes our board truly unapproachble and at an incredible price too. Join today!

For more information about joining, please call our BBS at (212) 740-8235, when connected please read the postings in the READ ME! section. If you wish to receive a free copy of the FirstClass Client, please email postmaster@intermac.com requesting either the Windows or Macintosh version.

Note: It is recommended that you either download or acquire the FirstClass Client (for Windows or Mac) because navigating this BBS is significantly easier with it. Both the Client and Settings software are available at NiteLife BBS and on America Online.

You can also use any communication program, set at N,8,1 (VT100).

Call N i t e L i f e  B B S today at 2 1 2 - 7 4 0 - 8 2 3 5 and register for a new account.

Thank you for your interest.

◇◇◇◇◇◇◇◇◇◇◇◇◇◇◇◇◇◇◇◇◇◇◇◇◇◇◇◇◇◇◇◇◇◇◇◇◇◇◇◇◇◇◇◇
N i T e L i f e  A d u l t  B B S        Intermac Corporation
A FirstClass BBS for Mac & Windows Users.   P.O. Box 140566
Modem: 212.740.8235 (8,N,1)              Staten Island, NY 10314
E-mail: hoopla@inx.net                   United States of America
◇◇◇◇◇◇◇◇◇◇◇◇◇◇◇◇◇◇◇◇◇◇◇◇◇◇◇◇◇◇◇◇◇◇◇◇◇◇◇◇◇◇◇◇

Message advertising an adult oriented BBS in the ALT.BBS news group on the Internet. This message has been edited to fit by changing the paragraph length. Notice they make their own picture files. Also notice the possibility of this BBS having Internet access.

Path: zimmer!nic-nac.CSU.net!usc!cs.utexas.edu!swrinde!emory!darwin.sura.net!mother.usf.edu!luna!jcollins
From: Jerrry CoLLiNs <jcollins@luna.cas.usf.edu>
Newsgroups: alt.bbs
Subject: 813 virus information BBS
Date: Fri, 14 Jul 1995 12:00:27 -0400
Organization: University of South Florida
Lines: 9
Message-ID: <Pine.SUN.3.91.950714115722.10668A-100000@luna>
NNTP-Posting-Host: luna.cas.usf.edu
Mime-Version: 1.0
Content-Type: TEXT/PLAIN; charset=US-ASCII
X-Sender: jcollins@luna

I ran across a BBS in the 813 area code(US) and they had quite an extensive collection of virii for educational purposes they also had lots of virii source the number is 813-920-2827

give it a call if you are interested or e-mail me for more info

Message advertising an adult oriented BBS in the ALT.BBS news group on the Internet. This message has been edited to fit by changing the paragraph length.

```
Xref: zimmer alt.sex:249845 alt.sex.motss:31110 alt.sex.homosexual:8955 alt.homosexual:47877 alt.bbs:47977 alt.bbs.ads:20872
alt.bbs.lists:13369
Message-ID: <121304Z13071995@anon.penet.fi>
Path: zimmer!csusac!charnel.ecst.csuchico.edu!olivea!spool.mu.edu!howland.reston.ans.net!EU.net!news.eunet.fi!anon.penet.fi
Newsgroups: alt.sex,alt.sex.motss,alt.sex.homosexual,alt.homosexual,alt.bbs,alt.bbs.ads,alt.bbs.lists,alt.cult.nudism,alt.sex.pedophilia
From: an266287@anon.penet.fi
X-Anonymously-To: alt.sex,alt.sex.motss,alt.sex.homosexual,alt.homosexual,alt.bbs,alt.bbs.ads,alt.bbs.lists,alt.cult.nudism,alt.sex.pedophilia
Organization: Anonymous forwarding service
Reply-To: an266287@anon.penet.fi
Date: Thu, 13 Jul 1995 12:03:49 UTC
Subject: Gay/Bisexual BBS with smooth/YOUNG guys!!!
Lines: 22


Finally!  A BBS for guys who like their men young and smooth!  Over 95% of our on-line pictures are of guys under 21!!!!!

Give us a call:

Electronic Male BBS
1-812-333-1912 -- 14.4K BPS
1-812-333-2937 -- 28.8K BPS

When on the BBS, leave a feedback message to the system operator mentioning the keyword 'chicken' to receive an initial 5 megs of downloading
credits!

We are NOT on the internet, you MUST have a modem and computer in order to use this service.

--------------------------------------------------------
To find out more about the anon service, send mail to help@anon.penet.fi.
If you reply to this message, your message WILL be *automatically* anonymized
and you are allocated an anon id. Read the help file to prevent this.
Please report any problems, inappropriate use etc. to admin@anon.penet.fi.
```

Message advertising an adult oriented BBS in the ALT.BBS news group on the Internet. The last paragraph in the message tells you it has passed through an anonymous message server. Finding the original sending ID of this message might require a court order from a Finnish court. This message has been edited to fit by changing the paragraph length.

```
Newsgroups: alt.bbs
Path: zimmer!csusac!csus.edu!netcom.com!instant
From: an139972@anon.penet.fi (Instant)
Subject: Online Orgasm
Message-ID: <steinwayDBow8H.6Mz@netcom.com>
Keywords: Adult Orgasm BBS
Sender: steinway@netcom15.netcom.com
Organization: NETCOM On-line Communication Services (408 261-4700 guest)
X-Newsreader: News Xpress Version 1.0 Beta #1
Date: Fri, 14 Jul 1995 05:04:16 GMT
Lines: 8

Ready for something exciting? looking for something different?
You should give our system a call... (404) 840-0907
We have over 30,000 adult Images, Animations, Games, and Erotic text files and we are in the process of installing a teleconferencing system so
that you can see and talk to beautiful women and have them do what ever you ask... Check us out!
```

Message advertising an adult oriented BBS in the ALT.BBS news group on the Internet. This message has been edited to fit.


## Subscribe to *Boardwatch* Magazine

*Boardwatch*, a monthly publication, features bulletin board systems all over the world. They publish lists of BBS and lists of systems that keep lists.

## Refer to Local Merchants

Check local bookstores, adult bookstores, magazine distributors, and smoke and curio shops for free newspapers, "zines" (cyberculture magazines), and regular cultural papers. Many of these sources have articles or advertising for colorful and even underground BBS which may advertise their illegal bent.

## Check for Strange Names

Look for BBS names that are satanic in nature, are typical of the H/P lifestyle, such as those using LaRgE and sMaLl letters in the same word or using "ph" in place of "f" in spelling common words (such as phun for fun) or those advertising or seeming to advocate illegal activity. This typing style is common for people wanting to be part of the underground cyberculture.

## Look for "Adult" Picture Collections

Look for BBS that advertise large collections of "young GIFs" or have sexually explicit questionnaires with questions asking about being under the legal age for sexual activity. Most of these picture collections are of people who just look like children. The only way to find out what is criminal and what is not is to download the pictures and have them analyzed by an expert in child development, usually a pediatrician.

## Law Enforcement Restrictions

Look for law enforcement disclaimers and banners which give warning to law enforcement agents or government employees. These banners say they must identify themselves as law enforcement or be subject to civil and criminal penalties. Some even challenge or threaten law enforcement if they attempt to access the board. Some may even state that members of law enforcement and other government agencies may not use the system at all. Many computerized criminals still have the idea that law enforcement people must identify themselves during investigations when asked if they are police or the case becomes entrapment. *Ignorance is bliss.* Let's just leave them ignorant.

## Meeting the Sysop

Be suspicious of BBS requirements to meet the sysop before they allow you access. Some of the more elite boards may want you to commit witnessed illegal or immoral acts before admittance to the board. These types of boards are a little more difficult to find.

## System Passwords

Be suspicious of BBS that demand the secret "system" password when you begin the login.

## Affiliations and References

Be suspicious of BBS that want your affiliation, the names of other boards you are on, or who referred you.

## Regular Systems with Restricted Areas

Bulletin boards where special areas are available only by meeting the sysop should always throw up a flag in your mind. This might be an indication of questionable activity.

## Prying Questionnaires

Distributing questionnaires regarding involvement in illegal activity such as hacking/phreaking or explicit sexual acts and preferences normally is not appropriate. You would think the sexual types of questionnaires would stop their line of questioning once a user states they are under age. The upstanding system will cut off underage users if it caters only to adults. If you go through a questionnaire as a minor and find the questions getting really personal, you might want to look into the system a little more.

## Frequent Chatting

Bulletin boards where the sysop breaks in during the login to question you about where you found the BBS number, system password, your sexual preferences, the meanings of underground acronyms, and other under-ground related activities are not normal. If this happens, you have stumbled upon either a new system or one that needs looking into further.

## Regular Systems with Many Users Online Simultaneously

Family-oriented systems such Prodigy, America Online, and Compuserve can have a dark side. Check activity in the areas designated for children. Some-times you might find topics for discussing alternate lifestyles or junior hack-ers. These areas may discuss the transfer of stolen or fraudulent credit card information and phone calling card information. Many adults pretend to be children to meet children for sex in areas such as these. Look for the exchange of pornography and sexually explicit mail or chat.

These few (well, more than a few) ideas are more than you need to get the hang of finding bulletin board systems that cater to the computer underground.

Finding things such as kiddie porn pictures might take a little digging, but they are there waiting for you to see.

## Initiating the Investigation

What would possess someone to start investigating a BBS of their own free will? Maybe someday the world will know. Brain damage? Delirium? Self-destructive tendencies? We just do not know. We sometimes suffer from the desire to investigate underground BBS systems ourselves. Sometimes the challenge, excitement, and pain are too much to resist. Warning — before you start, be aware of the pitfalls involved. Make sure your legal advisor is available to help with the legal challenges you will face and that your management understands what you are doing and supports the endeavor. There will be problems, complaints, and law suits filed against the investigator of these types of cases. Do not be hanging out there on your own without agency support. We will cover more of the dangers to investigators later in this chapter.

When you find BBS or areas on the Internet that appear suspicious, the next step is to establish your probable cause. If you do not find probable cause on one system, you can move onto another suspicious BBS and continue your search. This makes it easier to keep your undercover role intact. If you constantly change your focus and get involved with people online, you open yourself to additional mistakes and possibly giving yourself away, by omissions or slips.

Keep in mind that online investigations are not for everyone. Even those who have a gift for this type of investigation are not always good when they first start. Like everything else, practice makes perfect. To start out, try poking around various BBS, getting a feel for the way they look and work; try downloading information and sending messages to other members and the sysop. If you enjoy and understand what you are doing, you stand a good chance of being successful at online investigations. If you have problems that you cannot overcome, do not get discouraged; online investigations may not be your thing. Remember, this is role playing just like any other undercover operation. You must stay in character and not give yourself away.

## Tips to Avoid Traps, Snares and Pitfalls

From experience we have learned how to avoid certain errors we have made during investigations when we testify in court. Since computer crime investigation is new ground, we have made many errors in the eyes of the court. Thankfully, none of our errors has been devastating. Ways to avoid these errors are presented in the interest of your protection. When prosecuting an online case, a good defense attorney can seriously confuse a judge or jury as to certain aspects of your investigation by using accurate or inaccurate terminology or jargon. To help avoid this problem, keep some of the following suggestions in mind:

## Do Not Use ANSI Graphics

ANSI graphics may look good on the screen (if the creator of those graphics did a good job and has some artistic talent) but they take too much room on paper and do not print well. ANSI graphics have another common use by those who would damage computer systems and protect their own system: the ANSI bomb. Using ANSI escape codes, the suspect can reprogram the keyboard of the viewing computer to call a virus or format the hard drive. Always use a file viewer such as LIST (shareware) or XTreePro Gold™ to view text and binary files. This will protect you from any ANSI bomb. Remember: TYPE is not your type of viewer. ANSI bombs are not a problem while online. Communications software have their own ANSI graphics handlers.

## Playing the Role

There are many aspects to playing an undercover role while online; these may take months to master, if they can be mastered at all.

### Develop a "Biography"

Create a biography for the people (roles) you use in each investigation. List all personal information including your name, age, birthday, address, phone, other BBS you belong to, your knowledge of computers, your typing and spelling ability, friends, family members — anything and everything you need to remember what you tell people to appear as a real and consistent person. Log all the information you give out about your self on this biography. You never know when someone will remember when you went on vacation, where you attend school, and who your friends are. If you keep a log, this information is immediately available during later sessions when questions about your character comes up. See examples.

### Use Multiple Personalities When Working a Case

Make multiple biographies and use them to befriend and confirm each other on the BBS. At other times they may spar and get upset with one another. You may lose one or two during the course of an investigation. That's okay — if you have others in the works. Make sure you do not log on with each character in the same order each time, to avoid generating any suspicion.

## Use Multiple Investigators

The use of multiple investigators using multiple unique biographies, particularly if they are separated geographically, can relax suspicions and aid the speed of user acceptance and the gathering of evidence. A user calling from another city or state precludes the growing use of personal verification, where the sysop asks to meet the perspective members in person before allowing access to sensitive files.

## Know your Subject

Be it pedophilia (child-sex crimes), hacking, phreaking, credit fraud, counterfeiting, or Satanism, know what you are talking about. Know and use the language (jargon) of that particular crowd. If you are impersonating a homosexual pedophile, you should know what "bear" and "cub" mean. Do not bluff unless you have no choice. If you get caught bluffing, do not panic. Say you saw the terms elsewhere and thought they meant something else. Often the role of a beginner or naive novice works best, as most suspects want to brag about their knowledge to those with less experience. Some may also want to be your mentor.

## Identifying People during "Chat"

Several keys will eliminate confusion in identifying who said what (kind of like "Who's on First") during online chat sessions. Some programs (such as IRC or AOL Chat) make it easy by identifying who is typing. Frequently using the name of your suspect combined with always ending your paragraphs by hitting the enter key twice is a good way to distinguish your typing from your suspect's. This is also a commonly accepted way to participate in an online chat.

## Use of Terminal Software

Use terminal software that does not save ASCII control characters to the Capture file. For example, Procomm Plus saves every keystroke including back spaces, deletions and corrections caused by you, the suspect, and the bulletin board software. This makes for a very hard-to-read capture file and creates problems during testimony in court. The jury may have difficulty reading the printed files and determining who said what during a bulletin board chat. See below for an example. The ideal software will save what you see as a final product on the screen during chat mode conversations. See the example.

## Videotape Key Online Sessions

Using a video camera, you can capture the screen and keyboard as a chat or IRC session progresses. You can also make verbal comments on the tape to help during your review later. The videotape gives the investigator an eye witness (the tape) later in court. Just be careful of the audio comments you make, as they might be used against you during the trial or in the resulting civil suit.

### Make your Typing Different from Theirs

To help identify who is typing, use a typing style different from the person you are typing to. This can be as simple as making your case different. If the person you are typing to is using mixed case (the proper way of typing), you might use all upper or lower case. See the BBS Chat sample for additional information.

### Be Careful about What You Say to Other Users

Sysops often play multiple roles on their own BBS. Do not place your trust in anyone online while you are conducting an investigation.

### Keep your Language Consistent

If using street language or jargon, make sure you know the proper way to use each term you choose. Be consistent in their use. Obvious switching between language styles may give you away.

### Be Consistent in Typing Techniques and Spelling

If you are a beginning typist, stay that way. If you misspell words and use lots of typos, be consistent with that character. If you slip and get caught, mention you have been practicing with a typing tutor or something like that.

### Always Use a Capture or Log File

Your communications software creates log files and capture files. They record online activity between your computer and the remote system. How much information is contained in a capture or log file depends on the communications software. Some programs will capture every character that comes across the modem, while others will only capture plain ASCII text without any backspace or control characters. Confirm that your modem software is set up with a unique capture file name for each day or session. For example: 090393.cap or sept9-1.cap, sept9-2.cap, sept9-2.cap.

### Keep Up with Your Paperwork

When a session is finished, edit a *copy* of your capture file and identify who typed everything in the file. You can do this by using **bold** and <u>underline</u> or a combination of both. Do this immediately after you finish the session. Keep your reports up to date, showing the start and finish times and synopsis of that session's activity. Be sure to keep the original capture file unedited. The edited copy is for your use during the investigation and in court as part of your notes. Some cases have gone to court one to two years after the arrest. We always appreciate having little memory joggers. Keep in mind you might be altering original evidence if you modify the capture file and do not have a copy.

BBS Chat Sample

---

You are now in CHAT mode:

I've been watching you for a few minutes.

HOW CAN YOU DO THAT, MARK?

The BBS lets me look at everything going on all the time.

WOW! THAT'S GREAT! SO YOU CAN ALWAYS SEE WHAT I'M DOING?

Yea. I can do anything I want on this system. I can cut users off, I can change access levels and I can send messages. Great power. What a trip.

WOW! CAN ANYONE ELSE DO THAT BESIDES YOU?

No. Just me. By the way, you should not use all upper case. It is considered shouting. Use mixed case.

SORRY. WHEN I USE UPPER AND LOWER CASE I GET CONFUSED. I HOPE THIS IS OK.

Sure, no problem. If anyone else gives you any trouble, ignore them. If you have a problem, I'll take care of it for you.

THANKS. I APPRECIATE IT.

Well, I'll let you get back to using the BBS. I'll even give you a little more time on the system to look around.

THANKS. I'LL TALK TO YOU LATER.

Bye.

CHAT END.

Your time has been increased by 10 minutes.

---

### Use a COOL Phone Line

Every BBS we have encountered has requested a phone number for voice verification. Some are even asking for a phone number to do an automated callback verification where the BBS computer immediately calls you back. You will need to have one or two phone numbers available to give your suspect that they can call for verification. These phone numbers must not have a standard government prefix; this is a dead giveaway to the paranoid suspect. Some systems will not allow the same number to be used more than once, so do not plan on your single data line to work all the time. Consider forwarding other phones to yours for systems requiring a unique phone number.

## Obtain Adequate Identification

Identification may be in the form of driver's licenses, social security numbers, and credit references. School identification or other employment records may be necessary, depending on the character you are playing. Be sure that actual records are created in case the suspects attempt to verify your employment, school, or credit.

## Use Secure Credit

Some BBS want you to purchase a membership, time, pictures, or software over the computer. The most common method of payment is by credit card. If you choose to use a credit card, make sure the credit card cannot be traced back to the agency you work for or any of its employees. Another secure method of payment would be by money order. Both methods allow for fraudulent names yet maintain a trail of evidence.

## Use a Secure Address

Almost every BBS you encounter will want an address for their records. Sometimes a post office box is acceptable, but other times they require a real address. This address should not be related to your agency or any of its members. The general thought among computer criminals requesting information on your address is "No one lives in a P.O. Box."

## Have Voices Available

When impersonating a minor, a woman (sorry, ladies, we're assuming the male point of view), or someone you are not on a bulletin board, you will need to have someone with an appropriate voice to answer the phone for a voice verification. The person can say something like "My [blank] does not like me to use the phone … " to minimize the time spent on the phone with the suspect. Substitute wife, husband, parents, or whatever fits for [blank]. This person might be an officer or an informant or a private citizen. In any case, be sure to brief them thoroughly on their role, the biography designed for them, their manner of speech, and their level of knowledge. They should read the related capture files for the investigation to be able to speak appropriately when being verified by phone.

## Use Multiple Lines When Possible

Having multiple phone lines is common for a bulletin board. This allows a number of people to log onto the BBS at the same time. Some lines may be reserved for members and other special people. This can be useful by allowing you to have another officer on the BBS while you are also on to get messages from the sysop that may help your case.

### Use an Offline Mail Reader

Download your mail and prepare replies using an offline mail reader for later uploading to save time and avoid prolonged conversations with persons who are not your targets. You can use several programs to do this. Offline mail readers can be found on almost any BBS. Some systems (such as Wildcat) include the offline feature. The most popular offline reader format is QWK. Depending on the offline format, you may need to have several readers in your collection.

### Calling Hours

Take into account the type of case and your biography when determining how often and during what hours  to call the suspect BBS. Each character may be different. If you are portraying a child in school, keep track of when vacation starts and ends. Also make sure you are not available when you are supposed to be in class or sleeping.

## Identifying Your Suspect Before Arrest

### *Use Surveillance*

The only way you may be sure of the identity of the person you are chatting with on the computer is to have a surveillance team keeping an eye on who is coming and going from the location in question. Identification of the person actually using the bulletin board is one of the points the defense attorney will bring up when questioning your investigation. An accurate surveillance log is imperative. One person should keep the log throughout the investigation.

Get as much personal information from the suspect(s) as possible over the computer. This information can be corroborated from other sources.

1. Name: "Hi, who is this?"
2. Age or birthday: "My birthday is February 21; when is yours?"
3. Mailing addresses for pictures and/or personal letters; "I've got some cool pictures for you to scan. Where can I send them?"
4. Copy of preference, date, and log in scripts in which the suspect(s) describes themselves.
5. Personal talk about jobs, prior addresses, and family members.

### Routine Sources of Information

1. Department of Motor Vehicles (driver's license, a photograph, and prints)
2. Criminal history records
3. Utilities
   a. Gas
   b. Water
   c. Garbage
   d. Telephone subscriber information

4. Credit Bureaus
   a. CBI
   b. TRW
   c. Trans Union
5. Skip trace databases, i.e., CDB Infotek, Info America
   a. National phone directory
   b. National moving directory
   c. National subscriber information
   d. Criminal and civil filings
   e. Bankruptcy records
   f. Secretary of State records (corporations, limited partnerships)
   g. Real property
   h. Social Security tracking
   i. Change of address with 5 to 30 neighbors and their addresses, phone numbers, average income, and much more
   j. Birth, marriage, divorce and death records
6. Voter registration records

## Identifying the Suspects During Service of Arrest and Search Warrants

1. When possible, set up a reason to meet face to face, i.e., "date" with a pedophile, exchange of software or equipment with a hacker, drug buy or sale of chemicals with dealers, exchange of credit cards or related materials with fraud suspects.
   a. Pick a place providing good surveillance visibility.
   b. Pick a place that is quiet enough for recording equipment to work well.
   c. Pick a time and place where there are few people, yet your surveillance will not stand out.
2. Conduct surveillance before the meeting until suspect is in custody. *Note:* Be alert for counter surveillance.
3. Use video and audio tape of the meeting with suspect when possible.
4. Obtain evidence and statements from suspect during the meet which show intent to commit criminal acts.
5. Videotape and photograph the bulletin board location. Evidence which corroborates information you have already received may show up on film. A picture of a padlock on a bedroom door has saved us in court.
6. Interview other building occupants regarding ownership and use of the computer system.
7. Check documents, clothing, pictures, and other personal items in the room where the computer is located to figure out who uses the room and computer.
8. Check the computer software for any indication of ownership and use of the computer. It is possible you may find pirated software. Do not use the suspect's computer for this step; only check the registration documents.

## Cautions and Warnings

1. The possibility of counter surveillance

2. Caller identification capability, a feature implemented in some areas by the telephone company that reveals the phone number of the calling party
3. The use by suspects of multiple identities, just as the investigators are doing
4. Protection of the investigator's identity
5. Targeting of investigators after the arrest

## Investigators' Vulnerability (Sources of Personal Information)

1. Driver's license
2. Vehicle registration
3. Voter registration
4. Property ownership/tax rolls
5. Credit applications/inquiries
6. Telephone listing
7. Court records
8. Utility records
9. Insider information
10. Skip trace databases/subscription information

## Suggested Steps for Protecting Investigators

1. Use a P.O. Box for mail.
2. Use unlisted phone number.
3. Notify the Department of Motor Vehicles of your wish to not be on file.
4. Request that utility companies do not disclose subscriber information about your file.
5. Request credit reporting agencies to place an "alert" on your file to make your personal information unavailable and to contact you in case of an inquiry.

## Problems Encountered On One Pedophile Case

1. Telephone death threats
2. Computer (BBS) threats
3. Harassing phone calls (hundreds)
4. Five Internal affairs complaints
5. Complaints to district attorney, state attorney general, and FBI
6. Surveillance of officer
7. Videotaping of officer off duty (of officer giving presentation in church on subject of "dangers of unsupervised use of computers by juveniles")
8. Videocopied and sent to militant groups
9. Multimillion dollar civil suits filed
10. Tremendous media exposure initiated by suspects
11. Hate mail posted on Internet resulting in many phone calls
12. Investigator's plane tickets canceled by computer
13. Extensive files made on investigators and witnesses, including the above computerized information: name, address, spouse, date of birth, physical, civil suits, vehicle description, and license number
14. Above information posted on BBS

15. Witnesses' houses put up for sale and the bill for advertising sent to witnesses' home addresses by suspects
16. Witnesses receiving deliveries of products not ordered, with threatening notes inside
17. Hundreds of people receiving personal invitations to a witness's home for a barbecue (Put out by computer)

And much more ! After 18 months of this, when all was said and done, the suspect was sentenced to 6 years, 4 months in state prison. All the complaints against the investigator were found to be unfounded, and the investigator was exonerated of any wrong doing.

# "Elite Acronyms"

# 12

Hackers and phreakers (H/P) often refer to themselves as "elite", meaning they know more about the computer or telephone system than other people. They are probably right for the most part, as the H/P scene is their life. They refer to others as "lamers" and often screen the lamers (like cops) by asking for definitions of elite acronyms when someone signs onto an H/P/V/A/C/T bulletin board. To aid in the pursuit of criminal investigations into the elite scene, we include a few of the most common acronyms used by the "elite". More extensive lists are available on the Internet in the news groups under alt.2600 and other H/P titled areas, as well as on many "elite" BBS.

| | |
|---|---|
| AAB | Amazing Astrofest Bunch |
| AB2 | Anarchy Burger ][ |
| ACE | Arcane Corporate Elite |
| ACID | ANSI Creators in Demand |
| AE | ASCII Express |
| AFC | ANSI Factory |
| AHP | AcidHell Productions |
| AI | Artificial Intelligence |
| ALF | Anarchist's Liberation Front |
| AMIS | Atari Message and Information System |
| AMP | Ampere |
| ANI | Automatic Number Indentifier |
| BAD | Bitchin' ANSI Designers |
| BVN | Banned Vision |
| CBX | Cybrix |
| CCI | Cyber Crime International |
| CF | Cyber Force |
| CIP | CiPHER |
| CPU | Central Processing Unit |

| | |
|---|---|
| CTR | Contour |
| CUD | Computer Underground Digest |
| DDD | Dr. Death & Darkhawk |
| DMP | Dual Mod Player |
| DOD | Drink or Die |
| DOM | Dominators |
| DSP | Dead Smoking Punx |
| ECR | Electronic Rats |
| ETE | Eternity |
| EXT | Extortion PCBoard Magazine |
| FDN | Foundation |
| FLT | Fairflight |
| FSH | Flash |
| FTH | Faith |
| HEMP | Hardcore ELITE Mother Phuckers |
| ICE | Insane Creators Enterprise |
| INC | International Network of Crackers |
| IND | Independent |
| ITU | Infinity Trainers Unlimited |
| LGD | Legend Production |
| LOD | Legion of Doom |
| LOP | Lamers of Power |
| MP | Micro Pirates |
| MSI | More Stupid Initials |
| NCA | Number Calling Area |
| NEUA | National Elite Underground Alliance |
| NT | Needful Things |
| NTA | Nocturnal Trading Alliance |
| NUAA | National Underground Application Alliance |
| NX | Nexus |
| OTL | Outlaws |
| PBX | Private Branch Exchange |
| PCI | Power Crisis International |
| PE | Public Enemy |
| PHT | Phantasm |
| PIL | Pirates in Legion |
| PLC | POLICE |
| PSD | Psycho Squad |
| PSY | Psychosis |
| PTG | Pentagram |
| PW | Physical Wish |
| PWA | Pirates with Attitude |

| | |
|---|---|
| RISC | Rise in Superior Couriering |
| RZR | Razor 1911 |
| SIN | Software Innovation Network |
| SNB | Stones 'n' Bones |
| SWAT | Special Warez Acquisition Team |
| TDT | The Dream Team |
| TERR | TERRATRON |
| TFC | The Future Crew |
| TFYC | The Fuck You Crew |
| THG | The Humble Guys |
| THP | The Hill People |
| TOAO | The One And Only |
| TRI | Trinity |
| TRIC | The Really Insane Couriers |
| TRSI | TriStar & Red Sector |
| TSAN | The Sysop Association Network |
| TSD | The Shining Darkness |
| UHG | Ultimate Hacking Group |
| UID | Utilities in Demand |
| UNT | Untouchables |
| UTG | United Traders of Germany |
| VS | Virtual Shock |
| WC | Wild Cards |
| WSIWYG | What You See Is What You Get |
| WW | Wankers of Wimbledon |
| WWC | World-Wide Couriers |

# Networks

# 13

## I think I might need some help!

Many of your investigations will involve networks. We have great confidence in this statement. Many homes and most small businesses now have two or more computers. A computer connected to the Internet is considered networked. The printers, modems, and tape drives are important and often shared components in networking. A drop in the price of network cards and the advent of inexpensive, easy-to-install networking software has made networking for the masses possible.

Finding a network can be an added blessing or a tremendous curse. How the network has been configured and used will determine just how much of a blessing or a curse you must deal with when locating files of evidentiary value. Networks usually mean several people can use the same data storage from many different computers in many different locations; these may be in the same room, same floor, or same building. Network access in the same building is considered a local area network, or LAN. When access extends beyond the building, it is considered a remote or wide area network (WAN). Remote access means the interconnected computers can be anywhere in the world. With the ever-increasing speed of data communications, remote users (employees working at home or in distant offices) are becoming commonplace. Federal incentives exist for companies to reduce the driving employees do by encouraging them to telecommute. This involves setting up a computer at the employee's home and connecting it to the company network by high-speed modem.

## Network Ups and Downs

The downside to investigating networks involved in crimes includes:

- Difficulty in determining who had (or has) access to certain data
- Difficulty in securing multiple computers at multiple sites
- Difficulty in isolating and securing servers at multiple sites
- Large data storage capability
- Ease with which a remote user can completely wipe out all the data concerning your case
- Ease with which data that can be used as evidence can be hidden
- Large wire centers
- Additional expertise required
- Jurisdictional problems for large networks

The upside to investigating networks involved in crimes includes:

- Ease of determining who had access to certain data through built-in security
- Probability of regular backups
- The possibility of online surveillance of suspect activity
- Existing experts on staff
- Centralized data storage on servers

You might have noticed similar items on both lists. The variable that determines which list your situation falls under depends on the type of installation, network software, and the skills of the network administrator or installer. If good network security exists, the network just might be a blessing. If the security is terrible, you might not be able to accurately determine who created, edited, or deleted the data you are depending upon for evidence. You might be fortunate enough to have access to a networking expert who can make heads or tails out of the suspect system and who might be able to accurately narrow down your suspect. Also, software products are available that provide complete audit trails for those who access the network and specific files. This software will even tell you from which computer they accessed the network; this by itself can help identify your suspect. Network operating systems allow access rights to files and directories to be assigned by the network administrator, a fact which may also help you narrow down the possible suspects. System audit trails might also be available to track access by time and individual computer.

Jurisdictional problems come into play when you find evidence of a crime being committed on a computer network and the server is in another jurisdiction or where part of your evidence is stored in another jurisdiction. In cases like these, you may encounter resistance from your administration, since this situation tends to increase the cost of the investigation in both dollars and the time needed. Even worse, the location of the evidence could be in another country, where the deed is not even considered a crime. This would leave you and your case out in the cold.

## Network Parts and Pieces

Simply defined, networks are groups of computers linked together to share programs and data. This sharing can be word processing, database, spread sheets, electronic mail, World Wide Web pages, and Internet news. There are many types of networks, but they all have many aspects in common. Many terms specific to networking that you will encounter are discussed at the end of this chapter. You do not have to know them all, but a basic understanding will be useful when talking to witnesses, suspects, and informants who are familiar with networks.

### Servers

Think of a server as a waiter or waitress at a restaurant. They ask what you want, then get it for you if they can. Servers are computers which a person does not normally use; the computers may even be in closets and are set up to perform specific functions while unattended.

#### File Servers

A file server is a computer that services requests from other computers on the network for information stored on the server's one or more hard drives. A small server might have a 300-MB hard drive or a large disk array capable of holding hundreds of gigabytes, depending on its purpose. Servers might also have CD-ROM drives for sharing CDs across the network. File servers usually need a large amount of RAM proportional to the capacity of the installed hard drives. In large servers, you may see more than 100 MB of RAM. Do not be intimidated by these large amounts of RAM. You can conduct your investigation without as much RAM in your investigative computer.

#### Print Servers

Print servers are common in networks of all sizes. Print servers allow any type of printer — laser, matrix or ink jet — or a plotter to be attached directly to the network. All authorized users on the entire network can share these printers. This information might be useful if, say, your suspect is printing fraudulent checks or currency on a color printer. Using the network security, an expert could probably help you determine who has access to that particular printing device.

## Database Servers

Database servers are used to support client-server systems. This means you need special software to access the data on the server, as opposed to accessing data on a file server by looking at the directory. Since special software is needed to access the data on a database server, you can probably narrow down the possible suspects by determining who has access to the database server and the special software required to access the data on that server. To make a determination like this, you will need the help of an expert to decipher the software used on each networked computer.

## Tape Servers

Tape servers allow the use of multiple tape drives in a single server-type machine to back up multiple file servers, database servers, and workstations on a network. Tape servers are mostly found on large networks with many other servers. The software used to run the tape drives on a tape server usually will keep very detailed records of the files backed up during each backup job for each device. These logs may provide a clue about how long certain activities have been going on. Your best chance to reveal this information is to enlist the help of an on-site networking expert, if one is available and can be trusted.

## Routers

A router is a device used to connect multiple network topologies. This may sound complicated and highly technical, but the concept is fairly simple. Think of a router as a traffic signal controlling traffic coming from foot trails, roads of assorted sizes, superhighways, and airports. When someone coming from a foot trail wants to get on the superhighway, they are given a high-speed car. When they want to fly, they get a plane.

When you find a router in a network, you will need to immediately evaluate some additional possibilities. A router might be providing access to the Internet. This would mean your suspect's data could be anywhere in the world. Usually, a router is used to connect large networks. Branch offices connect to the main office using routers and various telecommunications devices to exchange all types of data. Many routers look like servers or regular personal computers. To make any sense of an active router, you will need to consult someone with experience in complex networks.

## Gateways

A gateway is used to connect one type of system to a totally different type of system. A gateway is used to connect networks to mainframes and minicomputers. This connection usually allows the computers on the network to emulate terminals on the mainframe or minicomputer connecting the two. Gateways add another layer of complexity to an investigation involving a minicomputer or mainframe, because suspects can access the larger system from anywhere on the network. Isolating access points to the mainframe may be a little harder depending on the security established on the gateway.

## Types of Networks

### Server Based

Server-based networks have at least one computer acting as a file server. The file server computer runs the network operating system and usually has a large hard drive. This computer holds all the shared data and programs for all users on the network. What you should know as an investigator is that most (if not all) the data you need for your investigation will be stored on a file server.

### Peer to Peer

Peer-to-Peer networks generally do not have a dedicated file; they use the resources of each workstation to provide shared programs and data to all other computers on the LAN. To an investigator, peer-to-peer networks add another level of complexity because the data you need might be on any of the peer computers set up as a peer server. The flip side to this is that access can be controlled. With the access control information, an expert may be able to tell you who has access to what and where.

### Bulletin Board Systems

Bulletin board systems (BBS) have become a very popular way to communicate. They usually do not charge a fee for access and provide a great deal of public domain and shareware software. Graphic images also have become extremely popular. These graphic images range from cartoons to photographs to pornography. Many bulletin board systems connect to each other over the telephone system. Special networks have been designed by those participating in bulletin board systems as a hobby that simplify the transfer of electronic mail and data. These transfers generally take place at night when the phone rates are low and the callers are usually in bed sleeping. Refer to Chapter 11 for the potential legal problems of dealing with private mail and confidential files.

## Physical Connections

Physical connections refer to the "wire" used to connect computers. Cables can alert you to the presence of networking. You should be familiar with the types of networks, hardware, and cabling for networks. These can show the number of servers, the number of users, and the distance between components of the network. Thus, your search might be of a single room, as often happens with two computers using peer-to-peer networking software and connected by thin Ethernet cabling, sharing a single printer. The other extreme might be when there are multiple servers, including mainframes, PC servers with routers, bridges, fiber optic cabling with modem racks, microwaves, and hundreds of connections to users, and when the information you are seeking could be hundreds of yards or thousands of miles away. The following are some examples of networking connections and systems with which you, as a computer investigator, should be familiar.

### Modems

The word "modem" stands for modulator/demodulator. Simply put, this device converts signals the computer understands (digital signals) into signals the telephone system understands (analog signals) and back again. Current technology allows for very high-speed data transfer rates using modems.

### Dedicated Modems

The fastest modems used on networks use dedicated telephone lines. Dedicated lines you are likely to encounter are 56-KB, Fractional T1, and T1. These modems only slightly resemble the standard modems you see on personal computers; they usually are larger and have more lights and buttons on the front.

### ARCnet

ARCnet was the first popular network topology. It provides a data transfer rate of 2 Mb/s (megabits per second, or, 2 million characters every 8 seconds). This topology can support 255 concurrent computers. ARCnet uses RG62 coax cable and can go as far as 2000 feet. The popularity of ARCnet has fallen almost to the point of extinction.

### Ethernet

Ethernet is the most popular network topology. Ethernet provides a data transfer rate of 10 Mb/s (or 10 million characters every 8 seconds). This topology has a limit of several thousand concurrent connections, but to maintain good speeds it is usually limited to between 40 and 100. Standard Ethernet is very affordable. Ethernet interface cards cost less than $20, which has helped it become the most popular network topology in use today.

### Thick-net

Thick-net is used for areas with excessive interference that might disable network communications. Thick-net uses RG8 coax cable and can go as far as 1800 feet. Due to the high cost of buying and installing this cable, it is mainly used for noisy buildings and for linking buildings that are close to each other.

### Thin-net

Thin-net is used for close areas and areas where interference is not a problem. Thin-net uses RG58 coax cable and has a maximum distance of 600 feet.

### 10Base-T

10Base-T is another form of Thin-net and uses unshielded, twisted-pair cable instead of coax. 10Base-T cabling runs from the workstation site to a central wiring box call a hub or concentrator. 10Base-T is somewhat more expensive than Thin-net, but the added cost can provide some very worthwhile benefits that are helpful in large networks. As you can see in Figure 48, the wire centers for a 10Base-T network can be intimidating; a good network specialist can help you make sense out of situations like these.

## Token Ring

Token ring has been around for quite some time but has not found acceptance like Ethernet because of its high cost and proprietary nature (IBM). Token ring is gaining in acceptance as additional manufacturers produce interface cards and wire centers. Traditionally, Token ring was found in IBM shops where a mainframe was found. Now, it is found in small networks, process control systems, and regular businesses.

Token ring comes in different speeds and cable types. Typical speeds are 4 and 16 Mb/s; higher speeds are being developed. Cable types include shielded and unshielded twisted pair and fiber optics. The connector for a Token ring interface card is a nine-pin connector resembling an EGA connector for the shielded, twisted-pair cable, an RJ-45 connector for the unshielded, twisted-pair, and the standard connector for fiber optic cable.

Figure 49 shows a small portion of a Token ring network using shielded, twisted-pair cable. The cables are plugged into a smart MAU (multistation access unit) that can be controlled remotely. Figure 50 shows the basics required to start a network using Token ring, including two network interface

**Figure 48**
A medium-to-large sized LAN running over 10Base-T Ethernet might have a wire center such as this.

cards; shielded, twisted-pair cable; and an IBM 8228 MAU. Figure 51 shows a wire center that includes Token ring.

## Microwave

Developments in microwave technology have created opportunities in networking for linking networks a distance of up to 16 miles, while achieving the full standard Ethernet speed of 10 Mb/s for less than $30,000. Microwave technology usually can be recognized by circular antennas ranging from 17 to 30 inches in diameter mounted on top of buildings or towers.

If you do not see a microwave dish on the roof of a site you are investigating, the computer room should have some definite signs of the presence of a microwave system. Since these systems are not common, the equipment

**Figure 49**
Token ring MAU using shielded twisted pair cable. Similar connections may be found in offices as plugs on the wall when the building is properly wired for the network.

used to service the microwave probably will say "microwave" on it in at least one visible area. The connection between the microwave system and the network will be through regular network topology. Older microwave systems act like fast modems and connect directly to a server or a router. In the upper right corner of Figure 51 is equipment used to support a microwave data communications system. The entire figure features a complex wire center.

## Integrated Services Digital Network

Integrated Services Digital Network (ISDN) is a new service being offered by telephone companies that provides a true digital interface from a home or office to the telephone system. ISDN has some developing data communications applications, but is not available in all areas at this time. The equipment used for ISDN communications is similar to that used on regular telephone lines with one major exception: the digital signal from the computer equipment does not need to be converted into sound to travel over the phone system; the ISDN phone system is already digital. A digital phone system is a better channel for data communications, since the data does not have to be changed from digital to analog and back again. Caution needs to be taken with ISDN. Do not, under any circumstances, plug your analog modem into a digital phone line; you might burn out your modem and not

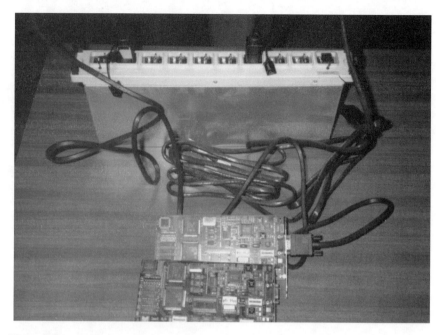

**Figure 50**
Using a portable MAU, cables, and Token ring cards, the authors can back up several computers at a time to a portable fileserver.

even know it. Most ISDN lines use an RJ-45 connector so it should be easy to avoid damaging your equipment.

## Operating Systems

Having all the hardware is nice; you might even say it is required. But that is not all you need for networking; you also need software. The software needed to make a network function is called the network operating system (NOS). This may be a dedicated software package or part of a desktop operating system. Larger networks often use a dedicated network operating system for its added performance, security, and reliability. Smaller networks sometimes use a nondedicated network operating system for its lower cost, ease of support, and ease of configuration.

### Novell

Novell Inc. makes NetWare®, a network operating system product line considered the industry standard for networking. Their network operating systems provides file and print services to workstations on the entire network.

**Figure 51**
The wire center for a large corporate network might look something like this. The racks shown include Token ring, UTP, STP, a fiber-optic patch panel, 3270 mainframe cables, 5250 minicomputer cables, and a microwave system.

The newer versions of NetWare can handle several terabytes of disk space, although the current technology cannot provide this amount of space. Many NetWare networks these days support several gigabytes of disk space on average servers.

## NetWare 2.x

The 2.x line of NetWare includes versions 2.1, 2.11, 2.12, 2.15, and the current version 2.2. NetWare 2.x is geared toward operating in small offices or departments. Although Novell no longer supports the 2.x line, it is still in use by some small businesses. The 2.x line can support a maximum of 100 concurrent users.

## NetWare 3.x

The 3.x line of NetWare includes versions 3.0, 3.1, 3.11, and the current version 3.12. NetWare 3.x supports entire corporations, while still being able to support smaller departments and remote offices. The 3.x line can support 1000 concurrent users on a single server (with a special licensed version from Novell) and several terabytes of disk space. The recent marketing effort has pushed version 3.12 to replace the 2.x line. This trend will end when Novell replaces the 3.x line with the 4.x line. NetWare 3.x is the most common line you will encounter at this time.

## NetWare 4.x

NetWare 4.1 is the newest version of NetWare, designed to provide enterprise-wide networking services with multiple file servers. Novell is promoting NetWare 4.1 as a replacement for the NetWare 3.x line almost entirely. Net-Ware 4.1 can support 1000 concurrent users on a single server and will provide support for capacities equal to or exceeding those provided by Net-Ware 3.12.

## NetWare Lite®/Personal NetWare®

NetWare Lite is a peer-to-peer network operating system. NetWare Lite allows each workstation to provide file and print services to other workstations on the network. This approach makes better use of computing resources at the expense of centralized data management and security.

## Banyan Vines®

Although Banyan Systems is not the most popular network operating system provider, it still enjoys a moderate-sized loyal following. Their network operating system provides a service called Street Talk™ that gives users a friendlier way to interface with the network and network resources.

## Lantastic®

Lantastic, a network operating system produced by Artisoft, is the most popular peer-to-peer network operating system on the market today. It can support several hundred concurrent users, allowing each workstation to provide file and print services. As an option, Lantastic also can supply voice communications over the network. This requires special hardware available from Artisoft at about $100 per computer. The Lantastic network operating system is a peer-to-peer operating system; this means any computer on the network can provide server functions, including disk storage and printer sharing. The e-mail system included with Lantastic allows the e-mail post office to be kept on any computer on the network. Lantastic runs with as few as 2 computers and has been known to support more than 100 computers on a single network.

### Microsoft Windows 95™

Can you imagine spending $12 million for a song to advertise one product? Microsoft spent this small amount of change to promote their new Windows 95 operating system. Microsoft has advertised Windows 95 as a complete graphical user interface, 32-bit operating system with built in networking. Microsoft has included many networking features in the operating system including peer-to-peer and access to assorted other server-based network operating systems. At the time of this writing, Windows 95 has been released for less than a week.

### Microsoft Windows for Workgroups™

Microsoft Windows for Workgroups is an enhancement of Windows 3.1 that provides peer-to-peer networking functions. These work even while using a server-based network without using the server. Computers running Windows for Workgroups have appeared on the Internet without the knowledge of the computer's user. This leads us to think there is almost no limit to the size of a Windows for Workgroups network when running in peer-to-peer mode. This can be a frightening proposition when PPP and SLIP connections are involved, since the Internet service provider dynamically assigns the addresses. Microsoft has designed the networking features in Windows for Workgroups to work with the Windows NT Advanced Server and other Microsoft networking products.

### Microsoft Windows NT Advanced Server™

Windows NT Advanced Server (NTAS) is Microsoft's product designed to compete with Novell NetWare. NTAS functions as a nondedicated network server providing file, print, and mail services for those Windows for Workgroups and Windows 95 computer users interested in taking advantage of them. NTAS needs a heavy-duty computer to function adequately. The size of the computer required (how much RAM, processor speed, and disk space) depends on the number of users and the types of applications the server is supporting.

### UNIX/Xenix/AIX

While most network operating systems provide file and print services to stand-alone workstations, UNIX and its variations provide central processing to attached terminals while also providing file and print services to other peer and client systems. These systems usually use a powerful computer such as a VAX, RS/6000, SUN, or other minicomputer or mainframe.

## So What Does This All Mean?

The main purpose of this somewhat technical summary is to give you some idea about what makes up a network and how large a group of connected computers can be. This is fine, but what good is it? Well, it tells you that you must be careful and find extra experts when you encounter a network. It also gives you an idea of how to spot a network and an idea of how far apart the computers in the network might be. It might be a few feet or many miles, and that information is necessary if you have to write a search warrant. Getting help from investigators in other agencies may be necessary if the network extends beyond your jurisdiction. You might also need to get extra help from both uniformed and plainclothes officers at your search sites if there are many computers to be secured to prevent suspects from removing all evidentiary data before you can get to it.

## The Bottom Line

If a network is involved in your investigation, *get competent assistance*. We often hire programmers and hardware and software experts who work under the direction of trained investigators during the investigation. The cost of hiring experts is a small price to pay compared with the potential civil law suits encountered if a business has its records destroyed or someone is injured or becomes ill while important records were unavailable because of inappropriate handling of a system. We strongly recommend joining professional organizations such as the High Tech Crime Investigators Association, where contacts with other investigators and computer hardware and software professionals will give you the resources necessary to be successful in this work.

# Ideal Investigative Computer Systems

A computer crimes investigator without special computer equipment is like a patrol officer without a notebook, pen, and a gun. You can investigate easy circumstances without these special tools, but the difficult instances will get away from you. The recommended equipment is expensive and you may have trouble getting such purchases approved but its justification is the time it will save in both your time and supporting officer time.

This equipment is cutting-edge technology (at least at the time we wrote this). The general rule for investigation is to get today's best technology to meet tomorrow's needs. This allows you to have equipment that should be usable for at least 3 years. It is understandable if you need to scale back these computers. We have run into problems obtaining even small supplies, such as diskettes, at times.

Each component has a brief description to aid in its justification. Keep in mind that these are *ideal* pieces of equipment: we are recommending the best available. If better equipment is available when you want to make a purchase, go for the better equipment. Being ideal also means you may not get what you want. If you are only able to get one computer system, choose the portable. The docking station with the portable will give you similar functionality to the desktop, while the desktop can only fill one role.

## Desktop

- *Pentium® 90, EISA and PCI bus, 64 MB RAM, full-sized tower case:* The Pentium 90-MHz processor provides a high-performance platform for all your investigative needs. The EISA bus has enough high-performance expansion slots for all the cards you might need for your regular operation. The PCI slots provide high-speed video expansion and high-speed disk expansion.

133

The tower case generally includes several drive bays and easier access to the cards and drives stored inside.

- *PCI SCSI card:* The SCSI card provides support for almost any SCSI device at the maximum speed of the device.
- *Internal 4-GB SCSI hard drive:* A 4 GB hard drive will have enough storage space for all of your applications and utilities. You should even have some space remaining for working on your investigations.
- *Iomega SCSI Zip drive:* The Iomega Zip drives work well for backing up computers in the field. The SCSI drive is a companion to the parallel version used with your investigative computer. The SCSI interface offers additional performance for your office work. The initial capacity of the Zip drive® is 100 MB on a small removable diskette.
- *Iomega Bernoulli 1-GB removable optical drive:* For long-term storage, a rewritable optical disk drive is an ideal medium for storing an entire case; it is not susceptible to erasure by magnetic fields. The disks are fairly inexpensive. You might also consider buying a large-capacity WORM (write once, read many) drive for storing data that is agreed to be original. (See Figure 52.)

**Figure 52**
Desktop components here include a CD-ROM, a 1-GB optical, and three Bernoulli drives.

- *8-mm tape backup:* You should keep constant backups of your computer to keep Murphy from byting you (ok, so I like computer humor) during important cases. The 8-mm tapes are the same as those used in modern video cameras and store a minimum of 5GB.

- *High speed serial card with a 16550 UART:* When it comes to telecommunications, the higher performance equipment easily pays for itself in time and long-distance savings. This serial card uses a modern high-performance chip (the UART) that can squeeze 5 to 20% additional speed from your modem. Many computers include this UART on the motherboard as standard equipment.

- *SVGA Multisync monitor with a 4-MB true color video card:* When investigating cases involving pictures on a computer, you will need a video system capable of showing graphics up to 1280 × 1024 pixels and 32 K, 64 K, *and* 16 million colors on the screen. A 17-inch or larger low-radiation monitor is no longer a status symbol. Larger monitors are easier on your eyes during extended periods of use.

- *Mouse or track ball:* This is included with almost every computer. Which you choose is a matter of personal preference.

- *External U.S. Robotics® Courier HST Dual Standard FAX/modem:* Of all the modems available, the HST Dual Standard is the Rolls Royce. It can connect to modems using V.32, V.34, and HST and even has ISDN capabilities. This is the only modem on the market capable of connecting this way. Its price is high compared to the new lines of V.34 modems, but it is worth every penny. The built in FAX allows you to send and receive FAX documents from your word processor or other applications on your computer.

- *Lexmark Optra R laser printer:* The Lexmark Optra line of printers can handle all your printing needs for reporting. The Optra line has a maximum printed resolution of 1200 × 1200 dots per inch (dpi). The toner cartridges last for several thousand pages. This printer is available in several speeds, including 12 and 16 pages per minute. Make sure you have at least 4 MB of RAM in the printer, with 8 being preferred. These printers feature both PostScript and PCL 5 emulation.

- *Epson LQ-2500 (or equivalent high-speed dot matrix printer):* Some cases will require a good quality, high-speed matrix printer. For these cases, a laser will not do. Many good matrix printers are available. The Epson is one of the more common, which means ribbons and parts are easier to obtain. A serial interface will also come in handy.

- *Canon BJC-600e color inkjet printer:* The Canon BJC-600e works great for producing color output for presentation in court or other special occasions. With the 600e, you can easily produce color overhead transparencies using special film. You will notice the supply of ink for these printers does not last very long when you print pages composed mostly of graphics. You should keep several refills on hand.

- *External SCSI CD-ROM drive:* Many applications and databases are becoming available on CD-ROM. CD-ROMs are available with hundreds of megabytes of nice and not-so-nice graphics. When you decide on a drive, select the fastest you can get. At the time of this writing, the 6x (six-spin) drives are just coming out and eight-spin drives are being discussed.

**Figure 53**
A laptop computer with a docking station containing a SCSI interface can be connected to
a miriad of peripheral devices and perform well as an investigative computer.

- *1200-VA online battery backup:* One of the greatest enemies of your computer
  is the power you are using to run it. A stray power spike or surge can destroy
  your investment in hardware and can erase software and data from your hard
  drives. A battery backup provides constant, filtered power no matter what
  the power company gives you. The computer can operate for several minutes
  on the battery in the event of a power failure.

## Portable

See Figures 53 and 54.

- *IBM ThinkPad® 755CE with a docking station:* The IBM ThinkPad is the best
  choice for an investigator. The 755 line is covered by a 3-year warranty. With
  the IBM Easyserve warranty, your computer should never be in the shop for
  more than a week if you happen to break it. The 755CE has an active TFT
  color matrix display capable of displaying 16-bit color. Available processors
  include the 486DX4/75, 486DX4/100, and Pentium®. Hard drives in the
  gigabyte range will soon be available; 20 MB of RAM should be your minimum purchase. The ThinkPad features two Type II PCMCIA slots. A

**Figure 54**
Portable investigative computers with SCSI interfaces can be connected to tape drives, Bernoulli drives, or optical drives and are easily transported to crime scenes.

FAX/modem is built in so you do not need a PCMCIA or external modem. The notebook has a 16-bit sound card on the motherboard and features an internal microphone and an internal speaker. An external stereo speaker jack and microphone jack are located on the side of the notebook. Other features of the ThinkPad are too numerous to list. The Dock I docking station for the ThinkPad lets your ThinkPad double as a desktop computer. Dock I has room for two 16-bit ISA slots and two half-height drives which can be floppy, CD-ROM, or hard drives. The docking station includes speakers for multimedia presentations; these can be useful for showing porn movies or other information in court or for parent groups.

- *ISA SCSI card:* One internal ISA slot should be used for a SCSI card to connect internal and external SCSI devices. This includes removable hard drives and tape drives.
- *Iomega parallel Zip® drive:* This removable drive is the companion to the SCSI version used on the desktop system. The parallel version will connect to almost any parallel printer port and copy data between the drive and the computer it is attached to. The disks are fully compatible with the SCSI version.
- *Xircom CE2 Combo:* The CE2 Combo is a PCMCIA Ethernet interface that includes both 10Base-T and 10Base-2 adapters. Drivers are included for DOS/Windows™ and OS/2. This adapter can run full duplex if the equipment to which you are connecting supports it.

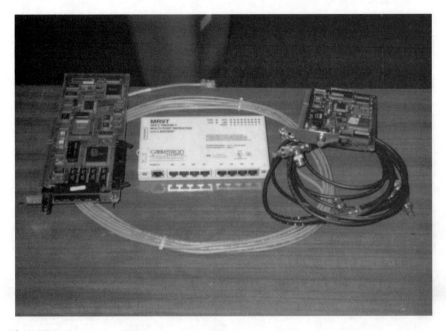

**Figure 55**
Cabletron E2212 Ethernet card (right), an 8-port Ethernet 10Base-T concentrator (center) and a Cabletron E2-HUB card (left) and cables.

- *Cabletron parallel port Ethernet adapter:* When backing up a computer such as a notebook, you will not be able to install a network interface card. The Cabletron interface will let you attach the suspect computer to your portable network through the parallel port. Performance will suffer, but you will still have the advantages of using a network for your backups. (See Figure 55.)
- *Cabletron E2212 Ethernet Card (3):* To connect a suspect computer to your portable network, you need one of these network interface cards installed in the computer.
- *Cabletron MR9TC 10Base-T Ethernet hub with coax connector:* The MR9TC is a small, somewhat portable 10Base-T hub with a coax connector.
- *Canon Bubblejet printer:* You will need a good portable printer, such as the Canon Bubblejet printer, which gives good quality output and is convenient to carry to crime scenes. This printer can be either color or black and white, depending on what you want to carry around with you.
- *400-VA online battery backup:* Battery backups of this size are heavy, but they can save you from power problems and keep you running in case the power fails. (See Figure 56.)
- *ThinkPad carry cases:* When transporting a notebook and docking station, make sure you have good carry cases; these will go a long way toward protecting your equipment. They also make travelling with your computer more pleasant.

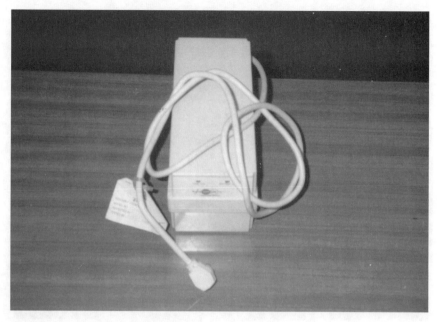

**Figure 56**
A small UPS (battery backup) can save your computer from power problems at the scene of an investigation. They are well worth the weight penalty to take with you everywhere you use a computer. It is the best insurance you can buy for any computer. They also are fairly inexpensive.

- *Equipment boxes:* Special boxes for all other equipment should be considered a necessity. We have lost equipment due to damage suffered from falls from the cart. A case or transportation box would have prevented the damage. Ideally, these cases should be made specifically for the intended use. If you cannot get specially made cases, check your property room for suitcases and briefcases that are about to be discarded. With the proper foam lining, these cases will do just fine.

## Tools

Tool kits for disassembling and reassembling computers and peripherals are a necessary part of your equipment. The vast majority of cases require only a set of screwdrivers. An electric screwdriver comes in handy when there is a lot to be done. More extensive kits may be useful, depending on the job to be done and the expertise of the investigators involved. We find that over a period of time we see equipment assembled with every screw, bolt, and part known to man. Some are very proprietary. For those occasions, you may need a more extensive tool kit. (See Figures 57, 58, and 59.)

**Figure 57**
All of the tools, computers, cameras, and other equipment needed for a major investigation can be easily packed in a few cases and transported in the trunk of a car.

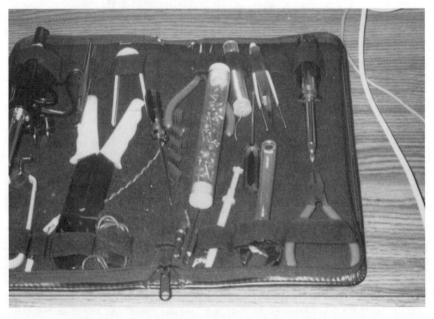

**Figure 58**
A simple tool kit. This kit is adequate for the vast majority of investigations.

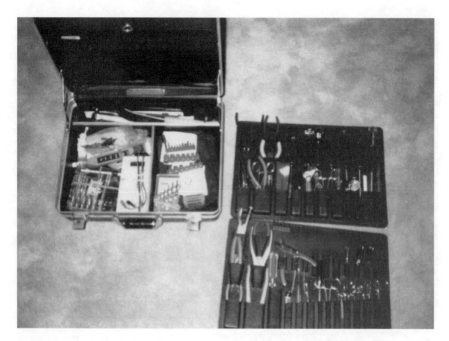

**Figure 59**
Depending on the systems to be seized and the expertise of the investigators and experts, a more extensive tool kit may be needed.

# Computer Cart

- *Heavy-duty collapsible computer cart:* The larger the better. Carts with a long wheel base provide more stability when loaded down. We have found it convenient to transport all our investigative equipment in one trip between the car and the suspect location.
- *Bungee cords:* Keeping your equipment secure on the cart is a high priority. Murphy (the guy who has all those funny laws) likes to toy with computer crime investigators who are not prepared.

# Media

Each time you use any of your high-capacity media, you should get replacements. Some cases require you to keep your evidence for months or years. As an investigator, you cannot afford to allow all your media to be tied up for these amounts of time (see Figure 60):

Minimum of 10 blank Zip® disks
Minimum of 2 removable optical disks
Minimum of 200 formatted 3.5" high-density diskettes

**Figure 60**
Backup media varies from diskettes to Bernoulli drives to gigabyte optical drives, depending on the size of the system to be backed up.

Minimum of 400 formatted 3.5" low-density diskettes
Minimum of 200 formatted 5.25" high-density diskettes
Minimum of 400 formatted 5.25" low-density diskettes

## Cables

See Figure 61.

Minimum of 4 25-foot or longer 10Base-T (unshielded, twisted-pair with RJ45 connectors)
Minimum of 2 50-foot or longer 10Base-T hub-to-hub cables
Minimum of 4 25-foot or longer 10Base-2 (RG-58 coax with BNC connectors)
Minimum of 2 20-foot DB25 to DB25 parallel cables
Cabletron DB9 and DB25 (male and female) connectors with RJ45 jacks for serial cables

## Bags

Collect and acquire all the antistatic packaging you can get your hands on. Long-term storage of computer equipment is normal in many cases involving

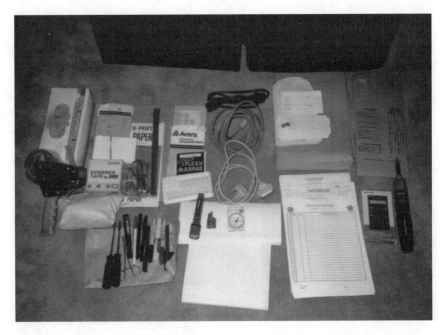

**Figure 61**
Cables, envelopes, gloves, and miscellaneous equipment necessary for tagging and marking evidence.

computers and can pose a real danger due to moisture and static electricity. Your property room may not know how to properly handle and store modern electronic equipment. Since it is your case, you should protect your evidence as best you can.

## Software

The following programs and operating systems should cover the majority of your software needs (see Figure 62). Some of these programs are shareware and should be registered with the author. Use caution when installing the same copy of your software on both computers to not violate the license agreement. Some software allows you to have it installed on more than one computer as long as it is only used one at a time, where others prohibit you from installing their software on more than one computer.

Software versions change rapidly. The software industry has learned that they can make a tremendous amount of money from their installed user base by charging for upgrades to the latest versions; keep this in mind. Also, make sure you get a copy of the latest version to be compatible with software you may find on a suspect's computer. Some of the software listed in this section includes a version number or two. For best compatibility, it is important to

**Figure 62**
Investigative software in soft carry folders. Includes DOS, device drivers, XTreePro GOLD, the Norton Utilities, Maresware, Fried Utilities, PC-Tools, LapLink, and networking software.

get the listed versions and the latest version. If no version is listed, just get the latest version.

The last suggestion about software is to collect all you can get your hands on. You never know when you might need even an outdated program. If your computer services group ever phases out old software, add it to your collection. You can gather a great deal of software after awhile. Following is a partial list of software you will find useful:

- WordPerfect®
- OS/2, version 3.0 (WARP)®: When it comes to doing several tasks at one time, OS/2 is the best way to go. With OS/2 you can run multiple DOS, Windows™ and OS/2 programs at the same time. This has some hidden benefits, such as being able to look at files from inside another application and not having to quit what you are doing to look for information for someone else who may happen to step into your office. (See Figures 63 and 64.)
- MS-DOS 6.22® or PC-DOS 6.3®
- Lantastic®, version 6.0 (five copies minimum)
- Quattro Pro®
- dBase® for Windows™
- XTreePro Gold™ for DOS: XTreeGold™ is one of the greatest disk utilities ever made. It allows you to see all the files on one or more diskettes and hard

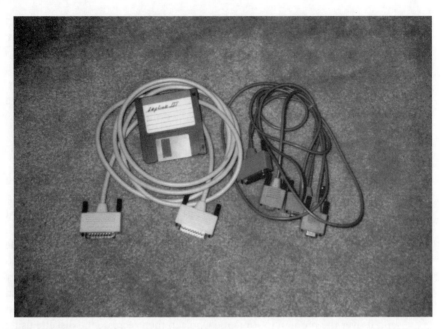

**Figure 63**
Small, stand-alone computers can be backed up using LapLink® via parallel or serial cables.

**Figure 64**
Using Ethernet to back up a seized computer can be as easy as having an Ethernet card in your investigative computer and bringing along a parallel port adapter, cable, and peer-to-peer networking software.

drives at the same time; view text, database, word processor, spreadsheet, and graphics files in their native format; view the contents of compressed files; copy, move, and delete single files or selected groups of files; and print listings of the files found on the drives.

- Qmodem Pro®: Version 1.5 of Qmodem Pro® supports the new RIP graphics. This graphics feature is similar to that found on Prodigy® and America Online®. The user can see the graphics while online without having to download any special graphics files.
- Display: Display allows you to view almost any graphic image or graphic animation; it is available on the Internet.
- Corel Draw™: Corel Draw®' versions 3.0 and up, includes a program called MOSAIC. This lets you catalog all the common images found on a computer. You can then print these images as a reference with the file names listed next to the image.
- Disk Copy Fast (DCF, shareware): DCF lets you copy any diskette in a single pass and make multiple copies. DCF uses your hard drive, EMS, and XMS memory to hold the diskette image during the copy process. DOS diskcopy uses only the conventional memory, requiring you to swap diskettes several times. DCF also allows you to save a diskette image to the hard drive and send it over the modem to someone who can then recreate the diskette using another copy of DCF. This allows you to avoid the mail for sharing floppy diskettes.
- Laplink®, Versions 3.0 and 5.0: Laplink® version 5.0 has some nice features including network support (Novell NetWare only). There have been some incompatibilities, however, which have necessitated the use of version 3.0. Version 4.0 was very user unfriendly and we have avoided it.
- Search Warrant Database program: The Search Warrant program allows you to print labels and print the usual reports required for the execution of a search warrant. This program can save a tremendous amount of time compared to the normal pen-and-paper method, but the program is somewhat difficult to use.
- PC-Tools® (all versions): The latest version of PC-Tools® for Windows™ contains an excellent backup program that will back up your system to floppy diskettes, removable disk drives, and tape drives.
- WP Crack: This program recovers the password used to protect a WordPerfect® document. It is very fast and, on a 386+, it can tell you the password used on a document within a few seconds. WordPerfect changed the encryption technique in version 6.x, resulting in this program working only with version 5.1 for DOS and 5.2 for Windows™.
- Compression Programs

| | |
|---|---|
| PKZIP (shareware) | USQ (shareware) |
| LHARC (shareware) | TAR (shareware) |
| PAK (shareware) | Compress (shareware) |
| ARJ (shareware) | GZIP (shareware) |
| ZOO (shareware) | LIST (shareware) |

# Court Procedures

# 15

## Expert Witnesses

Plan on using expert witnesses; good expert witnesses can convey complicated material to a judge and jury in a language they can understand. Spend time going over what you need covered. Have the expert work through questions directly from the prosecuting attorney to prepare them for what to expect when they are on the stand.

## Pretrial Preparation

Even though computers are common, they still are very complicated. Many people do not understand how a computer functions internally. Prosecuting attorneys are included in this group. They need to prepare as far in advance as possible for presenting computer evidence in court. Remember that even if the case is a pedophile or credit fraud case, if it involves a computer, online role playing, or capture files, it is a paper case and should be prepared as a paper case. That is, the documents required to prove the case from the computer will need to be printed, as will the capture files from your computer if this was a sting operation. These cases need to be prepared the same as any white-collar fraud case with all the documents printed out and the pages numbered sequentially, ie., 0000001 through 00001000. Copies of the numbered documents should be made for the prosecutor, investigator, defense, and court. Then everyone can refer to the proper page. Even the police reports should be included in this numbering system. We break up large cases by using one numbering system for the actual reports and a second system for the supporting documents. Even the simplest computer case can involve hundreds of pages of documentation. If you need to present a software

package in court, practice as much as you can. Get to the point where you
know the program well before presenting it in court.

## Speaking to the Judge and Jury

The judge and jury members are not computer professionals. They are everyday citizens who may or may not know anything about computers. When
you get the chance to talk, you have the opportunity to teach them everything
they need to know about what you are presenting. When speaking, keep the
following in mind:

1.  *Look at the people you are speaking to.* Make good eye contact. This is very
    important. It helps to convey your confidence in what you are saying. It also
    helps you determine if your audience is understanding what you are saying.
2.  *Speak slowly and clearly.* Sometimes technical information takes time to sink
    in.
3.  *Use hand gestures.* Unfortunately, you cannot always have a chalkboard in
    front of you to teach the judge and jury. To keep them interested, move a
    little inside the witness box. This will help to keep their attention.
4.  *Ask subliminal questions.* Since you cannot ask questions of the jury directly,
    ask little questions that may provoke a nod. This can give you good signals
    of how receptive your audience is. Look for kinesic feedback to determine if
    more needs to be said or if you need to be less technical.
5.  Explain the use of computer terminology in simple, everyday terms when
    possible.

## Terminology To Use in Court

Lawyers can be tricky critters. They can utterly confuse a judge and jury to
the point where they think you, as an investigator, have played some tricks
on the suspect to make them look guilty. An easy way to do this is to use
technical terms that the judge and jury do not understand. To help you defend
against these tactics, we have provided some terms to use and some terms
to stay away from.

If you must use technical terms, *know what they mean before you use
them.* If you do not know what a term means, say so. It is much better to say
you do not know than to pretend to know and get shot down. When you
speak, speak to the judge or jury. The attorney does not matter. The judge
and jury make the decisions. Before you get on the stand, try to arrange what
questions you want the prosecuting attorney to ask. Have them ask as many
open questions as possible to give you the opportunity to teach the jury.
*Translate, do not convert.* The term *convert* can take on the connotation of

altering the evidence. To avoid this, use the term *translate;* for example, "translate into human readable form."

## Resumes

Each expert witness needs to have a resume tailored to qualifying in court. The resumes in the preface can be used as examples.

## Equipment

For presentations in court, a color overhead projection panel to display the computer data relevant to the case can be very useful. Make sure the equipment works properly and as expected before you use it during your testimony.

# Search Warrants

## Case Law

At the time of this writing, there is very little case law in the area of computer crime. Even jury instructions are hard to come by. We are seeing investigators who are not specifically trained in the area of computer crime seizure and evaluation thrust into this very technical arena. These investigators do the best they can using traditional investigative methods.They by necessity are often forced to use non-law enforcement computer experts, who may be unaware of the rules of evidence and the need to preserve the same, to help in seizing and evaluating computer systems. The computer experts most often used by law enforcement are computer systems people with their particular agency who are technologically aware but may have no idea of how to obtain and preserve evidence in a criminal case. The end result can be bad case law and lost prosecutions.

We have received many calls from investigators and prosecutors across the country telling us this same story. "We served a warrant or arrested the suspect at his house or work place and found and seized a computer. We think there is evidence on the computer and we want to search it." Was the computer in the warrant? No. Fruit of the poison tree? Probably. Since we have an opportunity to make case law in a completely new area, let us make *good* case law. The fact that the investigators have a warrant for documents, drugs, or other items does not give blanket permission to seize and search other items, including computers, just because they are there.

The primary rule of search and seizure is that you need a warrant to search private property. We strongly recommend that "when in doubt, write a warrant". Then, in the service of any search warrant, if evidence or facts present themselves which would give probable cause to search for items not specifically documented in the original warrant, write an amendment to the warrant or obtain a warrant by telephone for the new items to be searched for.

## Writing a Warrant

Search warrants are not difficult to write. The problem for most investigators is the "legalese" of the warrant. The language used for search warrants in most jurisdictions is at best archaic. It is our opinion that attorneys purposely use this language to enhance their job security since, just like insurance policies, the average person cannot make heads or tails of them without an attorney's help. Grammatical programs often rate search warrants as being on a grade level of 22 to 26. The intent of the contents of search warrants is to put probable cause in a form acceptable to the court. One simply substitutes "your affiant" for the first person "I" and the result is acceptable language. When we first started writing search warrants in the early 1970s, we simply looked at what others had done, developed a template, and used present facts and circumstances for the new warrants. Today there are many excellent manuals on writing search warrants available to investigators.

The authors have written several hundred search warrants in California and other states, as well as federal search warrants. All search warrants have the same basic premises: *a search for specific items based on probable cause.* Only the form, not the information included in the warrant, changes from jurisdiction to jurisdiction. Included in this section are copies of various search warrants which we believe the reader will find useful, particularly the investigator who is new to this. In formulating the attached warrant forms, we met extensively with attorneys and investigators who are familiar with computer-related search warrants.

One clear warning is necessary: Make sure the judge understands the warrant. If the judge does not understand the warrant, it is not valid. This argument is being made in high-tech cases by defense attorneys. We make it a policy to explain the technical aspects of the case and the specific meaning of the computer jargon contained in the warrant to the court before the warrant is signed. We recommend seeking out a computer-literate judge to make this process easier. Just like attorneys, computer folks have a language all their own which the general public does not understand. We have to be understood both on the warrant and in court. We include the commonly accepted meanings of technical words in the affidavit itself. We also attach a dictionary (see the computer dictionary at the end of this book) to the warrant, explaining the generally accepted meaning of technical terms. This dictionary is part of this document and is constantly being modified to fit the case under investigation.

# Hacker Case

We will show the trail computer crimes investigators can follow and the types of search warrants needed by illustrating real cases. In the following case, information from one search warrant leads to the necessary probable cause for the next warrant and so on. Much of the information from the first warrant is used in the succeeding warrants. In our first illustration, hackers (crackers) entered a mainframe computer at Cellular One, temporarily shut down 20,000 telephone lines, and got access to the computer-controlled voice mail boxes. When a new voice mail box was opened, the hackers changed the default password and, using this method, took 35 voice mail boxes from their rightful owners. They used the stolen voice mail boxes to authorize long-distance phone calls for one another and to exchange stolen credit card and long distance access codes, as well as to brag about how smart they were while putting down other h/p people.

## Cellular Warrant

The first warrant was for access to the voice mail boxes the suspects were illegally using on the Cellular One system. This gave us information on the types of illegal activity taking place on the voice mail system as well as the suspects handles, such as "pyro", "uta", "imposter", "macho man", and others. Did we need a warrant for stolen voice mail boxes when Cellular One, who is the rightful owner of the system, wanted the suspects off their system? Cellular One had already captured the voice mail from several days' activity on these boxes and sent them to law enforcement. Could Cellular One legally record the voice mail from the suspect mail boxes and send it to law enforcement? Would they become agents of the police should they continue to record the mail and send it to the police? Could they become subject to the same laws of search and seizure as the police they were assisting? Several attorneys gave us vastly different answers which ranged from "no" to "yes" to "I don't know." Our response is always, *"When in doubt, write a warrant".* We did so, as the suspects had an "expectation of privacy" even when using the stolen boxes, as they had made the effort to change the password which was required to access the voice mail box and retrieve the mail. The fact that they took the trouble to change the password indicated the expectation of privacy. The warrant took less than 2 hours to get and helped ensure that we would not lose the case on a technicality at the end of a lengthy investigation.

We needed to identify the persons using the stolen voice mail boxes, so the next warrants were for a dialed number recorder (DNR) as well as trap-and-trace and subscriber information for the numbers calling into the voice mail boxes being investigated. These also included trap-and-trace orders for the telephone companies which is attached to the search warrant. Why did I say warrants? We had to write warrants for each telephone company providing service from Cellular One on down to the local phone company through the long-distance carrier to our suspect's phone in a dorm in Santa Barbara. There are lots of phone companies in this country, and often it is necessary to write warrants for several of them to trace a call back to its source. This can be a time-consuming project. Finally, we traced the calls to Cellular One from one of the suspects through GTE to the University of California at Santa Barbara's computerized telephone system. The caller was calling through a previously unknown backdoor in the system into the GTE system and eventually to Cellular One. So we wrote warrants for Pacific Bell and GTE and the university police, and computer folks traced the calls through their computerized phone system to a specific room in the campus dorms. The last warrant was for the room where the suspect lived. This is a lot of work to identify one suspect. We had 35 different suspects using the stolen voice mail boxes, some of which were in Germany and Holland, as well as different states in the U.S. Oh, yes, we did get to serve the last search warrant at UCSB; we arrested the suspect and seized his computer. Was it worth it? It was; kicking in doors and handcuffing suspects is a tremendous stress reliever.

These warrants show how one warrant can lead to another as evidence comes in from the previous warrant. A lot of the language and probable cause are similar for each succeeding warrant. We often can use the basic warrant and add the new information from each preceding warrant to write the next. One boiler plate listing for the information to search for and another for the investigator's expertise, combined with information from the police report, can all easily be imported into a search warrant template on the computer, which will greatly expedite the writing of search warrants, as demonstrated in the following.

## Search Warrant Sample 1

IN THE MUNICIPAL COURT OF THE FRESNO JUDICIAL DISTRICT

COUNTY OF FRESNO, STATE OF CALIFORNIA

STATE OF CALIFORNIA }                    AFFIDAVIT IN SUPPORT OF AND
                     } ss
COUNTY OF FRESNO     }                    PETITION FOR SEARCH WARRANT

NO._____

Personally appeared before me this 25th day of March, 1991, the affiant, Franklin Clark, a peace officer, who, on oath, makes complaint, and deposes and says that he had and there is probable and reasonable cause to believe, and that he does believe, that there is now on the premises located at and also described as Cellular One, **** N. Palm, City of Fresno, County of Fresno, State of California, the following personal property, to wit: Recorded voice mail messages on a computer harddisk from voice mail boxes 281-****, ****, ****, ****, ****, ****, ****, ****, ****, ****, ****, ****, ****, ****, ****, ****, ****, ****, ****, ****, ****, ****, ****, ****, ****, and **** which are part of a telephone switch owned and managed by Cellular One.

Your affiant says that there is probable and reasonable cause to believe and that he does believe that the access and use of said 281 prefix phone numbers constitutes;

stolen or embezzled property:

property or things used as the means of committing a felony:

property or things in the possession of a person with the intent to use it as a means of committing a public offense, or in the possession he may have delivered it for the purpose of concealing it or preventing its being discovered:

property or things which consists of an item or constitutes evidence which tends to show that a felony has been committed, or tends to show that a particular person has committed a felony.

Your affiant says that the facts in support of the issuance of the search warrant are as follows:

Your affiant has been a Police Officer for the past 22 years, 10 months, employed in such capacity by the Fresno Police Department and has acted and received the information set forth in this affidavit in that capacity.

Your affiant is now and has been for the past 4 years, 8 months assigned to the Economic/Computer Crimes Detail thereof.

Your affiant has received specialized training in computer use and investigations as well as telecommunications crime investigations as follows:

| | |
|---|---|
| Oct. 17, 1987 | 6 hr., Intro to micro-computers, Clovis West Adult School |
| Oct. 24 – Nov. 21, 1987 | 20 hr., Intro to micro-computers IBM, PC-DOS, Pc-Write, DBIII, PC-Tools and basic programming |
| Jan. – Feb., 1988 | 20 hr., Intro to Lotus 123, Clovis West Adult School |
| Jan. 31 – Feb. 3, 1989 | 36 hr. DOJ Computer Crime Investigation, micro & mini & main frame computers, techniques, hardware, software, law & search warrants |
| Aug. 7 – 11, 1989 | 5 days, Federal Law Enforcement Training Center, Glenco, GA, Federal Computer Investigators Committee Re: Computer Crimes Investigation/Investigative Software |

| Oct. 24 – 25, 1989 | 9 hr., City of Fresno info center, WP 5.0 ModII |
|---|---|
| Feb. 13 – 14, 1989 | 16 hr., Training Center, IBM PC/XT/AT trouble-shooting and repair |
| Feb. 28, 1989 | DEC Multi-Vendor Environments/LAN Systems |
| Aug. 21, 1990 | San Jose PD, High-Tech Crimes, IBM & FBI re: chip theft and ID of counterfeit chips |
| Sept. 12 – 14, 1990 | High-Tech Law Enforcement Seminar, Intel and Apple, Santa Clara |
| Dec. 3 – 14, 1990 | Federal Law Enforcement Academy, Glenco, GA, Investigations in an Automated Environment |

During the past 4 years your affiant has investigated numerous telecommunication frauds including "hacking" and illegal use and exchange of stolen Pacific Bell, U.S. Sprint, Com Systems, and other phone number providers long distance billing numbers, illegal use of and electronic exchange of stolen credit card numbers, and unauthorized entry into and use of business computers by telephone.

On the date of February 13, 1991, your affiant read Fresno Police Department report 91-***** where D******, the General Sales Manager for Cellular One at **** N. Palm, City of Fresno, State of California, reported that on or about February 8, 1991, a person or persons unknown called into the Cellular One voice mail system and left a message on approximately 800 customers' mail boxes stating "R**** W****, I know where you are and you're a dead man."

Your affiant called the General Manager of Cellular One, S*** J****. Mr. J**** told your affiant that a person using the name of "macho man" had called the 281 prefix voice mail computer at Cellular One and somehow found a seven (7) digit system password and electronically entered the computer controlling Cellular One's Fresno Voice Mail system. "Macho man" had gained access to customers' electronic mail boxes and changed the passwords and was using the mail boxes himself and was exchanging mail with other unauthorized users who are using the above 281 prefix mail boxes. Mr. J**** stated that after he listened to the recordings left on the stolen voice mail boxes he discovered that the suspects appeared to be using the voice mail boxes they had stolen from Cellular One to leave and solicit stolen telephone calling card numbers. Mr. J**** stated he listened to and recorded messages left on two mail boxes 281-**** and 281-* * * * after changing the password and locking the suspects out of the mail box. Recorded in these boxes were messages indicating that persons using the above stolen mail boxes were exchanging messages between the boxes on how to "hack" long distance calling card codes, how to send Western Union Mail Grams and bill someone else, and obtaining and use of stolen credit card numbers. Mr. J**** stated it sounded like the suspects were hacking MCI, Sprint, and AT&T systems for electronic mail and calling card numbers.

Mr. J**** stated that his company would like to change the passwords to the above illegally accessed 281 prefix mail boxes, shut the suspects out of them, give your affiant the new password, and allow the police to record the messages contained in these mail boxes to discover the phone codes and other evidence the suspects had exchanged on the Cellular One voice mail system. Then they could put these 281 boxes back in service and sell them to legitimate customers.

G*** C*****, the Switch Technician for Cellular One, at **** N. Palm, Fresno, California, told your affiant that what Cellular One operates in Fresno is actually 20,000 phone numbers using the entire 269 and 281 prefixes. These numbers are provided by Pacific Bell and come into his switch from Pacific Bell via a local route from the 209 area code and another tandem incoming call route for calls outside of the 209 area. The computer software at Cellular One controls and routes each of these calls to the appropriate line. Cellular One bought the entire 10,000 numbers of the 281 prefix, and 2000 or so of these numbers are set aside for use by the voice mail system. The entire Cellular One system is computer software controlled. The voice mail system is separate from the cellular phone traffic. When calls for voice mail come in, they are routed to a stand-alone machine which stores subscribers voice messages as well as voice messages for the subscriber from outside callers. These messages are digitally stored on a magnetic disk in the voice mail machine. Each subscriber to the voice mail system is given an individual phone number, i.e., 281-****.

A person identifying himself as "macho man" and some other persons have been getting into voice mail boxes and changing the passwords and leaving and receiving messages without authorization.

3-5-91 — Your affiant dialed 281-****, 281-*****, 281-**** and 281-**** and listened to and recorded the messages on these voice mail boxes.

281-**** — A male voice said "All third party billings accepted here for Tony C****** and Karen B*****."

281-**** — A male voice said "This is macho man; it's 11:49 eastern standard time, Thursday," and went on to say he had some virgin codes except for the one he was using on 800-288-**** system and he was looking for a pbx that dials the 900 number and any good CBI or TRW codes. Anyone that wanted any codes leave him a message.

281-**** — A male voice said "414-***-***-****" and was very hard to understand.

281-**** — A male voice said "Yo, this is macho man speaking; leave me a message, I'll get back to you."

3-6-91: 281-**** was changed to a male voice saying "Mike C********."

Your affiant, from experience and training, is familiar with the exchange of stolen telephone access numbers and the accessing of TRW and CBI to gather credit information and credit card numbers. TRW and CBI are two of the major U.S. credit reporting agencies, and with the proper codes persons can by computer via telephone enter these computers and then have access to all the credit reports in the system. The credit information obtained can then be used to obtain products on credit, apply for new cards, and send the bills to the unsuspecting victims and are often posted on computer bulletin boards for other criminals to use and are sent to voice mail boxes for exchange with other criminals in the same manner.

Based on the information received from Cellular One employees and your affiant's experience and training, your affiant believes the suspects using the Cellular One voice mail without authorization are violating PC 502 (b) and are in fact attempting to traffic in illegally obtained telephone access codes and seeking confidential passwords into credit agency computers. It is your affiant's experience that persons involved in this type of exchange of illegally obtained telephone access codes are also involved in the exchanging of stolen credit card numbers and this is consistent with the voice mail left by "macho man" on the 281 prefixes as described above. Your affiant believes that the above 281 prefix voice mail boxes contain evidence of these types of crimes covered under PC 502 and that the recordings contained therein will assist in this investigation in identifying other codes the suspects have illegally obtained and distributed as well as assist in identifying the suspects responsible.

Your affiant has reasonable cause to believe that grounds for the issuance of a search warrant exist, as set forth in Section 15243 of the Penal Code, based upon the aforementioned information, facts, and circumstances.

Good cause being shown, therefore, and that the same be brought before this magistrate or retained subject to the order of this Court, or of any other court in which the offense in respect to which the property or things taken is triable, pursuant to Section 1536 of the Penal Code.

Subscribed and sworn to before me _____
This    day of   , 19____
at    a.m.  p.m.

_____

JUDGE OF THE MUNICIPAL COURT

## Search Warrant Sample 2

IN THE MUNICIPAL COURT OF THE FRESNO JUDICIAL DISTRICT

COUNTY OF FRESNO, STATE OF CALIFORNIA

STATE OF CALIFORNIA }
                    } ss
COUNTY OF FRESNO    }

AFFIDAVIT IN SUPPORT OF AND

PETITION FOR SEARCH WARRANT

NO._____

Personally appeared before me this _____ day of Month, 1989, the affiant, *also* a peace officer, who, on oath, makes complaint, and deposes and says that he had and there is probable and reasonable cause to believe, and that he does believe, that there is now on the premises located at and also described as Cellular One, **** N. Palm, City of Fresno, County of Fresno, State of California, the following personal property, to wit: A telephone switch owned by Cellular One using prefix 281, including 281-****, 281-****, 281-**** and 281-**** which are Cellular One voice mail boxes. Said 281 prefix phone numbers are provided to Cellular One by Pacific Bell. Your affiant requests an Order for Pacific Bell to place a trap/trace device on the above 281 prefix phone numbers to determine the subscriber information on incoming calls based on this affidavit.

Your affiant says that there is probable and reasonable cause to believe and that he does believe that the access and use of said 281 prefix phone numbers constitutes;

stolen or embezzled property:

property or things used as the means of committing a felony:

property or things in the possession of a person with the intent to use it as a means of committing a public offense, or in the possession he may have delivered it for the purpose of concealing it or preventing its being discovered:

property or things which consists of an item or constitutes evidence which tends to show that a felony has been committed, or tends to show that a particular person has committed a felony.

Your affiant says that the facts in support of the issuance of the search warrant are as follows:

Your affiant has been a Police Officer for the past 22 years, 10 months, employed in such capacity by the Fresno Police Department and has acted and received the information set forth in this affidavit in that capacity.

Your affiant is now and has been for the past 4 years, 8 months assigned to the Economic/Computer Crimes Detail thereof.

Your affiant has received specialized training in computer use and investigations as well as telecommunications crime investigations as follows:

| | |
|---|---|
| Oct. 17, 1987 | 6 hr., Intro to micro-computers, Clovis West Adult School |
| Oct. 24 – Nov. 21, 1987 | 20 hr., Intro to micro-computers IBM, PC, DOS, Pc-Write, DBIII, PC-Tools, and basic programming |
| Jan – Feb, 1988 | 20 hr., Intro to Lotus 123, Clovis West Adult School |
| Jan 31 – Feb 3, 1989 | 36 hr. DOJ Computer Crime Investigation, micro & mini & main frame computers, techniques, hardware, software, law & search warrants |

| | |
|---|---|
| Aug. 7 – 11, 1989 | 5 days, Federal Law Enforcement Training Center, Glenco GA, Federal Computer Investigators Committee Re: Computer Crimes Investigation/Investigative Software |
| Oct. 24 – 25, 1989 | 9 hr. City of Fresno info center, WP 5.0 ModII |
| Feb. 13 – 14, 1989 | 16 hr., Training Center, IBM PC/XT/AT troubleshooting and repair |
| Feb. 28, 1989 | DEC Multi Vendor Enviroments/LAN Systems |
| Aug. 21, 1990 | San Jose PD, High-Tech Crimes, IBM & FBI re: chip theft and ID of counterfeit chips |
| Sept. 12 – 14, 1990 | High-Tech Law Enforcement Seminar, Intel and Apple, Santa Clara |
| Dec. 3 – 14, 1990 | Federal Law Enforcement Academy, Glenco, GA Investigations in an Automated Environment |

During the past 4 years your affiant has investigated numerous telecommunication frauds including "hacking" and illegal use and exchange of stolen Pacific Bell, U.S. Sprint, Com Systems, and other phone number providers long distance billing numbers, illegal use of and electronic exchange of stolen credit card numbers, and unauthorized entry into and use of business computers by telephone.

On the date of Febuary 13, 1991, your affiant read Fresno Police Department report 91-***** where D*** F***, the General Sales Manager for Cellular One at **** N. Palm, City of Fresno, State of California, reported that on or about February 8, 1991, a person or persons unknown called into the Cellular One voice mail system and left a message on approximately 800 customers' mail boxes stating "R**** W****, I know where you are and you're a dead man."

Your affiant called the General Manager of Cellular One, S**** J****. Mr. J**** told your affiant that a person using the name of "macho man" had called the 281 prefix voice mail computer at Cellular One and somehow found a seven (7) digit system password and electronically entered the computer controlling Cellular One's Fresno voice mail system. "Macho man" had gained access to customers' electronic mail boxes and changed the passwords and was using the mail boxes himself. In addition, "macho man" had locked Cellular One employees out of the computer and changed the computerized recorded message given to customers of "Hello, you've reached the voice mail system" to a scream. Mr. J**** told your affiant that his technicials did not know how to change the computer program controlling the voice mail system the way "macho man" had and he felt "macho man" had used a computer to "hack" into their computer via telephone in order to obtain the seven-digit system password whereby he gained control of the computer. Mr. J**** stated that after listening to the recordings left on the stolen voice mail boxes, the suspect appeared to be using the voice mail boxes he had stolen from Cellular One to leave and solicit stolen telephone calling card numbers. Mr. J**** stated he would contact Pacific Bell to initiate the placing of a phone trap/trace on the numbers "macho man" was using without authorization.

G*** C*****, the Switch Technician for Cellular One, at **** N. Palm, Fresno, California, told your affiant that what Cellular One operates in Fresno is actually 20,000 phone numbers using the entire 269 and 281 prefixes. These numbers are provided by Pacific Bell and come into his switch from Pacific Bell via a local route from the 209 area code and another tandem incoming call route for calls outside of the 209 area. The computer software at Cellular One controls and routes each of these calls to the appropriate line. Cellular One bought the entire 10,000 numbers of the 281 prefix and 2000 or so of these numbers are set aside for use by the voice mail system. The entire Cellular One system is computer software controlled. The voice mail system is separate from the cellular phone traffic. When calls for voice mail come in they are routed to a stand-alone machine which stores subscribers voice messages as well as voice messages for the subscriber from outside callers. These messages are digitally stored on a magnetic disk in the voice mail machine. Each subscriber to the voice mail system is given an individual phone number, i.e., 281-8871.

A person identifying himself as "macho man" has been accessing the Cellular One main computer and getting into voice mail boxes and changing the passwords and leaving and receiving messages without authorization. G*** C***** has installed tracking software programs as of 3-4-91 where now every call to the stolen voice mail box 281-**** is recorded as to the time and duration of the call. He will try to set up the same program for the other 281 prefix numbers that have been entered by "macho man" without authorization.

D*** F******, Customer Care Supervisor for Cellular One, told your affiant that she and two other women in her section actually set up customers with voice mail boxes and activate the phone numbers by computer.

D*** F****** stated that the person identifying himself on voice mail as "macho man" had gotten into Cellular One's main computer in February by locating and using the default password *******, changed the password, changed the voice message system welcome message to a scream, and had access to all the phone numbers for all their voice mail boxes. They had been locked out of their own system for awhile but had gotten back in and changed the password. They were still having trouble with the system, as 3-4-91 she had activated 3 voice mail boxes for new customers and the message welcoming the customers to the system was just a scream which the suspect had recorded in the computer. The normal procedure for a customer to purchase a voice mail box would be for them to purchase same from her section. Then a 281 prefix phone number would be assigned to that customer. The computer would be accessed and given the command to activate that customer's 7-digit phone number. The customer would be given a temporary password of ***** and he would call his voice mail box, hit the # sign and *****, then enter his own password of 1 to 15 numbers. Then the customer would record his own welcome message and could send and receive voice mail. The suspect seems to know when new boxes are sold and gets into the voice mail boxes before the legitimate customers can put in their own passwords and takes over the box by putting in his own password. The computer does not allow them to see the password and they cannot kick the suspect out of the box and can only turn off the phone number. In every case where "macho man" has gained access to a voice mail phone box he has entered into a newly activated box using the temporary access code ***** and changed it before the legitimate purchaser of the box could put in his password. D*** F****** stated that the messages are erased by the box owner by hitting #7 and are saved for 5 days by hitting #9 and are erased by the system after one week.

Your affiant commenced the actual physical mechanics of preparing this affidavit and attached search warrant at   a.m. p.m. of   , 19___, and your affiant affixed his signature under oath to this affidavit before the undersigned magistrate at the time and date attested by said magistrate; the elapsed time reflected herein has been diligently utilized by your affiant in the mechanics of physically preparing these documents, locating the appropriate magistrate, and transporting these documents to the magistrate for his official action in connection therewith.

Your affiant has reasonable cause to believe that grounds for the issuance of a search warrant exist, as set forth in Section 15243 of the Penal Code, based upon the aforementioned information, facts, and circumstances.

Your affiant prays that a search warrant be issued, based upon the above facts, for the seizure of said property, or any part thereof in the daytime, good cause being shown therefore, and that the same be brought before this magistrate or retained subject to the order of this Court, or of any other court in which the offense in respect to which the property or things taken is triable, pursuant to Section 1536 of the Penal Code.

Subscribed and sworn to before me _____
This   day of    , 19___
at   a.m. p.m.


_____
JUDGE OF THE MUNICIPAL COURT

## Search Warrant Sample 3

IN THE MUNICIPAL COURT

COUNTY OF FRESNO, STATE OF CALIFORNIA

Re: Order Authorizing Telephone Trap/Trace No:_____

### ORDER

This matter having come before the Court pursuant to the request for a search warrant, and that an Order be issued (1) authorizing the installation and/or use of equipment to trap/trace and identify the telephone numbers of certain parties placing calls to telephone numbers (209) 281-****, 281-****, 281-**** and 281-**** located at **** N. Palm, Fresno, California, and subscribed to by Cellular One, and (2) directing Pacific Bell, a public utility as defined in California Public Utilities Code Section 234, to forthwith furnish Officers of the Fresno Police Department with all of the information herein described, and (3) requiring said utility to produce certain records.

It appearing that the application has been made in good faith in furtherance of a pending criminal investigation, and it appearing there is probable cause that the telephone(s) from which incoming telephone calls are to be trapped/traced and identified are being used in connection with criminal activity, and Pacific Bell having received notice of this application on _____, is hereby authorized and ordered to:

(1) Program and/or use equipment in order to trap/trace and identify the telephone number(s) and/or provide the name and address of the subscriber of record, whether published or unpublished, of each identified incoming call to telephone number(s) (209)281-****, 281-****, 281-**** and 281-**** and, where possible, provide the time and duration of each call; and

(2) Continue the operation of such trapping/tracing activity for a period not to exceed ten (10) days from the date of this Order;

Provided, that the trap/trace operation can be conducted nonobtrusively, with a minimum of disruption to normal telephone service.

It is further ordered that:

(1) Pacific Bell will give to the Fresno Police Department all information gathered by reason of this Order at reasonable intervals while this Order is in effect.

(2)  The Subscriber (Cellular One) will compensate and/or reimburse Pacific Bell for all charges and/or expenses incurred in complying with this Order.

(3)  Pacific Bell, its agents, and employees shall not disclose to the subscriber(s) of the telephone service described herein, or those subscribers identified as calling the above mentioned number(s), the existence of this Order or of this investigation, unless otherwise ordered by this Court.

This Order, unless renewed or terminated by the Court, will terminate _____ days from now at _____ on_____ or on a date agreed to before the above mentioned date by the Fresno Police Department and Pacific Bell.


_____              _____
Date                                             Judge of the Municipal Court


## Search Warrant Sample 4

IN THE SUPERIOR COURT OF THE FRESNO JUDICIAL DISTRICT

COUNTY OF FRESNO, STATE OF CALIFORNIA

| STATE OF CALIFORNIA } | AFFIDAVIT IN SUPPORT OF AND |
|---|---|
| } ss | |
| COUNTY OF FRESNO } | PETITION FOR SEARCH WARRANT |

NO._____

Personally appeared before me this 28th day of May, 1991, the affiant, Franklin Clark, a peace officer, who, on oath, makes complaint, and deposes and says that he had and there is probable and reasonable cause to believe, and that he does believe, that there is now on the premises located at and also described as room number 4*** San ****** Hall, University of California, Santa Barbara, California. Room number 4*** is located on the 4th floor of San ****** Hall, a pink 8-story concrete and glass building, trimmed in off white and pink tone block brick. Said room has the numbers 4*** clearly attached to the door at eye level. The name San ****** is displayed on the building face.
    The following personal property, to wit:

1.  Any and all telephones including memory devices and associated peripheral equipment, including automatic dialers, speed dialers, programmable telephone dialing or signalling devices, electronic tone generating devices;

2. Computers, central processing units, external and internal drives and eternal storage equipment or media, terminals or video display units, together with peripheral equipment such as keyboards, printers, modems or acoustic couplers, automatic dialers, speed dialers, programmable telephone dialing or signalling devices, electronic tone generating devices;

3. Any and all computer or data processing software, or data including, but not limited to: hard disks, floppy disks, cassette tapes, video cassette tapes, magnetic tapes, integral RAM or ROM units, and any other permanent or transient storage device(s);

4. The following records and documents, whether contained on paper in handwritten, typed, photocopies or printed form, or stored on computer printouts, magnetic tape, cassettes, disks, diskettes, photooptical devices, or any other medium: telephone and communications activity and service billing records, computer electronic and voice mail system information, access numbers, passwords, personal identification numbers (PINs), telephone and address directories, logs, notes, memoranda and correspondence relating to theft of telephone and communications services, or to unauthorized access into computer, electronic and voice mail systems;

5. Any computing or data processing literature, including, but not limited to: printed copy, instruction books, notes, papers, or listed computer programs, in whole or in part;

6. Indicia of occupancy, including, but not limited to: bills, letters, invoices, personal effects, rental agreements tending to show ownership, occupancy, or control of the premises, or the above described items one through three.

7. Any confirmation numbers, purchase numbers, and purchase information reflecting the use of a credit card to obtain property, goods, or services;

8. Neutralize and seize degaussing equipment located at the search location.

This affidavit recognizes that some of the above described property is data contained on cassette tapes and videotapes and in electronic and machine readable media which is not readable by your affiant in its present state. Authorization is given to searching officers to seize, listen to, read, review, copy, and maintain the above described property and to convert it to human readable form as necessary. Being advised that data stored in computers and telephone memory machines may be lost if it is disconnected from an electrical power source. Authorization is given to make human readable copies or recordings of this data at the search location in order to preserve and protect the information and to thereafter seize, read, listen to, copy, and maintain the described property.

Any and all evidence seized to be held in Evidence at the Fresno Police Department, 2323 Mariposa, City of Fresno, County of Fresno, State of California, until disposition is authorized by a magistrate in said County.

Your affiant says that there is probable and reasonable cause to believe and that he does believe that the said property constitutes;

stolen or embezzled property:
property or things used as the means of committing a felony:
property or things in the possession of a person with the intent to use it as a means of committing a public offense, or in the possession he may have delivered it for the purpose of concealing it or preventing its being discovered:
property or things which consists of an item or constitutes evidence which tends to show that a felony has been committed, or tends to show that a particular person has committed a felony.

Your affiant says that the facts in support of the issuance of the search warrant are as follows:

Your affiant has been a Police Officer for the past 22 years, 11 months, employed in such capacity by the Fresno Police Department and has acted and received the information set forth in this affidavit in that capacity.

Your affiant is now and has been for the past 4 years, 9 months assigned to the Economic/Computer Crimes Detail thereof.

Your affiant has received specialized training in computer use and investigations as well as telecommunications crime investigations as follows:

| | |
|---|---|
| Oct. 17, 1987 | 6 hr., Intro to micro-computers, Clovis West Adult School |
| Oct. 24 – Nov. 21, 1987 | 20 hr., Intro to micro-computers IBM, PC DOS, Pc-Write, DBIII, PC-Tools and basic programming |
| Jan. – Feb., 1988 | 20 hr., Intro to Lotus 123, Clovis West Adult School |
| Jan. 31 – Feb. 3, 1989 | 36 hr., DOJ Computer Crime Investigation, micro & mini & main frame computers, techniques, hardware, software, law & search warrants |
| Aug. 7 – 11, 1989 | 5 days, Federal Law Enforcement Training Center, Glenco, GA, Federal Computer Investigators Committee Re: Computer Crimes Investigation/Investigative Software |
| Oct. 24 – 25, 1989 | 9 hr, City of Fresno info center, WP 5.0 Mod II |
| Feb. 13 – 14, 1989 | 16 hr., Training Center, IBM PC/XT/AT troubleshooting and repair |
| Feb. 28, 1989 | DEC Multi Vendor Environments/LAN Systems |
| Aug. 21, 1990 | San Jose PD, High-Tech Crimes, IBM & FBI re: chip theft and ID of counterfeit chips |
| Sept. 12 – 14, 1990 | High-Tech Law Enforcement Seminar, Intel and Apple at Santa Clara |

Dec. 3 – 14, 1990          Federal Law Enforcement Academy, Glenco, GA
                           Investigations in an Automated Environment Train-
                           ing, including investigations in mainframe, mini, and
                           PC environments, telecommunications frauds

During the past 4 years your affiant has investigated numerous telecommunication frauds including "hacking" and illegal use and exchange of stolen Pacific Bell, U.S. Sprint, Com Systems, and other phone number providers long distance billing numbers, illegal use of and electronic exchange of stolen credit card numbers, and unauthorized entry into and use of business computers by telephone.

On the date of February 13, 1991, your affiant read Fresno Police Department report 91-***** where D*** F******, the General Sales Manager for Cellular One at **** N. Palm, City of Fresno, State of California, reported that on or about February 8, 1991, a person or person(s) unknown called into the Cellular One voice mail system and left a message on approximately 800 customers mail boxes stating "R**** W****, I know where you are and you're a dead man."

Your affiant called the General Manager of Cellular One, S**** J****. S**** J**** told your affiant that a person using the name of "macho man" had called the 281 prefix voice mail computer at Cellular One and somehow found a seven (7) digit system password and electronically entered the computer controlling Cellular One's Fresno voice mail system. "Macho man" had gained access to custom-ers' electronic mail boxes and changed the passwords and was using the mail boxes himself and was exchanging mail with other unauthorized users who are using the above 281 prefix mail boxes. S * * * J * * * * stated that after he listened to the recordings left on the stolen voice mail boxes he discovered that the suspects appeared to be using the voice mail boxes they had stolen from Cellular One to leave and solicit stolen telephone calling card numbers. S*** J**** stated he listened to and recorded messages left on two mail boxes, 281-8805 and 281-8895, after changing the password and locking the suspects out of the mail box. Recorded in these boxes were messages indicating that persons using the above stolen mail boxes were exchanging messages between the boxes on how to "hack" long distance calling card codes, how to send Western Union Mail Grams and bill someone else, and obtaining and use of stolen credit card numbers. S*** J**** stated it sounded like the suspects were hacking MCI, Sprint, and AT&T systems for electronic mail and calling card numbers.

3-20-91 — S*** J**** called me and stated that a review of the Cellular One voice mail boxes showed the following voice mail boxes have been illegally accessed and the passwords changed by "macho man" and other suspects: 281-* * * *,  * * * *,  * * * *, * * * *,  * * * *, * * * *,  * * * *,  * * * *,  * * * * .

G*** C****, the Switch Technician for Cellular One, at **** N. Palm, Fresno, California, told your affiant that what Cellular One operates in Fresno is actually 20,000 phone numbers using the entire 269 and 281 prefixes. These numbers are provided by Pacific Bell and come into his switch from Pacific Bell via a local route from the 209 area code and another tandem incoming call route for calls outside of the 209 area. The computer software at Cellular One controls and routes each of these calls to the appropriate line. Cellular One bought the entire 10,000 numbers of the 281 prefix and 2000 or so of these numbers are set aside for use by the voice mail system. The entire Cellular One system is computer software controlled. The voice mail system is separate from the cellular phone traffic. When calls for voice mail come in they are routed to a stand-alone machine which stores subscribers' voice messages as well as voice messages for the subscriber from outside callers. These messages are digitally stored on a magnetic disk in the voice mail machine. Each subscriber to the voice mail system is given an individual phone number, i.e., 281-8871.

A number of persons identifying themselves as "macho man", "imposter", "AK-47", "doc solo", "gold hawk", "pyro", and some other persons have been getting into voice mail boxes and changing the passwords and leaving and receiving messages without authorization.

3-5-91 — Your affiant dialed 281-****, 281-****, 281-**** and 281-**** and listened to and recorded the messages on these voice mail boxes.

281-**** — A male voice said "All third party billings accepted here for Tony C**** and Karen *****."

281-**** — A male voice said "This is macho man; it's 11:49 eastern standard time, Thursday," and went on to say he had some virgin codes except for the one he was using on 800-***-**** system and he was looking for a pbx that dials the 900 number and any good CBI or TRW codes. Anyone that wanted any codes, leave him a message.

281-**** — A male voice said "414-***-***-****" and was very hard to understand.

281-**** — A male voice said "Yo, this is macho man speaking; leave me a message, I'll get back to you."

3-6-91 — 281-**** was changed to a male voice saying "Mike C*****."

3-7-91 — Your affiant obtained a search warrant for a trap/trace on 281-****, ****, ****, ****. The results of this/trap trace show numerous calls coming into the above numbers from outside the 209 area code, and subscriber information which would identify the caller's phone and name were not available through PT&T.

3-25-91 — Your affiant obtained a search warrant for the above (22) 281-prefix voice mail boxes which the suspects were known to be using. Your affiant listened to several hours of recorded voice mail recordings per the search warrant and recorded the messages on audio tape. One of these boxes, 281-****, was used as a personal voice mail box by a male who identified himself as "the imposter" and T***. "Imposter" bragged on the voice mail system that he had been busted by U.S. Sprint for hacking their phone system 3 years ago in November 1988 and nothing happened to him. He bragged about hacking calling card numbers and left 3 recorded hacking songs on the voice mail system in which "imposter" bragged about hacking calling card codes using his computer which hacked random or sequentially while he was at school. He talked about the penalties for hacking and advised others on the mail system that basically the phone companies did not pursue criminal prosecution but tried to get money from the hackers, sometimes by telling the hackers they were responsible for all the illegal use of the hacked numbers. "Imposter" also talked about hacking with his computer, living in a dorm on campus, using a phone at Sizzler near his place. He asked for anyone having any AT&Ts to send them to him. "Imposter" told others on the voice mail system about rumors that the (800)***-**** number they were using was not MCI but "tele-connect". He was replying to other messages that those using the system were being investigated by MCI.

In a telecommunications fraud control magazine your affiant read that J*** E******, an investigator for Com Systems was working a telephone fraud by a suspect using the code name "R**** W****". Your affiant called J*** E****** to see if the R**** W**** using Cellular One's system was the same person E****** was working.

J*** E****** told me that he did not have an active case on R**** W**** but R** C*****, investigator for GTE, was working cases on "imposter" and has a DNR running right now.

I called R** C*****, who stated he was working "imposter" whose true name is T. W**** who lives on campus at UCSB. W**** is a known hacker who had been arrested approx. 2 to 3 years ago by U.S. Sprint. C**** stated he had a DNR on "imposter's" home phone now and that "imposter" was calling (209)-281-**** often. R** C**** stated that he has been working telecommunications investigations for approx. 15 years and that he reviewed the DNR records on the W**** phone per his investigation and there was evidence of repetitious number hacking taking place on that phone number indicating the use of a computer to dial phone numbers. R** C***** stated he had put the DNR on "imposter's" phone per a complaint by a GTE customer, Wells Fargo Bank. "Imposter" had hacked Wells Fargo's phone system and was charging long distance calls to Wells Fargo's numbers.

R** C***** also told your affiant that "imposter" was being investigated by Brookfield Wisconsin Police Department for extortion by phone and by the UCSB Police for illegal use of their telephone system.

4-4-91 — Your affiant talked to Officer M***** of the University of California at Santa Barbara Police Department. Officer M***** told your affiant that they had a investigation going on T. W****, who uses the name "imposter" and that W**** is living on campus at San ***** Dorm #4*** using a university phone number of (805)***-**** since September 20, 1990. This number is part of a university-operated phone system and their evidence shows that W**** is calling long distance and illegally charging his calls to the university. Officer M***** is also following up on an extortion case against W**** by Detective S***** of the City of Brookfield Police Department as well as the illegal use of the University's phone system.

4-4-91 — Your affiant talked with Officer S*****. Officer S***** stated that he has been working an extortion against W**** known as the "imposter", who lives on campus at the University of California at Santa Barbara. The victim is a juvenile in his jurisdiction who is receiving threats and demands for money from W****, their case 91-****. Officer S****, stated his investigation shows W**** is making the calls to his victim and even to his office and charging the calls to other people's phone numbers. Officer S***** gave me W****'s name, address, CDL, and a condensed copy of their report.

Based on the information received from Cellular One employees, the above investigators, and your affiant's experience and training, your affiant believes the suspects using the Cellular One voice mail without authorization are violating PC 502 (b) and are in fact attempting to traffic in illegally obtained telephone access codes and seeking confidential passwords into credit agency computers. It is your affiant's experience that persons involved in this type of exchange of illegally obtained telephone access codes are also involved in the exchange of stolen credit card numbers and this is consistent with the voice mail left by "imposter" and other unauthorized users on the 281 prefixes as described above. Your affiant believes that the dialed number recording information in possession of GTE on phone number (805)***-**** during the period of February 8, 1991, through March 27, 1991, will show that the telephone (805)***-****, which is listed to T. W****, was used to illegally access the Cellular One 281 voice mail boxes and the DNR information will assist in identifying the person(s) responsible for said illegal access of the phone system.

This DNR information also will provide information necessary for a search warrant for the originating location of illegal access calls to the 281 Cellular One voice mail boxes. Your affiant has probable cause to believe that grounds for the issuance of a search warrant exist, as set forth in Section 15243 of the Penal Code, based upon the aforementioned information, facts, and circumstances.

Your affiant from experience and training is familiar with the exchange of stolen telephone access numbers and the accessing of TRW and CBI to gather credit information and credit card numbers. TRW and CBI are two of the major U.S. credit reporting agencies and with the proper codes persons can enter these computers by computer via telephone and then have access to all the credit reports in the system.

The credit information obtained can then be used to obtain products on credit, apply for new cards and send the bills to the unsuspecting victims, and are often posted on computer bulletin boards for other criminals to use and are sent to voice mail boxes for exchange with other criminals in the same manner.

Good cause being shown, therefore, and that the same be brought before this magistrate or retained subject to the order of this Court, or of any other court in which the offense in respect to which the property or things taken is triable, pursuant to Section 1536 of the Penal Code.

Subscribed and sworn to before me _____
This    day of    , 19 at    a.m. p.m.


_____
JUDGE OF THE MUNICIPAL COURT

## Hacker Residence Warrant

This next warrant is for a typical hacker/phreaker residence. The hacker is suspected of using a computer program with his modem to dial telephone numbers and PIN numbers in order to locate valid long-distance calling card numbers. The hacking programs used to commit these types of crimes are readily available on bulletin boards and the internet in Cyberspace and are easy to use.

Nearly everyone has received a telephone bill with long-distance charges for calls they did not make. Many of these calls are the result of hackers/phreakers using these programs. This crime costs telephone companies many millions of dollars annually. Remember that as with most computer crimes you need an expert to testify to the probable cause in your warrant. In this case, we used the expertise of the telephone company's investigator.

> *Note:* Civilian experts who accompany sworn investigators in the service
> of a search warrant need to be identified in the warrant and their expertise
> and their purpose during the service of the warrant explained in the affi-
> davit.

Pay particular attention to the expertise of the civilian expert and the dictionary of terms used in the search warrant used here. We are qualifying a civilian expert in order to describe the probable cause for the warrant and defining terms so the court is aware of the meanings of words peculiar to this industry.

## Search Warrant Sample 5

IN THE MUNICIPAL COURT OF THE FRESNO JUDICIAL DISTRICT

COUNTY OF FRESNO, STATE OF CALIFORNIA

| | | |
|---|---|---|
| STATE OF CALIFORNIA  ) | | AFFIDAVIT IN SUPPORT OF AND |
| | ) ss | |
| COUNTY OF FRESNO     ) | | PETITION FOR SEARCH WARRANT |

NO._____

Personally appeared before me this 29th day of August,1989, the affiant, L**** B****, a peace officer, who, on oath, makes complaint, and deposes and says that he has and there is probable and reasonable cause to believe, and that he does believe, that there is now on the premises located at and also described as **** NORTH ***** AVENUE, CITY OF FRESNO, COUNTY OF FRESNO, STATE OF CALIFORNIA, described as a single-family dwelling located on the east side of North ***** Avenue, the fifth lot north of R****** Avenue. The dwelling is pale green stucco in color with aluminum window shades on the front west-facing windows. The dwelling has a cedar shake roof. Located on the front, west-facing wall is an address lamp with a white lens and the numerals "****" in black on the cover of the lamp lens. The numerals "****" are located directly south of the front door to the dwelling. Including all rooms, storage areas, garages, and outbuildings assigned to or part of the above described residence.

FOR THE FOLLOWING PROPERTY:

1. Any computing or data processing device(s) and associated peripheral equipment, including but not limited to: computer units, keyboards, display screens, printers, hard or floppy disk drives, cassette recorders, interconnection cables, modems, whether acoustic or electrical, associated telephone sets, speed dialers, and any other controlling devices.
2. Any computing or data processing software, stored on any type of medium such as: hard disks, floppy disks, cassette tapes, integral RAM or ROM units, or other permanent or transient storage medium.
3. Any computing or data processing literature, including, but not limited to instruction books, manuals, or listed computer programs in whole or in part, or any materials printed or otherwise, which make reference to the following telephone and/or billing authorization codes:

A. Com Systems access number: 209-\*\*\*-\*\*\*\*
   Com Systems billing authorization codes:

\*\*\*\*\*\*\*   \*\*\*\*\*\*\*   \*\*\*\*\*\*\*   \*\*\*\*\*\*\*   \*\*\*\*\*\*\*
\*\*\*\*\*\*\*   \*\*\*\*\*\*\*   \*\*\*\*\*\*\*   \*\*\*\*\*\*\*   \*\*\*\*\*\*\*

7112085 and any other seven-digit Com Systems billing
authorization code.

B. Telephone numbers:

| | | |
|---|---|---|
| 201-\*\*\*-\*\*\*\* | 201-\*\*\*-\*\*\*\* | 206-\*\*\*-\*\*\*\* |
| 206-\*\*\*-\*\*\*\* | 209-\*\*\*-\*\*\*\* | 209-\*\*\*-\*\*\*\* |
| 209-\*\*\*-\*\*\*\* | 209-\*\*\*-\*\*\*\* | 209-\*\*\*-\*\*\*\* |
| 209-\*\*\*-\*\*\*\* | 301-\*\*\*-\*\*\*\* | 313-\*\*\*-\*\*\*\* |
| 412-\*\*\*-\*\*\*\* | 419-\*\*\*-\*\*\*\* | 504-\*\*\*-\*\*\*\* |
| 516-\*\*\*-\*\*\*\* | 602-\*\*\*-\*\*\*\* | 609-\*\*\*-\*\*\*\* |
| 614-\*\*\*-\*\*\*\* | 615-\*\*\*-\*\*\*\* | 615-\*\*\*-\*\*\*\* |
| 616-\*\*\*-\*\*\*\* | 619-\*\*\*-\*\*\*\* | 713-\*\*\*-\*\*\*\* |
| 718-\*\*\*-\*\*\*\* | 916-\*\*\*-\*\*\*\* | |

4. Records of occupancy for \*\*\*\* NORTH \*\*\*\*\* AVENUE, FRESNO, CALIFORNIA, which show dominion, ownership, or control of said premises and any of the items to be seized, including, but not limited to, utility bills, credit card bills, insurance receipts, photographs, property tax receipts, postmarked envelopes addressed to \*\*\*\* NORTH \*\*\*\*\* AVENUE, FRESNO, CALIFORNIA, bills of sale for a computer or modem, repair bills for a computer or modem, and sales receipts for floppy disks. Any and all evidence seized to be held in Evidence at the Fresno Police Department, 2323 Mariposa, City of Fresno, County of Fresno, State of California, until disposition is authorized by a magistrate in said County.

Your affiant says that there is probable and reasonable cause to believe and that he does believe that the said property or things which consists of an item or constitutes evidence which tends to show that said property;

\_\_X\_\_  was stolen or embezzled
\_\_X\_\_  was used as the means of committing a felony
\_\_X\_\_  is possessed by a person with the intent to use it as a means of committing a public offense, or is possessed by another to whom he may have delivered it for the purpose of concealing it or preventing its discovery
\_\_X\_\_  is evidence which tends to show a felony has been committed or a particular person has committed a felony

Your affiant says that the facts in support of the issuance of the search warrant are as follows:

Your affiant has been a Police Officer for the past 21 years, employed in such capacity by the Fresno Police Department and has acted and received the information set forth in this affidavit in that capacity.

Your affiant is now and has been for the past 8 years assigned to the Investigations Detail thereof. On the date of August 28, 1989, at approximately 9 a.m., your affiant received information from ***** Y*****, Technical Investigations–Senior Investigator, for the Pacific Bell Telephone company. Y***** developed the information contained within this affidavit.

Your affiant relied on information supplied by ***** Y*****, in the writing of this search warrant.

***** Y***** is employed by Pacific Bell Telephone company, in the capacity of an Investigator within the Security Division, and has so been employed since May of 1983. Y***** is currently a Senior Investigator within the Technical Investigations Unit. Y***** received his Bachelor of Science degree in Business Administration, with a specialization in Accounting, from the California State University, Sacramento, in January of 1983.

Y***** completed an intensive eighty-hour criminal investigative course in November of 1983. This course was certified by the Northern California Criminal Justice Training and Education Center and devoted approximately twenty-four hours to criminal fraud investigation. Y***** has received over forty hours in telephone operations training.

Y***** has received extensive training on the various methods used by individuals employing electronic devices to defraud the telephone network, including the use of computers in violation of California Penal Code (CPC) sections 484e, 502 and 502.7.

During Y*****'s employment with Pacific Bell, he has also received intensive, on-the-job training in the principles of electronic toll fraud investigation and computer abuse. Y***** has become knowledgeable in the workings and operations of personal computers and microcomputers as well as the following programming languages and software: DOS, CP/M, MP/M, BASIC, dBASE II, dBASE III, Word-Star, BASIC, and COBOL.

Y***** has been the primary investigator in over sixty completed fraud investigations involving electronic equipment to detect abuse of the telephone network, thirty-five of which have resulted in arrests and/or complaints being filed for computer crimes (CPC Section 502) and/or fraudulently obtaining telephone service (CPC Section 502.7).

The words used in this search warrant and affidavit have the following meanings:

HARDWARE                    A term describing the physical equipment asso-
                            ciated with a computer system. Hardware may
                            include, but is not limited to, the following
                            items: central processing unit(s) (CPU), video
                            display monitor(s) (VDT), keyboard(s),
                            printer(s), hard disk(s) — whether internal

and/or external to the CPU, floppy (or soft) disk(s), modem(s), autodialer(s), telephone(s), other storage medium(s) used to store data outside of the CPU, and any container(s) used to store such medium(s).

SOFTWARE
A term used to describe the written instructions or programs which may be used to operate the computer hardware.

COMMON CARRIER
An inter-exchange (IEC) carrier or telephone company (e.g., Com Systems, AT&T, MCI, U.S. Sprint) that provides long distance telephone service to its customers.

HACKING
A generic term used to describe the persistent and continuous attempt to gain access and/or knowledge of another's informational database. Such information may include passwords and/or billing authorization codes used to bill legitimate IEC customers.

ACCESS NUMBER
A local, usually toll-free, telephone number provided by a common carrier to its customers to connect them to the common carrier's network. Once the access number is dialed, the customer will then enter (dial) their unique billing authorization code as assigned by the respective common carrier. The call is then billed to that code.

AUTHORIZATION CODE
A series of numbers that represent the billing/account number to a specific authorized customer of a common carrier. The authorization code allows calls to be completed through the telephone network and enables the common carrier to bill the originator of the call(s).

MODEM
An electrical device which enables the transference of computer data over the telephone network. A modem makes it possible for one computer to communicate with another by a telephone line.

DIALED NUMBER
RECORDER (DNR)
A device capable of monitoring the activity (incoming and outgoing calls) of a single telephone line. The DNR will record all digits dialed on outgoing calls, along with the date and time the call was begun and ended by the calling party. The DNR records the date and time of an incoming call; however, no digits are recorded. DNR are sometimes referred to as "pen registers".

NUMBER SEARCH        A printout generated from official accounting
                     billing tapes. A number search will identify call
                     information pertaining to activity on a specific
                     telephone number. Pacific Bell Telephone, pur-
                     suant to tariffs approved by the California Pub-
                     lic Utilities Commission (CPUC), owns, installs,
                     and maintains all its telephone facilities and
                     services and charges for the use of its facilities
                     and services at prescribed rates. Pacific Bell,
                     pursuant to CPUC tariffs, is the authorized
                     agent to investigate electronic toll fraud, code
                     billing abuse, computer abuse, and billing eva-
                     sion activity for other common carriers (tele-
                     phone companies) such as Com Systems which
                     provide telecommunications services to its
                     customers.

Com Systems' long distance company is a communications common
carrier and is regulated by both the Federal Communications Commission and the California Public Utilities Commission. Y*****, through
his employment with Pacific Bell, has become familiar with the services
of various common carriers including Com Systems.

Com Systems essentially operates as follows: First the user dials
a local and usually toll-free access number to connect with the nearest
network. (Quite often these access numbers are assigned by Pacific
Bell and are designed so that more than one person can call them at
the same time and not get a busy signal). Once the access number is
dialed, a tone similar to a dial tone is returned to the caller. Next, the
caller inputs an authorization code provided to him by the common
carrier for identification and billing. (Depending on the company, the
code may be five to fourteen digits). Finally, the caller dials the
telephone number to be called. If a valid authorization or billing code
is input, then the call is routed through the common carrier's network.
If the authorization or billing code is invalid, the common carrier will
ask the caller to redial the call with a valid number. Until a valid
authorization number is dialed, the call will not go through. Computerized billing equipment owned by the common carrier determines the
length of the call and the rates and bills the person whose authorization
code was used to make the call. The use of a common carrier billing
or authorization code is similar to the use of a Pacific Bell/AT&T
"Calling Card". Most common carrier networks and associated computers cannot, at this time, determine the origination point of the calls
placed throughout their network, only the termination point. The common carrier, therefore, is only aware of fraudulent and illegal use of
their customer's authorization codes after the customer receives the
bill for the fraudulent calls and so informs the common carrier.

Y***** is aware, from training and experience, that it is possible
to create a program for a computer that instructs it to continuously

dial any telephone number and supply continuously variable series of codes or numbers in an effort to acquire an authorization code, password, or billing number. Such programs are relatively simple and are published in a number of sources, some of them computer bulletin boards. This kind of computer program is called a "hacker" because its function is to "hack" or break down a code by trying all possible codes until the correct one is reached. Y***** is further aware that "hacking" programs are programmed to attempt various codes by calling a terminating telephone number, usually connected to a computer and answered with standard modem tone. This is done because it is the sound (tone) of the distant computer modem connection that is the signal to the calling ("hacking") computer making the call that the call went through and the authorization code used for that particular code is valid.

A computer set to "hack" need not be attended, for the entire results of its efforts will be listed out for the computer operator when he or she returns. The operator can easily determine how many calls were placed, how many were completed, and what the valid codes are that were used in the completed calls.

Frequently, if it is a seven-digit code that is being hacked, the operator of the computer may start at code 1000000, then on the next attempt try 1000001, and so on. Some of the more sophisticated programs will periodically re-randomize the code increment scheme, so as to not be obvious to office switching personnel who may be observing their computers during the time of the hacking.

Hacking programs are usually set to put through approximately 120 code trials per hour, depending on the program, and often run from several hours to days at a time. Once the valid codes are determined, they are used in a variety of ways to make fraudulent, unauthorized telephone calls. The valid codes that are found by the computer are displayed on the computer screen, and are stored in the memory of the computer and on external media such as hard disks, floppy disks, cassette tapes, and paper media, such as notepads and loose paper sheets.

An investigative method used by Pacific Bell to discover the source of "hacking" is referred to as a "number search." A number search printout will identify "to" and "from" telephone numbers, date, connect time, duration, whether the call was completed or not, and the type of billing method used.

Y***** knows from training and experience that the common carrier switching personnel know when a "hacker" is accessing their network because an unusually high number of invalid codes are used in an attempt to place calls. Common carriers will routinely request Pacific Bell to generate number searches in an attempt to identify the telephone number of the "hacker".

On August 23, 1989, Y***** was advised by G*** M*******, Senior Investigator–Technical Investigations with Pacific Bell Security, of the following:

On July 19, 1989, M******* was contacted by J*** E*****, Network Security Investigator, Com Systems, requesting DNR assistance on subscriber telephone number of 209-439-****. E***** had identified "hacking" activity originating from 209-439-**** into the Com Systems switch number of 209-950-0266.

M******* told Y***** that E***** had obtained this information as a result of reviewing a number search that he had requested from Pacific Bell Security on alleged "hacking" into the Com Systems computer switch located in Fresno, California.

A check of Pacific Bell records revealed that telephone number 209-439-**** is listed to H. W. M***, **** N. ***** Avenue, Fresno, California, and billed to H. M*** at the same address.

On July 21, 1989, a DNR was connected to telephone number 209-439-****.

On July 26, 1989, Senior Investigator M******* reviewed the printouts generated from the DNR. M******* noted that there were no indications of any fraudulent calls being made from telephone number 209-439-****. Moreover, there were no calls placed from telephone number 209-439-**** into the Com Systems long distance network.

M******* checked official Pacific Bell records and discovered that a second telephone service had recently been established at the same residence. The new telephone number is 209-439-****. A check of official Pacific Bell records revealed that telephone number 209-439-**** is listed to K. K***, **** North ***** Avenue, Fresno, California, and billed to H. M*** at the same address.

On July 26, 1989, at the request of E*****, a DNR was connected to the new telephone number 209-439-****.

On August 8, 1989, the DNR was removed from telephone number 209-439-****.

On August 23, 1989, M******* turned the case over to Y*****.

On August 23, 1989, Y***** reviewed the printouts resulting from the DNR placed on telephone number 209-439-****. Y****** noted that on July 26th, between 2:32 p.m. and 9:58 p.m., thirteen calls were made from 209-***-**** into the Com System computer network via access number 209-950-****. Three different seven-digit billing authorizations codes (*******, *******, and *******) were used to place the unauthorized calls.

Y***** observed from the DNR printouts that on July 27th, beginning at 12:41 a.m., a continuous series of calls were made from ***-***-****. The first five calls were captured by the DNR as follows:

| Called Number | Authorization Code | Called Number |
| --- | --- | --- |
| 950-**** | ******* | 209-233-**** |
| 950-**** | ******* | 209-233-**** |

| Called Number | Authorization Code | Called Number |
|---|---|---|
| 950-* * * * | * * * * * * * | 209-233-* * * * |
| 950-* * * * | * * * * * * * | 209-233-* * * * |
| 950-* * * * | * * * * * * * | 209-233-* * * * |

The calls continued in this pattern (with the authorization code being incremented by a factor of one) every 24 to 25 seconds until the "hacking" ended on July 27th at 10:56 a.m. At the rate of one code tried every 24 to 25 seconds, approximately 1257 codes were "hacked" to determine their validity.

Y***** checked official Pacific Bell records and found out that telephone number 209-233-**** is a computer access number listed to T******* C************** Corporation, **** T****** Street, Fresno, California. Y***** dialed 209-233-**** and heard a standard computer modem tone. Further inspection of the DNR print-outs revealed additional "hacking" originating from 209-439-****. A "hacking" sequence began on July 28th at 1:44 a.m. The first five calls were captured by the DNR as follows:

| Called Number | Authorization Code | Called Number |
|---|---|---|
| 950-* * * * | * * * * * * * | 209-233-* * * * |
| 950-* * * * | * * * * * * * | 209-233-* * * * |
| 950-* * * * | * * * * * * * | 209-233-* * * * |
| 950-* * * * | * * * * * * * | 209-233-* * * * |
| 950-* * * * | * * * * * * * | 209-233-* * * * |

The calls continued in this pattern (with the authorization code being randomly generated by the "hacking" computer) every 24 to 25 seconds until the "hacking" ended on July 28th at 11:22 a.m. At the rate of one code tried every 24 to 25 seconds, approximately 930 codes were "hacked" to determine their validity.

Y***** observed another "hacking" sequence in which seven-digit Com System authorizations codes were "hacked". The "hacking" began on July 29th at 2:47 a.m. and ended on July 29th at 9:53 a.m. Approximately 877 additional codes were "hacked" to determine their validity.

Y***** noted the following billing authorization code abuse generated from 209-439-****. Starting on July 27th at 10:56 a.m. and ending on August 11th at 3:12 a.m., Y***** observed the following unauthorized calls:

| Authorization Code Used | Number of Times Used |
|---|---|
| * * * * * * * | 101 |
| * * * * * * * | 23 |
| * * * * * * * | 19 |
| * * * * * * * | 6 |

```
* * * * * * *                              2
* * * * * * *                              1
* * * * * * *                              1
* * * * * * *                              1
* * * * * * *                              1
* * * * * * *                              1
```

Y***** noted that the following telephone numbers were dialed using Com System billing authorization codes, all without the permission of Com System:

```
201-* * * -* * * *  201-* * * -* * * *  206-* * * -* * * *  206-* * * -* * * *
209-* * * -* * * *  209-* * * -* * * *  209-* * * -* * * *  209-* * * -* * * *
209-* * * -* * * *  209-* * * -* * * *  301-* * * -* * * *  313-* * * -* * * *
412-* * * -* * * *  419-* * * -* * * *  504-* * * -* * * *  516-* * * -* * * *
602-* * * -* * * *  609-* * * -* * * *  614-* * * -* * * *  615-* * * -* * * *
615-* * * -* * * *  616-* * * -* * * *  619-* * * -* * * *  713-* * * -* * * *
718-* * * -* * * *  916-* * * -* * * *
```

On August 24, 1989, Y***** contacted E***** of Com Systems. E***** stated that none of the billing authorization codes were assigned to anyone residing at **** North ***** Avenue, Fresno, California. E***** provided the following information:

Code# *******   Norman Stanbler & Company
                *** W. Redondo Beach Blvd.
                * * * * *, C A * * * * *
                Contact: J. S***** @ 213-* * * -* * * *
Code# *******   R. J****
                ***** Woodland Drive
                * * * * *, C A * * * * *
                Contact: R. J***** @ 714-* * * -* * * *
Code# *******   McCaslin Oil Company, Inc.
                P.O. Box ***
                * * * * * * *, C A * * * * *
                Contact: J. M****** @ 805-* * * -* * * *
Code# *******   W. B********
                *** Hodencamp Road
                T * * * * * * * * * *, C A * * * * *
                Contact: W. B******** @ 805-* * * -* * * *
Code# *******   Schneider Publishing Company
                **** Third Street Promenade
                * * * * * * * * *, C A * * * *
                Contact: T. S****** @ 213-* * * -* * * *

At the time of this writing, Com Systems was unable to determine the amount of fraud that had been accumulated due to unauthorized usage.

On August 24, 1989, your affiant, drove by **** North *****
Avenue, Fresno, California, and obtained a description of the residence.

Y***** has maintained possession and control of the aforementioned DNR printouts as generated from telephone number
209-439-**** at the Pacific Bell Security office, 180 New Mont-
gomery Street, Room 250, San Francisco, California. Pacific Bell
Telephone company, pursuant to a California Public Utilities Commission
tariff, is the authorized agent to investigate toll fraud and computer
related fraud over common carrier telephone lines for Com Systems.

Y*****, based on his investigation of suspect telephone number
209-439-****, believes that someone residing at **** North
***** Avenue, Fresno, California,

initiated over 3050 calls through the Com Systems computer access
port located in Fresno, California, using a computer-generated
"hacking" program.

made and/or attempted to make over 165 illicit calls, using at least
eleven (11) different Com System billing authorization codes,
none of which were assigned to anyone residing at said address.

made and/or attempted to make calls using stolen Com System
billing authorization codes to the following telephone numbers:

201-* * * - * * * *
201-* * * - * * * *
206-* * * - * * * *
206-* * * - * * * *
209-* * * - * * * *
209-* * * - * * * *

Y***** checked a Pacific Bell White Pages directory, which
revealed the following information:

| Area Code | State Served |
|-----------|--------------|
| 201 | New Jersey |
| 206 | Washington |
| 209 | California |
| 301 | Maryland |
| 313 | Michigan |
| 412 | Pennsylvania |
| 419 | Quebec |
| 504 | Louisiana |
| 516 | New York |
| 602 | Arizona |
| 609 | New Jersey |
| 614 | Ohio |

| 615 | Tennessee |
| 616 | Michigan |
| 619 | California |
| 713 | Texas |
| 718 | New York |
| 916 | California |

Based on training, experience and information contained in this affidavit, ***** Y***** has formed the opinion that:

1. There is at least one computer installation of some complexity located within the premises known as **** North ***** Avenue, Fresno, California.
2. The computer is capable of receiving and transmitting data over the telephone lines and can dial telephone numbers automatically using programmed software.
3. There is a computer program, contained in some sort of storage device or medium, located within the premises at **** North ***** Avenue, Fresno, California, the sole function of which is to "hack" valid billing authorization codes from long distance common carrier companies in violation of CPC Section 502.7.
4. The person(s) responsible for the operation of the computer system at **** North ***** Avenue, Fresno, California, is in violation of California Penal Code Section 502 (c) in that they are knowingly and without permission using a computer system to execute a scheme to defraud and to wrongfully obtain data.
5. Someone at the above address is using common carrier billing authorization codes, without express approval of Com Systems, to place illicit telephone calls in violation of 502.7 P.C.
6. Someone at the above address is in violation of California Penal Code Section 484(e) in that, within a consecutive 12-month period, he or she acquired four or more fraudulently obtained common carrier billing authorization codes.

Based on the investigation conducted by Y***** described herein, your affiant has reasonable cause to believe that the involved numbers named in this affidavit and search warrant will be recorded in some form, such as on hard disks, floppy disks, cassette tapes, RAM units, paper mediums, notepads, or loose paper sheets, at **** North ***** Avenue, Fresno, California.

The above described investigation has not revealed the identity of the user or users of the above described computer hardware or software or the fraudulent user or users of the billing numbers. Items tending to show dominion and control are needed to establish that identity.

In your affiant's experience, utility bills, credit card bills, insurance receipts, photographs, property tax receipts, postmarked envelopes addressed to the address of the location being searched, bills of sale for a computer or modem, repair bills for a computer or modem, and sales receipts for floppy disks are commonly found in the residence and tend to indicate either directly or circumstantially the identities of the occupants of the premises or the owner and user of the computer hardware and software.

Your affiant prays that a search warrant be issued, based upon the above facts, for the seizure of the property, as described herein or any part thereof, between the hours of 7:00 a.m. and 10:00 p.m., good cause being shown thereof, and that the same be brought before this Magistrate or retained subject to the order of the court, or of any other court in which the offense(s) in respect to which the property or things taken, is triable, pursuant to Section 1536 of the Penal Code.

_____
(Signature of Affiant)

Subscribed and sworn to before me this _____ day of _____, 19__.

_____
(Signature of Magistrate)
Judge of the Municipal Court Fresno Judicial District

## Prodigy® Services Warrant

The next warrant is for business records for Prodigy Services Company, a major online service provider. The authors had received child pornography in GIF format via Prodigy e-mail from a suspect unknown. These pictures depicted a young boy (7 or 8 years old) who appeared to be unconscious, who was being sodomized. This warrant is typical of the items and records needed to identify suspects using online services for illegal purposes.

The authors have found that many businesses will comply with the exact wording of the search warrant, if not the intent. Thus, if you do not ask for the items you want by the name the organization uses for them, you will often end up writing another warrant for the desired items using their industry's words to describe the evidence/documents you are looking for. Save yourself some time and ask them for the names of the documents they use for their business records and double check the list with more than one employee just in case something inadvertently was left out by the first employee. Be particularly careful if you are getting your information from a company attorney! They may well have a different agenda from yours.

## Search Warrant Sample 6

SW NO. _____

STATE OF CALIFORNIA — COUNTY OF FRESNO

SEARCH WARRANT AND AFFIDAVIT

(AFFIDAVIT)

Franklin Clark, being sworn, says that on the basis of the information contained within this Search Warrant and Affidavit and the attached and incorporated **Statement of Probable Cause**, he/she has probable cause to believe and does believe that the property described below is lawfully seizable pursuant to Penal Code Section 1524, as indicated below, and is now located at the locations set forth below. Wherefore, affiant requests that this Search Warrant be issued.

_____, NIGHT SEARCH REQUESTED: YES( ) NO(XX)

(SEARCH WARRANT)

**THE PEOPLE OF THE STATE OF CALIFORNIA TO ANY SHERIFF, POLICEMAN OR PEACE OFFICER IN THE COUNTY OF FRESNO:** proof by affidavit having been made before me by Franklin Clark that there is probable cause to believe that the property described herein may be found at the locations set forth herein and that it is lawfully seizable pursuant to Penal Code Section 1524 as indicated below by "X"(s) in that it:

_____   was stolen or embezzled.
XX      was used as the means of committing a felony.
_____   is possessed by a person with the intent to use it as means of
        committing a public offense or is possessed by another to whom
        he or she may have delivered it for the purpose of concealing
        it or preventing its discovery.
XX      tends to show that a felony has been committed or that a
        particular person has committed a felony.
XX      tends to show that sexual exploitation of a child, in violation
        of P.C. Section 311.3, has occurred or is occurring.

**YOU ARE THEREFORE COMMANDED TO SEARCH:**
Between the hours of 7:00 a.m. and 10:00 p.m. or at any time of the day or night to make immediate search, Prodigy Services Company, 445 Hamilton Avenue, White Plains NY 10601

**FOR THE FOLLOWING PROPERTY:**
Records kept in the normal course of business including, but not limited to, subscriber information on the following Prodigy customer IDs: D. L**** DJEC49A, J. S**** YXNW82A, S**** G**** NVSE43A, K*** G**** NVSE43B, and B**** G**** NVSE43C, including name, address, telephone number(s), date of birth, gender, martial status, date of enrollment, billing information, associated account number information, mail cover information identifying to whom the above IDs sent electronic mail by ID and the associated identifiers of these IDs, session records including the PLS code showing the Prodigy phone line location from where the above IDs originated their calls, any and all phone records from Prodigy's 800 Membership Support lines showing calls from D. L**** DJEC49A and J. S**** YXNW82A, and any and all memos, notes or written reports regarding these 800 line calls by Prodigy Services Company employees.

Said records to be provided to the Fresno Police Department within 10 days by B*** S******, Attorney for Prodigy Services Company.

And if you find the same, or any part thereof, to retain it in your custody, subject to order of court as provided by law. Given under my hand, and dated this_____day of_____A.D. 19_____, at _____ _____ a.m./p.m.

Judge of said

Court_____Attest:_____Clerk

## STATEMENT OF PROBABLE CAUSE

Your affiant, Franklin Clark, is a Detective with the Fresno Police Department and has been so employed for the last 25 years. Your affiant has been assigned to the Economic/Computer Crimes Unit for approx. 8 years. Your affiant has received extensive training in the area of micro computers and telecommunications over the last 8 years, from California Department of Justice, Federal Law Enforcement Training Center, Federal Computer Investigators Committee, The High Tech Crime Investigators Association; he has attended computer classes at Clovis West Adult School, City of Fresno software classes, and hardware and software classes, at The Training Center Fresno. Your affiant has taught covert bulletin board investigation classes for the Federal Law Enforcement Training Center, Canadian Police College, and the Federal Computer Investigators Committee.

Your affiant has written over two dozen search warrants for computers and computer systems. Your affiant is familiar with microcomputers, software, and telecommunications hardware and techniques. Your affiant has investigated over a dozen computer bulletin board systems, including those involved in pedophilia, distribution of pornography including "child pornography" (pornographic pictures sent over the computer involving minors).

Since August 1993 your affiant has been investigating reports of grand theft (use of fraudulent credit cards), stalking, online harassment, and possible pedophilia on Prodigy bulletin boards. This investigation was initiated at the request of Prodigy Security.

Your affiant was given Prodigy ID NDDA67A to use while investigating the online abuse of Prodigy bulletin board services.

February 10, 1994, at 11:28 a.m. your affiant posted a message on the Prodigy Bulletin Board under the Members Exchange BBS in the subject Stalkers Advisory**** (see attachments A1 and A2). Stalker refers to persons believed to be responsible for the theft of services from Prodigy Services Company, a national computer bulletin board service. The suspect(s) obtain free starter kits consisting of a computer disk, ID, and password to allow the computer and modem to connect to Prodigy's computers. When the user signs on they have 30-day limited access to Prodigy services and limited use of the electronic mail system. When the 30 days or the mail service limit is exceeded, the user must pay for the service. In this case, the 30-day period and/or the mail limit was exceeded, causing charges to be placed against the account and related fraudulent credit card numbers which went unpaid.

The second part of the stalker investigation involved what appears to be a group of connected persons receiving perhaps hundreds of theses starter kits, dozens of which were being sent to *** W. *******, Fresno, CA. This address is known by your affiant to be the mailing address of M**** J. who, for over three years, has been known by your affiant to use many fraudulent names and addresses, as well as listing fraudulent credit card numbers for their billing which circumstantial evidence suggests are being used by the same person(s) using the multiple kits and running up costs on the Prodigy system exceeding $3000.

These same persons are variously described as "Vito and company" and the "Stalker" and are suspected of being involved in sending vulgar and threatening electronic messages to other persons on the Prodigy system as well as using multiple Prodigy startup kits and running up unpaid bills on Prodigy using fraudulent credit card numbers when logging onto Prodigy systems. This second group, which is receiving the vulgar and threatening messages from "Vito" and the "Stalker", is sometimes known as COLD, which is an acronym for Coalition for Online Decency and is used to describe the victims of harassing e-mail and public posted messages on Prodigy.

On February 15, 1994, your affiant was contacted by S***** R********, a reporter from the *Fresno Bee,* who had received your affiant's Prodigy posts A-1 and A-2 and responses from Prodigy member J. S**** YXNW82A.

On February 16, 1994, your affiant read his personal e-Mail on the Prodigy Bulletin Board. The e-mail included twenty messages asking your affiant for "gifs". GIF is known to your affiant to be a standard file format for graphic images on computers. These images look like photographs and often are photos taken with a video camera or digital camera which is connected to a computer; the photograph is then stored digitally in the computer as a GIF file. These GIF files can be displayed on the computer screen and printed or placed on disk or sent via modem and viewed on another compatible computer. These mail messages are attached to this warrant as attachments B-1 through B-10.

In addition to the above messages, there were two GIF image files in your affiant's mail box which the mail header identified as being sent by S**** G**** Prodigy ID NVSE43A. This mail header lists the ID of the person being sent the message, the sender of the message, the subject, and the date. The sender and date are put on the mail automatically by Prodigy's computer, which reads the ID off the software being used to log onto Prodigy Services. These two GIFs were downloaded (copied from your affiant's Prodigy mail box to your affiant's computer in the Fresno Police Department) and viewed on screen. These two GIFS were named Scotty's.gif and THEGUYS.gif and are attached to this affidavit as attachments C1 and C2, respectively. Scotty's.gif shows two nude young boys, one having anal intercourse with the other. THEGUYS.gif shows three nude young boys lying on their backs touching their own penises. These two GIFs were sent to your affiant by S**** G**** NVSE43A according to the mail header on the GIFs. The e-mail sent to your affiant by S**** G**** NVSE43A is attached to this affidavit as attachment D-1.

Your affiant contacted Sex Crimes Investigator J*** P****** of the Fresno Police Department. J*** P****** has been a police officer for over 27 years and has worked on sex crimes for over 14 years. He investigates in excess of 400 sex crimes a year, many of which involve children. Your affiant showed Detective P****** the printed picture of the above GIFs, which were sent electronically to your affiant. Detective P****** stated that in his opinion, based on his training and experience, the boys in these GIFs are no older than 10 years of age.

Your affiant contacted Prodigy Information Security Officer, A*** B****** and Prodigy's Security Attorney B*** S****** regarding the above-listed e-mail and GIFs sent to your affiant.

A*** B****** told your affiant that notes were posted on Prodigy by D. L**** DJEC49A and J. S**** YXNW82A stating something to the effect that ID NDDA67A (your affiant's ID on Prodigy) had lots of GIFs and to send your affiant mail asking for the pictures they wanted and NDDA67A would send them the pictures. Mr. B****** stated that the prodigy posts by D. L**** and J. S**** had been pulled by Prodigy but could be obtained from their archive files, as could the other information requested in this search warrant. He stated that these two IDs used the same address of \*\*\* L. Street, Sacramento, California. J. S\*\*\*\* had recently called Prodigy's 1-800 number for Customer Support several times asking for Prodigy IDs and had on one occasion claimed to be the "Stalker". Mr. B\*\*\*\*\*\* stated that he can determine the originating phone number of the calls to Prodigy's 1-800 number by D. L\*\*\*\* and J. S\*\*\*\* by their phone bill.

Mr. B\*\*\*\*\*\* stated that Prodigy's records show that S\*\*\*\* G\*\*\*\* NVSE43A is a valid ID and they have a billing address for the ID. D. L\*\*\*\* and J. S\*\*\*\* do not appear to be paying members of Prodigy services but were using temporary startup ID kits. The use of the startup kits and the \*\*\* L. Street, Sacramento, California, address and the phone calls to Prodigy are consistent with the "stalker" who is already under investigation for the use of fraudulent credit cards.

Your affiant has been in regular contact with M\*\*\*\* J. of Fresno in person and by phone and e-mail since August 1994. M\*\*\*\* J. has described himself to your affiant as a frequent user of lots of names and IDs on Prodigy using free Prodigy startup kits. He had bragged about harassing Prodigy members, including the COLD group, and admits that they accuse him of being "vito" and the "Stalker". M\*\*\*\* J. has told your affiant that he is now using numerous Prodigy IDs which do not require a credit card and that all he does is call Prodigy services to obtain a new ID and password. Two of these latest e-mails from M\*\*\*\* J. are attached to this case; see attachments E-1 through E-4.

Based on your affiant's training and experience, your affiant believes that the business records of Prodigy Services Company contain information that will provide the identity and address of the person responsible for sending your affiant the attached "child pornography" pictures through Prodigy electronic mail via computer. Your affiant also believes that information in the business records of Prodigy Services Company will identify the phone number and personal information on D. L\*\*\*\* and J. S\*\*\*\* who posted the messages telling people to send mail to your affiant asking for GIFs. Further investigation is needed to determine if said archived Prodigy messages by these two subjects constitute procurement or conspiracy to transmit child pornography. This information may also tend to identify the "Stalker" who has been involved in credit fraud on Prodigy for the last year.

## Credit Card Warrant

The next warrant is for the home of a suspect using fraudulent credit cards to obtain services through an online service provider. He also was suspected of online stalking and having illegal sex with a minor. This warrant covers the basic "boiler plate" of items to search for when seeking computers and computer-related hardware.

## Search Warrant Sample 7

SW NO. _____

STATE OF CALIFORNIA — COUNTY OF FRESNO

SEARCH WARRANT AND AFFIDAVIT
(AFFIDAVIT)

Franklin Clark, being sworn, says that on the basis of the information contained within this Search Warrant and Affidavit and the attached and incorporated **Statement of Probable Cause**, he/she has probable cause to believe and does believe that the property described below is lawfully seizable pursuant to Penal Code Section 1524, as indicated below, and is now located at the locations set forth below. Wherefore, affiant requests that this Search Warrant be issued.

_____, NIGHT SEARCH REQUESTED: YES( ) NO( )

(SEARCH WARRANT)

**THE PEOPLE OF THE STATE OF CALIFORNIA TO ANY SHERIFF, POLICEMAN OR PEACE OFFICER IN THE COUNTY OF FRESNO:** proof by affidavit having been made before me by Franklin Clark that there is probable cause to believe that the property described herein may be found at the locations set forth herein and that it is lawfully seizable pursuant to Penal Code Section 1524 as indicated below by "X"(s) in that it:

| | |
|---|---|
| ____ | was stolen or embezzled. |
| XX | was used as the means of committing a felony. |
| XX | is possessed by a person with the intent to use it as means of committing a public offense or is possessed by another to whom he or she may have delivered it for the purpose of concealing it or preventing its discovery. |
| XX | tends to show that a felony has been committed or that a particular person has committed a felony. |
| XX | tends to show that sexual exploitation of a child, in violation of P.C. Section 311.3, has occurred or is occurring. |

**YOU ARE THEREFORE COMMANDED TO SEARCH:**
Between the hours of 7:00 a.m. and 10:00 p.m. or at any time of the day or night to make immediate search of \*\*\* W. C\*\*\*\*, City of Fresno, County of Fresno, State of California, located between T\*\*\*\* and A\*\*\*\*\*\*, a single story beige wood-sided building with a gray asphalt roof. The numbers \*\*\* appear above the front south-facing door. And further described as having a detached garage. Said search to include a vacation trailer parked on the west side of the house and

numerous vehicles parked in the backyard, driveway, and garage of said residence and any and all outbuildings attached or unattached.

**FOR THE FOLLOWING PROPERTY:**
Description of Personal Property to be seized:

1.  Any and all telephones, including memory devices and associated peripheral equipment, including automatic dialers, speed dialers, programmable telephone dialing or signalling devices, electronic tone generating devices;
2.  Computers, central processing units, external and internal drives, external storage equipment or media, terminals or video display units, together with peripheral equipment such as keyboards, printers, modems or acoustic couplers, scanners, automatic dialers, speed dialers, programmable telephone dialing or signalling devices, electronic tone generating devices;
3.  Any and all computer or data processing software or data, including, but not limited to, hard disks, floppy disks, cassette tapes, videocassette tapes, magnetic tapes, integral RAM or ROM units, and any other permanent or transient storage device(s);
4.  The following records and documents, whether contained on paper in handwritten, typed, photocopied, or printed form or stored on computer printouts, magnetic tape, cassettes, disks, diskettes, photo optical devices, or any other medium: telephone and communications activity and service billing records, computer electronic and voice mail system information, identification numbers, access numbers, passwords, personal identification numbers (PINS), telephone and address directories, logs, notes, memoranda and correspondence relating to theft of telephone and communications services, or to unauthorized access into computer services or electronic and voice mail systems;
5.  Any computing or data processing literature, including, but not limited to, printed copy, instruction books, notes, papers, or listed computer programs, in whole or in part;
6.  Indicia of occupancy, including, but not limited to, bills, letters, invoices, personal effects rental agreements tending to show ownership, occupancy, or control of the premises, or the above described items one through three.
7.  Any confirmation numbers, purchase numbers, and purchase information reflecting the use of a credit card or credit services to obtain property, goods or services;
8.  Neutralize and seize degaussing equipment located at the search location.
9.  Any and all FAX machines.
10. Pictures, whether on film, slides, printed, photographs, electronic media, or on magnetic media, depicting nude minors.

This affidavit recognizes that some of the above described property is data contained on cassette tapes, videotapes, and in electronic and machine-readable media which is not readable by your affiant in its present state. Authorization is given to the searching officers to seize, listen to, read, review, copy, and maintain the above-described property and to convert it to human-readable form as necessary, being advised that data stored in computers and telephone memory machines may be lost if disconnected from an electrical power source. Authorization is given to make human readable copies or recordings of this data at the search location in order to preserve and protect the information and to thereafter seize, read, listen to, copy, and maintain the described property.

And if you find the same, or any part thereof, to retain it in your custody, subject to order of court as provided by law. Given under my hand, and dated this_____day of_____A.D. 19_____, at _____ _____ a.m./p.m.

Judge of said

Court_____Attest:_____Clerk

## STATEMENT OF PROBABLE CAUSE

Your affiant, Franklin Clark, is a Detective with the Fresno Police Department and has been so employed for the last 25 years. Your affiant has been assigned to the Economic/Computer Crimes Unit for approx. 8 years. Your affiant has received extensive training in the area of microcomputers and telecommunications over the last 8 years from California Department of Justice, Federal Law Enforcement Training Center, Federal Computer Investigators Committee, The High Tech Crime Investigators Association; he has attended computer classes at Clovis West Adult School, City of Fresno software classes, and hardware and software classes at The Training Center Fresno. Your affiant has taught covert bulletin board investigation classes for the Federal Law Enforcement Training Center, Canadian Police College, and the Federal Computer Investigators Committee. He has taught Computer Search Techniques classes for investigators with the Internal Revenue Service, Fresno Police Department, Fresno Sheriff's Office, and the Secret Service. He has taught classes in computer hardware and troubleshooting for investigators with the Internal Revenue Service.

Your affiant has written over two dozen search warrants for computers and computer systems. Your affiant is familiar with microcomputers, software, and telecommunications hardware and techniques. Your affiant has investigated over a dozen computer bulletin board systems, including those involved in pedophilia and distribution of pornography, including "child pornography" (pornographic pictures sent over the computer involving minors).

Since August 1993 your affiant has been investigating reports of grand theft (use of fraudulent credit cards), stalking, online harassment, and possible pedophilia on Prodigy bulletin boards. This investigation was initiated at the request of Prodigy Security.

This case involves the theft of services from Prodigy Services Company, a national computer bulletin board service. The suspect(s) obtain free starter kits consisting of a computer disk and/or an ID# and password, which allows a person using a computer and modem to connect to Prodigy's computers and obtain limited use of Prodigy's services. When users sign on, they have 30-day limited access to Prodigy services and limited use of its electronic mail system. When the 30 days or the mail service limit is exceeded, the user must pay for the service. In this case, the 30-day period and/or the mail limit was exceeded, causing charges to be placed against the account, which went unpaid. Also involved in this case is what appears to be suspect(s) receiving hundreds of the starter kits and using many names and addresses, as well as listing fraudulent credit card numbers for billing, which circumstantial evidence suggests are the same person(s) using the multiple kits and running up costs on the Prodigy system exceeding $4000.

These same persons are variously described as "Vito and company" and the "Stalkers" and are suspected of being involved in sending vulgar and threatening electronic messages to other persons on the Prodigy system, as well as using multiple Prodigy startup kits and running up unpaid bills on Prodigy using fraudulent credit cards.

In July 1993, the suspect M**** J., who is known to your affiant, came by my office regarding the conviction of M**** F***** on a sexual assault case. M**** J. told me about his activities on Prodigy Services' Bulletin Board and the fun he was having with a bunch of Saturn car owners in one section of Prodigy. He advised me that Prodigy sends him hundreds of starter kits which are good for 30 days free use. He uses these kits for 30 days or less and then uses another, and meanwhile gives the Saturn owners a bad time and they give him a bad time about Volkswagens.

M**** J. told me he used the name "Vito" on Prodigy and now everyone who gives the Saturn folks a bad time is called "Vito". M**** J. stated that Prodigy just keeps sending the kits and he never goes over their limits or incurs charges and the online stuff is just having fun.

At the end of July, your affiant received a call from B*** S., an attorney for Prodigy. Mr. S stated that there was a stalker on Prodigy who used the name "Vito". This person was harassing and threatening persons on the Saturn Board on Prodigy. This person was also signing onto Prodigy with false credit card numbers, exceeding the free service provided by the startup kits, and incurring charges against the fraudulent credit card numbers.

They suspected that the person lived in Fresno, as most of the Prodigy kits being used by the stalker used a Fresno PLS (Prodigy local service) phone number. Also, dozens of the free startup kits were being sent to *** West C***** in Fresno, and one name kept coming up, a M**** J., but they did not know if the address and name were legitimate or not. B*** S. stated that Prodigy's Security, A. B*****, had the evidence of the stalking.

In late July and early August, after a couple of phone calls with B*** S. and later A. B*****, Mr. S. stated that what they wanted right now was for M**** J. to cease and desist. If he would leave Prodigy and stop the stalking, they would not press charges.

Your affiant called M**** J. and advised him of the complaint by Prodigy. M**** J. stated he was not using Prodigy anymore, that he would immediately erase any Prodigy information from his hard disk and would not use the service anymore. He stated Prodigy had continued to send him approx. 500 startup kits and he would throw them away.

About 2 weeks later, your affiant received a call from A. B*****, who stated that the suspect in Fresno was back at it again. He was using many startup kits, using fraudulent credit card numbers, and stalking Prodigy members.

On December 6, 1993, your affiant reviewed some 19 pounds of computer printouts from Prodigy. Included was a list of suspected "Stalker" IDs, names used, and the credit card numbers along with the loss to Prodigy for the use of their services which were charged against fraudulent credit cards. This list is attached to this affidavit as attachments A-1 and A-2.

Your affiant then called M**** J. again and asked him to come in and talk about this list of IDs and names and false credit cards your affiant had received from Prodigy. M**** J. told me he is the one being harassed and there are different Vito's on Prodigy. M**** J. went on to say that he had not been on Prodigy since your affiant talked to him so if any of this stuff was since August it was not him, as he was not on Prodigy, and that someone was trying to set him up. He told me he wanted to talk to his attorney before he came in to talk to me and he could prove Prodigy wrong about his using the kits and credit cards.

On December 13, 1993, B. M******* called your affiant and stated she understood from M**** J. that I wanted to talk to her about Prodigy and that she was a suspect in the Vito/Stalking case. She said she wanted me to know she had a legal ID on Prodigy and that M**** J. was using her ID, DGKJ12B, under the name of R. M*****.

She said she met R. S******* and M**** on Prodigy. They met on the Saturn board. She, R. M****, and M**** J. were labeled the "Vito" crowd, and people who liked Saturns, consisting of L.G., L.P., I.F., E.M., P.B., C.F. and C.B., were known as COLD, or Coalition for Online Decency and seemed to be giving them a bad time. The COLD group threatened law suits and accused her of harassing and getting a woman fired who worked for Saturn. Now there were accusations of "Vito" being a stalker and pedophile and she was afraid things were getting out of hand.

L.P., L.G., and numerous others on Prodigy called your affiant in December and continue to call about the ongoing threats and harassment by the Stalker/Vito to this date, April 12, 1994. They complained that the Vito/Stalker personalities were sending e-mail bombs — that is, sending hundreds of copies of the same message to their e-mail and filling it up and forcing them to check through hundreds of messages before they could get to their real mail, thus depriving them of a mail service they had paid for — and that they receive vulgar and threatening e-mail and messages from the Stalker/Vito IDs.

L.G. told your affiant that he works for H******* Productions, and on November 18, 1993, his employer G*** S**** received an "extortion" letter by FAX, claiming that L.G. was a convicted pedophile, and if he was not terminated the writers were going to withdraw all financial support from the company. This FAX is attached to this affidavit. L.G. had posted information on his job on Prodigy, and the letter is very similar to other online messages of Vito/Stalkers.

On December 28, 1993, M**** J. and his attorney E** P***** came into my office. I advised M**** J. that I had reviewed the information sent to me by Prodigy and the names of victims who had received hate mail, death threats, and vulgar mail. I only wanted to know a couple of things from him. Did he use fraudulent credit card numbers when signing onto Prodigy using the free kits? The second question was, did he send the vulgar mail and death threats to the COLD victims?

M**** J. denied even being on Prodigy except to lurk. (That means he just read the public messages, he did not post messages or send mail.) He stated he has not even used Prodigy or sent mail since I talked to him in August. His attorney confirmed that, saying he knows personally that his client has not been on Prodigy. I explained that what they had just said was not the truth as I had witnesses that M**** J. had been using R.M.'s ID.

M**** J. admitted lurking but denied posting or mailing messages since August and stated several times that he had never used credit cards when logging onto Prodigy. M**** J. said he would go home and remove anything to do with Prodigy from his computers and his attorney could watch him to make sure it was done. M**** J. again confirmed he was getting rid of all Prodigy material and said he had never used credit cards or sent the threats or vulgar messages.

On February 16, 1994, your affiant read my e-mail on Prodigy and several people were asking me to send them GIFs (graphic information format for computer pictures). One person, S**** G**** NVSE43A, had sent me two GIFs. Both were sexually explicit nude photos of young boys (8 to 11 years old). Your affiant wrote and served a search warrant on Prodigy for the ID and personal information on

the suspect who had sent the GIFs of the young boys. A.*****
B****** had told me that this person was a regularly billed member
of Prodigy. The information supplied pursuant to the search warrant
showed that the suspect had used fraudulent information, had never
paid his Prodigy bill, and his information was not verified.

Your affiant did find that the persons who had posted on Prodigy
in the TEENS.BBS under Alternate Lifestyles, where my ID had lots of
GIFs, were J. S********** YXNW82A and associated family members and D. L**** DJEC49A. Both of these IDs were later identified
as calling from a Fresno PLS and using a password of "diesel". A
citizen informant listed in this affidavit as "the victim" told your
affiant that "diesel" was M**** J.'s most common password on
Prodigy.

A.***** B******, Information Security for Prodigy, and B***
S., Prodigy's attorney, told your affiant that there is no verification
process in place to check on the name, address, or credit card number
of a customer signing onto Prodigy with one of the free startup kits.
They are normally verified in that, when the billing cycle comes around,
a bill is sent to the customer and if it is not paid or the information is
incorrect, the account is closed. They are also unable to do a trap-
and-trace on subscribers dialing into Prodigy.

On March 10, 1994, your affiant received a phone call from
R***** D******. She said she had read in the *Fresno Bee* on March
7, 1994, that I was investigating a case on Prodigy involving "Vito".
She knew who "Vito" was and wanted to talk to me.

R***** D****** said she is the regional coordinator for EF
(Educational Foundation for Foreign Study), an organization which
places foreign exchange students. August 1993 M**** J. applied with
EF as a host family for a foreign exchange student. M**** J. stated
that he was a teacher and custodial father with three sons, 14, 15,
and 18 years of age, the oldest of whom graduated in June and moved
to Fullerton for college. He expressed interest in a Nordic boy. In fact,
as a host family, M**** J. was allowed to review applications and
photos of the prospective students. M**** J. specifically asked for
a Nordic boy because his family roots were Norwegian and it would
please his parents. M**** J. then reviewed the applications and
pictures and when he saw the picture of a 17-year-old blond, M****
J. immediately stated, "That's him, that's the one I want."

R***** D****** met and talked to M**** J. numerous times
during the next few months, both in person and over the computer via
Prodigy. She thought he met the criteria for placement of a student
and placed the victim with him in mid-August 1993.

Later she found out that M**** J. had given false information in
his application to be a host family and that he was in fact a part-time
substitute teacher and part-time raisin inspector for the Federal Government. She found out from the mother of M**** J. that M**** J.
had only one child, a 9-year old boy, and that M**** J.'s mother had
custody of the child.

M**** J. for some reason became very trusting of R*****
D****** and told her that he enjoyed "pushing people's buttons".
He admitted he spent time on Prodigy harassing women. He went on
the Saturn board because a lot of women like Saturns and that was a
good place to meet them. He would meet them electronically, then start
giving them a bad time using the name "Vito". He told her once that
there was a possibility that the FBI was looking for him, but that he
had a friend who was a Lieutenant of the Fresno Sheriff's Office, who
would let him know if anyone made inquiries about him.

In October 1993 she was asked by the victim to move him from
M**** J.'s home. He told her that M**** J. was too busy for him
and was angry all the time. She contacted M**** J. and by mutual
agreement the victim was moved to another host family.

On April 5, 1994, your affiant interviewed the victim, whose name
is not in this affidavit as he was a minor at the time he lived with
M**** J. He reported to your affiant that he was the victim of
repeated sexual advances by M**** J. It should be noted that the
victim's first language is not English and he has difficulty with some
terms, thus making the interview process a slow one. The victim is
very intelligent and told me that his language skills in English have
improved in the last several months, but slang and specific sexual
terms are not part of his English vocabulary. He also was very uncom-
fortable talking about sexual things.

The victim told me that he was 17 years old when he went to stay
with M**** J. at *** West C***** in Fresno. He lived with M****
J. from about the 17th of August to the end of October 1993.

M**** J. was on the computer virtually all the time he was at
home. M**** J. went to bed at 8 or 9 p.m. and got up early, usually
between 5 and 7 a.m. M**** J. would often wake up in the middle of
the night and work on the computer and the first thing he did upon
waking was to get his mail on Prodigy and the other online services.

The victim stated that he knows M**** J. is doing something
wrong on the computer. He took two years of computer and computer
programming in Norway and was a member of a computer club there
before coming to the U.S. and understands computers fairly well. He
explained that M**** J. spent time explaining what he was doing on
Prodigy as he worked on the computer.

M**** J. explained that he was giving people a bad time and
enjoyed upsetting them while using free Prodigy 30-day startup kits.
M**** J. bragged that he was "Vito" to these people and used lots
of IDs and fraudulent names and made-up addresses to give them a bad
time to trick them, and to have fun with them and enjoyed getting them
upset. M**** J. told him the Saturn people were favorite targets and
that they were not as intelligent as he was. The victim said that M****
J. liked to use the name Vito because that was the name of M****
J.'s cat. He liked the name "Vito" so much that his license plate on
his Volkswagen bus was "VITO ***". M**** J. told the victim that
he liked to use "Vito" because no one would ever know it was him.

"Vito" was a Mafia name in old movies and M**** J. liked the connection. M**** J. often griped about the "wannabes", that is, people who acted like "Vito" on Prodigy.

M**** J. bragged about beating the Prodigy system in that he would upload 500 messages at a time when the limit was much less for the free kits and he enjoyed filling up people's mail boxes like that because they had to read through all of them to get to their real mail.

The victim watched M**** J. log on (that is, to use a computer and modem and call Prodigy's local service number) to Prodigy using numerous IDs in August, September, and October 1993 using many startup kits. M**** J. would often invent a name to sign on with, often pulling a name straight out of the Fresno telephone book. M**** J. would then enter a credit card number for this account. M**** J. told him he would use his own credit card as a base and change the last four digits until the computer accepted the number and then would get all excited because he tricked Prodigy into accepting a false credit card number. M**** J. would use a false name, false credit card number, and an address in another city to log on this way. M**** J. also had a legitimate account he used to look around on Prodigy.

The victim stated that M**** J. only used three passwords when logging onto the bulletin board systems and that they were "diesel", "Molly", and "Molly Dog". M**** J. used "diesel" because all of his cars were diesels, and Molly was the name of his dog, which he often called Molly Dog. The primary password he used was "diesel."

The victim stated that M**** J. showed him how he got new kits from Prodigy. He would log off with an old ID and get another ID and password while still on the computer or could order two more new IDs any time he wanted. He knew a lot about Prodigy and bragged about how he tricked them into giving him all the IDs he wanted. In fact, M**** J. had between 500 and 1000 IDs in a cardboard box in the trunk of his green Maverick parked in the garage behind the house at *** West C*****. M**** J. showed him this box and explained he was hiding the IDs there. M**** J. would often print out the messages he received and sent by Prodigy and would hide them in books and boxes in shelves and up high in the garage. M**** J. also made backups of the Prodigy data on disks, which he keeps in cabinets in the dining room. The victim stated that M*** J. was very secretive and hid things important to him. The victim told your affiant that M**** J. had a trailer, motorcycle, and six different automobiles in his yard including a Volkswagen bus with the license VITO ***, a green Volkswagen Rabbit, a blue Rabbit pickup, a green Maverick, a Nissan pickup, and a Volkswagen Dasher.

M**** J. would get up early on Saturday, after sending hundreds of copies of the same message to people on Prodigy the night before, and say to the victim, "Well, let's see if I pissed enough people off last night." M**** J. often made copies of the files he considered "funny" from Prodigy. He would break loose laughing while reading them and would say things like "all hell broke loose last night because of Vito."

M**** J. warned him that some day the police might come to the house looking for him. If he was to come home from school and find the police there and M**** J. was not home, he was to tell them to go away and he would take care of it later.

M**** J. also had a gray cable decoder box used to get cable television. M**** J. told him it was illegal and not to tell anyone about it or show it to anyone. M**** J. told him to put it away if anyone came to the house, and if anyone came over M**** J. would put the box away.

The victim stated that M**** J. started talking to him about sex when he had been there a month. M**** J. explained that he was bisexual and that women were for emotional love and men for physical sex. He explained that he was especially attracted to blond men (note: the victim is a Nordic blond). M**** J. told him that in his house they could go around undressed because there were no doors with locks and no one there but them. He would not force himself sexually on the victim because he had self control. The victim said M**** J. specifically asked him to have sex with him, but the victim had problems with the English words M**** J. had used, but it was clear to him that M**** J. meant for them to have sex the way men have sex together.

M**** J. showed the victim nude photos of his son when the boy was about 5 years old and talked about he and the victim being just like family and they did not need to hide things from each other by closing or locking doors.

M**** J. had camouflage nets in the backyard so he could go out to the clothes line and get underwear off it without getting dressed and no one could see him.

The victim stated that M**** J. would sit around in his underpants working on the computer and often talked to him about sex. M**** J. pressured him to have sex about twice a week, but he always turned M**** J. down and M**** J. never forced himself on him.

M**** J. stated he started having sex with boys very young when he was in a school band because his parents did not care about him.

On April 4, 1994, your affiant compared a list of suspected "Stalker/Vito" Prodigy names with fraudulent credit card numbers received in October from Prodigy Security against the Fresno telephone book and found ten of them.

Your affiant called A. B****** at Prodigy and asked him to check their database for IDs using the passwords "diesel", "Molly", and "Molly Dog" against this list of suspected IDs.

On April 7, 1994, Mr. B****** faxed me a list containing 43 suspected IDs which the A ID was "diesel". Many of the B IDs under the same name used BBBBBBBBBB for a password, and the C ID used CCCCCCCCCC, and so on. Some of the B,C,D,E, and F IDs used the password "diesel" and there were many similarities between the IDs. They used fraudulent credit cards, called Prodigy from a Fresno PLS phone number, were involved in the Saturn board, etc. This list is attached to this affidavit as attachment B.

Of all 53 of the IDs using the password "diesel" and giving credit card numbers on this list, only two used legitimate credit card numbers. Those IDs were FRTE48 and GERY83 listed to M**** J. and M**** J. at *** West C*****, respectively. The legitimate credit card number of M**** J., ****-****-****-*, is very similar to the numbers of the fraudulent credit card numbers used by the suspected "Stalker/Vito" IDs on this list, which is also consistent with the information supplied by the victim about M**** J.'s use of names from the phone book, using the passwords "diesel", "Molly", and "Molly Dog", and the means by which M**** J. chose credit card numbers he used when calling Prodigy services. The total theft from Prodigy using just these IDs totals $5,231.34.

Your affiant has probable cause to believe and does believe that M**** J. used numerous free 30-day limited use Prodigy startup kits and logged on with false names, fraudulent addresses, and fraudulent credit card numbers. He used the same password for his A ID ("diesel") and often used names from the Fresno phone book. He exceeded the free usage agreement of the startup kits and caused at least $5,231.34 in charges to be made against the fraudulent credit card numbers, thus violating PC 487(a), Grand Theft, 484g(a) Fraudulent use of Credit Card, PC 532(a) Obtaining Money or Property by False Pretenses, PC 532a Making a False Financial Statement (which Prodigy relied on to provide credit for services rendered), PC653m(a) Threatening and Obscene Phone Calls, Using a computer and modem over the phone to complete said calls repeatedly over a period of over a year amounting to hundreds and perhaps thousands of calls.

Your affiant checked Fresno Police Department records, which show M**** J. used the address of *** West ***** since 1987.

Your affiant checked real estate records with the County of Fresno, which show the owners of the property at *** West ******* to be P. and C. J. at *** F***** Avenue, Clovis, CA. R*** D**** told your affiant that these persons were M**** J.'s parents.

DMV records show vehicles registered to M**** J. as:

1982 Volkswagen, License*****
1971 Mercury, License ******
1981 Volkswagen, License *******
1983 Nissan, License *******
1981 Volkswagen, License *******
1978 Yamaha, License *******

Detective P****** is a sex crimes investigator with the Fresno Police Department. Detective P****** has been a police officer for 28 years and has worked sex crimes for 16 years. He has investigated thousands of sex crime cases. Detective P****** advised your affiant that M**** J. acted toward the victim in a manner typical of persons sexually assaulting minors, in that, when becoming a host family for a foreign exchange student, M**** J. specifically asked for and picked out a blond Nordic boy. He befriended the victim, lowered his suspicions about nudity and sexual things, and showed him nude child photos to desensitize him. He then stated he was sexually attracted to blond boys, and then started pressing the victim for sex in violation of PC288.2, Exhibiting Harmful Matter to a Minor for the purpose of sexually arousing him, Attempt PC286(b)1, Sodomy and PC288(a)(b)1, Oral copulation.

Based on your affiant's experience and the above information, your affiant has probable cause to believe and does believe that evidence of the above crimes exists at *** West C*****, City of Fresno, State of California.

## Search Warrant Examples

We have also included two search warrants used in our one-week computer search training classes given for the IRS and U.S. Secret Service computer crimes investigators. Both warrants are for a fictitious place of business (Fresno City Hall computer training room), but they give a good idea of places to be searched and things to search for. The warrants also list the expertise of a civilian expert and the reason why law enforcement would take them on the service of the search warrant. They are completely different scenarios and are good background material for the investigator who is new to search warrants and computer-related crimes in general. We offer a note of apology here to the contractor who built the new Fresno City Hall. We mention in the warrant that the building we are searching is described as Madonna's Bra or a Ferengi warship. Search warrants require that the building or place to be searched be described in such a manner that there is no doubt as to the place to be searched and we tried to do so here. You have to see the large shiny building to fully appreciate the humor and factual nature of our description.

## Search Warrant Sample 8

SW NO. _____

STATE OF CALIFORNIA — COUNTY OF FRESNO

SEARCH WARRANT AND AFFIDAVIT
(AFFIDAVIT)

Franklin Clark, being sworn, says that on the basis of the information contained within this Search Warrant and Affidavit and the attached and incorporated **Statement of Probable Cause**, he/she has probable cause to believe and does believe that the property described below is lawfully seizable pursuant to Penal Code Section 1524, as indicated below, and is now located at the locations set forth below. Wherefore, affiant requests that this Search Warrant be issued.

_____, NIGHT SEARCH REQUESTED: YES( ) NO( )

(SEARCH WARRANT)

**THE PEOPLE OF THE STATE OF CALIFORNIA TO ANY SHERIFF, POLICEMAN OR PEACE OFFICER IN THE COUNTY OF FRESNO:** proof by affidavit having been made before me by Franklin Clark that there is probable cause to believe that the property described herein may be found at the locations set forth herein and that it is lawfully seizable pursuant to Penal Code Section 1524 as indicated below by "X"(s) in that it:

_____   was stolen or embezzled.
XX      was used as the means of committing a felony.
XX      is possessed by a person with the intent to use it as means of committing a public offense or is possessed by another to whom he or she may have delivered it for the purpose of concealing it or preventing its discovery.
_____   tends to show that a felony has been committed or that a particular person has committed a felony.
_____   tends to show that sexual exploitation of a child, in violation of P.C. Section 311.3, has occurred or is occurring.

**YOU ARE THEREFORE COMMANDED TO SEARCH:**
Between the hours of 7:00 a.m. and 10:00 p.m. or at any time of the day or night to make immediate search.

City Hall Business Complex, 2600 Fresno St. Suite #123, City of Fresno, County of Fresno, State of California. Further described as a 5-story tall Ferengi Warship, Madonna's Bra, and a Circus Tent for Clowns. Suite #123 is located on the first floor, east wing, and has a 8.5-in. by 11-in. blue sign on the front door at eye level with the name ABC Computer Services City Hall Business Complex, 2600 Fresno St., Suite 123 plainly affixed to the front door.

**FOR THE FOLLOWING PROPERTY:**
Description of personal property to be seized:

1.  Any and all telephones, including memory devices and associated peripheral equipment, including automatic dialers, speed dialers, programmable telephone dialing or signalling devices, electronic tone generating devices;

2.  Computers, central processing units, external and internal drives and external storage equipment or media, terminals or video display units, together with peripheral equipment such as keyboards, printers, modems or acoustic couplers, automatic dialers, speed dialers, programmable telephone dialing or signalling devices, electronic tone generating devices;
3.  Any and all computer or data processing software, or data including, but not limited to, hard disks, floppy disks, cassette tapes, video cassette tapes, magnetic tapes, integral RAM or ROM units, and any other permanent or transient storage device(s);
4.  The following records and documents, whether contained on paper in handwritten, typed, photocopied, or printed form or stored on computer printouts, magnetic tape, cassettes, disks, diskettes, photo optical devices, or any other medium: telephone and communications activity and service billing records, computer electronic and voice mail system information, access numbers, passwords, personal identification numbers (PINS), telephone and address directories, logs, notes, memoranda and correspondence relating to theft of telephone and communications services or to unauthorized access into computer, electronic, and voice mail systems;
5.  Any computing or data processing literature, including, but not limited to, printed copy, instruction books, notes, papers, or listed computer programs, in whole or in part;
6.  Indicia of occupancy, including, but not limited to: bills, letters, invoices, personal effects, rental agreements tending to show ownership, occupancy, or control of the premises, or the above described items one through three.
7.  Any confirmation numbers, purchase numbers, and purchase information reflecting the use of a credit card or credit services to obtain property, goods or services;
8.  Neutralize and seize degaussing equipment located at the search location.
9.  Any and all copy machines.
10. Samples of computer and copier paper.
11. Any and all documents paper which are representations of currency of the United States of America.

This affidavit recognizes that some of the above described property is data that will be contained on cassette tapes, video tapes, and in electronic and machine-readable media which is not readable by your affiant in its present state. Authorization is given to searching officers to seize, listen to, read, review, copy, and maintain the above-described property and to convert it to human-readable form as necessary, being advised that data stored in computers and telephone memory machines may be lost if disconnected from an electrical power source. Authorization is given to make human-readable copies or recordings of this data at the search location in order to preserve and protect the information and to thereafter seize, read, listen to, copy, and maintain the described property.

And if you find the same, or any part thereof, to retain it in your custody, subject to order of court as provided by law. Given under my hand, and dated this ____ 9th day of August____A.D. 19__, at ____ a.m. p.m.

Judge of said

Court_____Attest:_____Clerk

## STATEMENT OF PROBABLE CAUSE

Your affiant, Franklin Clark is a Detective with the Fresno Police Department and has been so employed for the last 25 years. Your affiant has received extensive training in the area of microcomputers and telecommunications over the last 7 years from the California Department of Justice, Federal Law Enforcement Training Center, Federal Computer Investigators Committee, the High Tech Crime Investigators Association, and he has attended computer classes at Clovis West Adult School, City of Fresno, and software and hardware classes at The Training Center Fresno.

Your affiant has written over two dozen search warrants for computers and computer systems. Your affiant is familiar with microcomputers, software, and telecommunications hardware and techniques.

This statement of probable cause will show that the property described to be seized consists of computers, copy machines, computer software (programs), and paper. This statement of probable cause has statements from witnesses who state that the suspect in this case, Jay Bitthief, who is the owner of ABC Computing, is a computer expert. Jay Bitthief is running a computer bulletin board — that is, a computer connected to a modem which is connected to a telephone. This computer is then called by telephone by other persons with a computer connected by modem to a telephone line. This computer bulletin board requires the caller to have a pre-approved name and password before he can get into the system. The person calling can then access Mr. Bitthief's computer, view and copy files to his computer, and send files to Mr. Bitthief's computer. This affidavit will show that Mr. Bitthief has hidden information which is evidence of a felony on the computers using various passwords and other devices and is using a color printer connected to this computer to print counterfeit U.S. currency.

Your affiant requests permission of the court to take the below-listed computer expert, Ken Diliberto, to assist your affiant during the service of this search warrant under your affiant's direction. Your affiant has first-hand knowledge that Ken Diliberto has extensive experience in computer networks, computer bulletin boards, and bypassing of password protection devices, as Ken Diliberto has assisted your affiant in over a dozen computer related investigations including the investigation of four computer bulletin board cases, where, under your affiant's direction, Ken Diliberto was able to bypass password and encryption schemes and bring up the data stored on the computer in human-readable form. Ken Diliberto has training and experience in these areas which will greatly assist your affiant in the efficient investigation of this case.

Ken Diliberto is employed as a network systems specialist for the City of Fresno Information Systems Division and has been employed in said position for 2 years. Ken Diliberto attended Fresno City College as a Data Processing major and was employed by Fresno City College to provide programming and technical assistance to instructors. He was employed by Argos Software for 1 year as a hardware/software/network specialist and previously with Everything Goes, Inc., as a programmer and computer specialist and with West Hills College as a programmer/Operator computer specialist. Ken Diliberto has over 14 years experience in the use of computers, computer networks, telecommunications, and computer bulletin boards. He has experience in programming in BASIC, Xbase, C, and COBOL and is a licensed HAM operator.

Ken Diliberto has assisted your affiant in the seizure and examination of computers in evidence in over 12 cases. Ken Diliberto's expertise in computer languages and systems has allowed law enforcement to obtain information from password-protected programs and to convert proprietary systems while protecting the integrity of the original computer data. Ken Diliberto was able to convert the information into human readable form, which would not have been otherwise possible for the investigators.

On August 6, 1993, your affiant was contacted by Ken Rom, a repair technician for ABC Computer Services. Ken Rom told your affiant that his boss and owner of ABC Computing is named Jay Bitthief. Ken Rom stated that ABC Computing is a computer consulting firm which is just starting in business. In fact, he is the only employee. He was hired June 1, 1993, and his job has been to contact local businesses and offer the company's services to set up local area networks, repair and optimize hardware, and consult in the area of computer software and security issues. Mr. Rom stated that Mr. Bitthief does very little field work and spends most of his time at the office running a computer bulletin board system (BBS) called "Anarchy". Mr. Rom stated that he has never been allowed to look at or log onto the BBS and Mr. Bitthief is very secretive of the BBS. Mr. Rom knows that the numbers of the BBS are 498-0000, 498-0001, 498-0002, and 498-0003, as the phone numbers are marked on the four modems connected to the BBS computer. Mr. Rom told your affiant that he opens the mail and often pays the bills for the company and has paid the telephone bills for these four numbers. The phone numbers stuck in his mind due to the unusual number sequence. In fact, he became suspicious of the business and "Anarchy" BBS at the end of July when he tried to call the Anarchy BBS at 498-0000 from his personal computer at home. The computer screen came up telling Mr. Rom that this was a closed BBS and to log on you must have a name and password assigned by the sysop. If you were part of "Anarchy" you would already know the name and password. The only way to get a name and password was to send a letter to the sysop with a copy of your driver's license to "Anarchy", 4974 N. Fresno St., Suite 135, Fresno, CA 93704, along with a self-addressed stamped envelope. The notice stated you would then be contacted in person by the sysop after the appropriate background checks were made.

August 6, 1993, Mr. Rom returned to the business at approximately 1700 hours and as he walked in the front door Mr. Rom saw Mr. Bitthief arguing with two women about some documents Mr. Bitthief was printing on the high resolution color printer. The women stated they wanted their share and Mr. Bitthief was yelling that, "He did not want any more of them passed in Fresno for a while." Mr. Bitthief and the two women got into a shoving match and went out the back door arguing. Mr. Rom stated that he has seen Mr. Bitthief talking to these women on several other occasions, and he knows them as Karen and Nancy. Mr. Rom looked at the papers on and in the printer and found that the documents were, in fact, copies of $20 and $50 bills. He stated there was a pile of copied money approx. 10 inches thick on a table by the printer. He took two pages of this pile of copied money from the printer and put them in his briefcase. Mr. Rom immediately brought the two copies of the $50 and $20 bills to your affiant at the Fresno Police Department and contacted your affiant at 1740 hours. Copies of these papers are attached to this warrant as attachments 1-A and 1-B. Mr. Rom described the women arguing with Mr.Bitthief as follows: Karen is a white female adult, 30 to 35 years old, 5' 6", 125 lbs., dark hair, dark eyes. Nancy is a hispanic female adult, 30 to 35 years old, 5' 4", 118 lbs., dark hair, dark eyes. Both almost always have silly guilty grins on their faces.

Mr.Rom told your affiant that he had looked at the computer which was connected to the color printer where the money was being printed. He saw a $20 bill on the computer screen which looked just like the ones being printed. He then got out of the program displaying the money on the screen and the screen came up to the "Anarchy" BBS menu screen. On this screen he saw submenus and remembers submenus called "Hacking", "Phreaking", "Make a Buck" and "Forgeries". He then restarted the program displaying the money, which was under "Make a Buck", and left the business without Mr. Bitthief seeing him.

Mr. Rom stated he has a Master's degree in Computer Science and is a Novell Certified Technician. He is familiar with programming languages and has talked many times with Mr. Bitthief about computers, hardware, software, and even BBS Systems. Mr. Rom stated that he considers Mr. Bitthief to be very knowledgeable in these areas.

Your affiant contacted Special Agent Rick Nelson of the Secret Service and showed him the copies of the $50 and $20 bills Mr. Rom had brought to your affiant. S.A. Nelson, who has extensive training and experience in the investigation of counterfeiting U.S. currency and knows more than any other person in the world about this kind of stuff, told your affiant that the copies were very good copies, considering they came off a computer printer. The serial numbers and other identifiers for these bills are consistent with counterfeit bills that have been showing up with increasing frequency across the United States. S.A. Nelson stated that the bills started showing up in the Central Valley of California in June 1993 and within days were being passed in New York City; Philadelphia, Pennsylvania; Austin, Texas; and Portland, Oregon. Now they are being passed in at least 50 cities across the country. The recorded losses to date are in the tens of millions of dollars.

Your affiant checked the City of Fresno Business Records and found that Jay Bitthief was listed as the sole owner of ABC Computer Services at 2600 Fresno St., Suite #123, City of Fresno, County of Fresno, State of California.

Fresno City Utilities and Pacific Gas and Electric both show the customer ABC Computing at 2600 Fresno St., Suite #123, and the responsible party as Jay Bitthief. Pacific Bell lists four phone lines going to ABC Computing: 498-0000, 498-0001, 498-0002, and 498-0003, all of which are in the name of Jay Bitthief of ABC Computing.

Your affiant checked with Patricia Hoffman, U.S. Postal Inspector, who stated that they have a card on file for 4974 N. Fresno St. Suite #135. This suite is actually a mail drop (private business mail box service) at Sam's Mail Call, 4974 N. Fresno, which comes back to Jay Bitthief at 2600 Fresno St., Suite #123.

Based on your affiant's training and experience and the above information, your affiant has probable cause to believe and does believe that Jay Bitthief is running a four-line BBS in ABC Computing which is involved in counterfeiting U.S. currency, the collection and distribution of counterfeit U.S. currency, and the exchange of programs and data commonly known in the computer world as "hacking and phreaking" programs and information. Phreaking/hacking programs allow a computer user to run checks on telephone numbers and their associated PIN number (access codes) and record these numbers to a disk for later use. Your affiant believes and has probable cause to believe that there will be contained within the BBS computer telephone numbers and PIN numbers which allow the unauthorized use of said phone numbers and credit card numbers and their associated PIN numbers, as these two types of unauthorized use of access/credit cards are, in your affiant's experience, nearly always found together on computers which are involved in hacking and phreaking, hacking being the unauthorized access into computer systems and phreaking the unauthorized access and use of phone numbers, as used here. Your affiant also believes that the BBS computer will contain a log of the BBS users which may list the names, passwords, dates, and times they logged onto the computer as well as a list of files they uploaded (sent) to the BBS and files they downloaded (copied) from the BBS which may indicate the distribution of copies of U.S. currency and or trafficking in stolen credit card and phone number information.

## Search Warrant Sample 9

SW NO. _____

STATE OF CALIFORNIA — COUNTY OF FRESNO

SEARCH WARRANT AND AFFIDAVIT
(AFFIDAVIT)

Franklin Clark, being sworn, says that on the basis of the information contained within this Search Warrant and Affidavit and the attached and incorporated Statement of Probable Cause, he/she has probable cause to believe and does believe that the property described below is lawfully seizable pursuant to Penal Code Section 1524, as indicated below, and is now located at the locations set forth below. Wherefore, affiant requests that this Search Warrant be issued.
_____, NIGHT SEARCH REQUESTED: YES( ) NO( )

(SEARCH WARRANT)

**THE PEOPLE OF THE STATE OF CALIFORNIA TO ANY SHERIFF, POLICEMAN OR PEACE OFFICER IN THE COUNTY OF FRESNO:** proof by affidavit having been made before me by Franklin Clark that there is probable cause to believe that the property described herein may be found at the locations set forth herein and that it is lawfully seizable pursuant to Penal Code Section 1524 as indicated below by "X"(s) in that it:

_____  was stolen or embezzled.

__XX__  was used as the means of committing a felony.

__XX__  is possessed by a person with the intent to use it as means of committing a public offense or is possessed by another to whom he or she may have delivered it for the purpose of concealing it or preventing its discovery.

__XX__   tends to show that a felony has been committed or that a
         particular person has committed a felony.
_____   tends to show that sexual exploitation of a child, in violation
         of P.C. Section 311.3, has occurred or is occurring.

## YOU ARE THEREFORE COMMANDED TO SEARCH:

Between the hours of 7:00 a.m. and 10:00 p.m. or at any time of the
day or night to make immediate search.

City Hall Business Complex, 2600 Fresno St., Suite #123, City of
Fresno, County of Fresno, State of California. Further described as a
5-story tall Ferengi Warship, Madonna's Bra and a Circus Tent for
Clowns. Suite #123 is located on the first floor, east wing, and has
an 8.5 in. × 11 in. blue sign on the front door at eye level with the
name ABC Computer Services City Hall Business Complex, 2600 Fresno
St., Suite 123 plainly affixed to the front door.

## FOR THE FOLLOWING PROPERTY:

Description of personal property to be seized:

1.  Any and all telephones including memory devices and associated
    peripheral equipment, including automatic dialers, speed dialers,
    programmable telephone dialing or signalling devices, electronic
    tone generating devices;
2.  Computers, central processing units, external and internal
    drives and external storage equipment or media, terminals or
    video display units, together with peripheral equipment such as
    keyboards, printers, modems or acoustic couplers, automatic
    dialers, speed dialers, programmable telephone dialing or sig-
    nalling devices, electronic tone generating devices;
3.  Any and all computer or data processing software, or data
    including, but not limited to: hard disks, floppy disks, cassette
    tapes, videocassette tapes, magnetic tapes, integral RAM or ROM
    units, and any other permanent or transient storage device(s);
4.  The following records and documents, whether contained on paper
    in handwritten, typed, photocopied, or printed form or stored
    on computer printouts, magnetic tape, cassettes, disks, dis-
    kettes, photo optical devices, or any other medium: telephone
    and communications activity and service billing records, com-
    puter electronic and voice mail system information, access num-
    bers, passwords, personal identification numbers (PINs),
    telephone and address directories, logs, notes, memoranda, and
    correspondence relating to theft of telephone and communications
    services, or to unauthorized access into computer, electronic,
    and voice mail systems;
5.  Any computing or data processing literature, including, but not
    limited to, printed copy, instruction books, notes, papers, or
    listed computer programs, in whole or in part;

6. Indicia of occupancy, including, but not limited to, bills, letters, invoices, personal effects, rental agreements tending to show ownership, occupancy, or control of the premises, or the above described items one through three.
7. Any confirmation numbers, purchase numbers, and purchase information reflecting the use of a credit card or credit services to obtain property, goods, or services;
8. Neutralize and seize degaussing equipment located at the search location.

This affidavit recognizes that some of the above described property is data that will be contained on cassette tapes, and videotapes and in electronic and machine-readable media which is not readable by your affiant in its present state. Authorization is given to searching officers to seize, listen to, read, review, copy, and maintain the above described property and to convert it to human readable form as necessary, being advised that data stored in computers and telephone memory machines may be lost if disconnected from an electrical power source. Authorization is given to make human readable copies or recordings of this data at the search location in order to preserve and protect the information and to thereafter seize, read, listen to, copy and maintain the described property.

And if you find the same, or any part thereof, to retain it in your custody, subject to order of court as provided by law. Given under my hand, and dated this 23rd day of February, A.D. 1993, at 10:00 a.m.

Judge of said

Court_____Attest:_____Clerk


STATEMENT OF PROBABLE CAUSE

Your affiant, Franklin Clark, is a Detective with the Fresno Police Department and has been so employed for the last 25 years. Your affiant has received extensive training in the area of microcomputers and telecommunications over the last 7 years from the California Department of Justice, Federal Law Enforcement Training Center, Federal Computer Investigators Committee, the High Tech Crime Investigators Association and he has attended computer classes at Clovis West Adult School, City of Fresno, software and hardware classes at The Training Center Fresno.

Your affiant has written approx. two dozen search warrants for computers and computer systems. Your affiant is familiar with microcomputers, software, and telecommunications hardware and techniques.

This statement of probable cause will show that the property described to be seized consists of computers and computer software (programs), and said computers are connected to a network which has its own operating system. This statement of probable cause has statements from witnesses who state that the suspect in this case, Jay Bitthief, who is part owner of ABC Computing, is a computer expert and that he has hidden information which is evidence of a felony on the computers using various passwords and other devices.

Your affiant requests permission of the court to take the below-listed computer expert, Ken Diliberto, to assist your affiant during the service of this search warrant under your affiant's direction. Your affiant has first-hand knowledge that Ken Diliberto has extensive experience in computer networks and bypassing of password protection devices, as Ken Diliberto has assisted your affiant in five computer-related investigations where, under your affiant's direction, Ken Diliberto was able to bypass password and encryption schemes and bring up the data stored on the computer in human-readable form. Ken Diliberto has training and experience in these areas which will greatly assist your affiant in the efficient investigation of this case.

Ken Diliberto is employed as a network systems specialist for the City of Fresno Information Systems Division. Ken has been employed in said position for 11/2 years. Ken Diliberto attended Fresno City College as a Data Processing major and was employed by Fresno City College to provide programming and technical assistance to instructors. He was employed by Argos Software for 1 year as a hardware/software/network specialist and previously with Everything Goes, Inc., as a programmer and computer specialist and with West Hills College as a programmer/operator computer specialist. He has over 14 years experience in the use of computers, computer networks, and computer telecommunications. He has experience in programming in BASIC, Xbase, C, and COBOL and is a licensed HAM operator.

Ken Diliberto has assisted your affiant in the seizure and examination of computers in evidence in five cases. Ken Diliberto's expertise in computer languages and systems has allowed law enforcement to obtain information from password-protected programs and convert proprietary systems while protecting the integrity of the original computer data. Ken Diliberto was able to convert the information into human-readable form, which would not have been otherwise possible for the investigators.

On February 22, 1993, your affiant was contacted by Ken Rom and Jerry Scsi, part owners of ABC Computer Services. Ken Rom told your affiant that he and Jerry Scsi have a third partner in ABC Computing named Jay Bitthief. Ken Rom stated that approx. 3 months ago he overheard a conversation between Jay Bitthief and someone Jay called at the IRS, Fresno. Jay was offering this person $10,000 to "fix" the tax bills of one of ABC Computing's clients. The client's name is James Kilgore. Mr. Rom further stated that this is one of several conversations he has heard where Mr. Bitthief has stated he has a connection at the IRS who "fixes" tax problems for a fee. Mr. Rom stated that yesterday he talked to his partner Jerry Scsi about his suspicions that Mr. Bitthief may be bribing an IRS employee and receiving kickbacks, that one of their clients may be paying Mr. Bitthief to bribe an IRS employee, and that Mr. Bitthief may be obtaining a fee for his part from the client. He and Mr. Scsi then checked the company computers for the account of James Kilgore and found that the account was password protected. Their company, ABC Computing, provides computerized bookkeeping and payroll services for clients all over the country. None of their files are ever password protected, as any one of them may have to look up the data for a customer. They then found a letter to their client Mr. Kilgore which was written by Jay Bitthief, who signs his letters "Big J". This letter stated that Big J knew about an IRS employee who was being bribed by someone at Niemela Construction and that Big J might be able to do the same thing for Niemela Construction for a fee. Niemela Construction is a client of ABC Computing and is in debt to the IRS for over $400,000. They checked Niemela Construction's account in the ABC Computer services computers and found it was password protected now, also.

Jerry Scsi stated that he had overheard a conversation last week between Jay Bitthief and his son Mac Bitthief about Mac taking unsigned money orders out of the mail room from his employer's business. Mac Bitthief works in the mail room at the IRS Service Center at Butler and Chesnut in Fresno. Mr. Rom and Mr. Scsi both told your affiant that Jay Bitthief and his son Mac are members of a militant anti-IRS group called "Down with Organized Crime, Eliminate the IRS", or DWOCETIRS for short, and talk in the office weekly about their attempts to get the IRS any way they can. In fact, Mr. Scsi stated that on or about the 18th of February he saw some computer viruses on the company computer system and Jay Bitthief put one of these viruses in a customer's tax return file and sent it by modem to the IRS. The virus programs are still on the computer. (A modem is a device which connects a telephone line to a computer and allows the computer to call another computer with a modem. The two computers can then exchange data over the phone lines.)

Mr. Scsi stated that he and Ken Rom are computer novices and that their computer system, which consists of four IBM clones on a Novell network, was set up and managed by Jay Bitthief who is very expert in computers, networks, computer languages, and programming, as well as password protecting files, denying access to files which are password protected. Ken Rom stated that Jay Bitthief uses all four computers in the office and so does Mac Bitthief. Jerry Scsi stated that only he, Ken Rom, and Jay and Mac Bitthief use the computers. There are no other employees in the business. Jay and Mac Bitthief both keep many records on the computer and Mac even has a diary on the computer which he has password protected. He has seen Mac Bitthief type into this diary and last week, approx. Tuesday the 16th, he saw Mac type in the diary something about finding an unsigned check in the mail room which, Mac wrote, he endorsed and cashed. He does not know for sure which mail room, but Mac Bitthief works in the mail room at the IRS. Mr. Scsi stated that he and Mr. Rom do not use the computer modems or Mr. Bitthief's speed dialing phone from which he contacts IRS and his special clients.

Your affiant checked the City of Fresno Business Records and found that Ken Rom, Jerry Scsi, and Jay Bitthief are listed as joint owners of ABC Computer Services at 2600 Fresno St., Suite #123, City of Fresno, County of Fresno, State of California.

Fresno City Utilities and Pacific Gas and Electric both show the customer ABC Computing at 2600 Fresno St., Suite #123 and the responsible parties as Ken Rom, Jerry Scsi, and Jay Bitthief. Pacific Bell lists four phone lines going to ABC Computing: 498-0000, 498-0001, 498-0002, and 498-0003, all of which are in the name of Jay Bitthief of ABC Computing.

# Conclusion

It is probably impossible to cover every aspect of computer crime investigations in a single book, and computer technology changes very rapidly. Unfortunately, the public often can be victimized by this new technology before law enforcement has time to catch up with it. We urge you to constantly seek new training from competent and qualified instructors. Your best classes most often will taught by those who are actively investigating or have experience investigating computers involved in crime.

# Glossary

The following are definitions of terminology that may be found in a search warrant:

**10Base-T**   A form of Ethernet using unshielded, twisted-pair cable.

**286 or 80286**   A central processing chip created by Intel, Inc., used in the 286 AT line of personal computers.

**386 or 80386**   A central processing chip created by Intel, Inc., used in the 386 AT line of computers.

**486 or 80486**   A central processing chip created by Intel, Inc., used in the 486 AT line of computers.

**Acoustic Coupler**   A device used to attach a modem to the telephone system by placing the telephone handset on a set of rubber cups.

**Arcnet**   An older networking topology using RG62 coax achieving 2 Mb/s.

**AUTOEXEC.BAT**   A text file generally found in the root directory of a bootable floppy disk or hard disk on a computer running MS/PC-DOS or OS/2 that establishes the second level of the operating environment as the computer boots up.

**Back up or Backup**   Either the act of creating a duplicate copy of working programs and data or the actual copy of programs and data, used for disaster recovery. Ideally, such copies are stored off site.

**Banyan Vines**   A network operating system produced by Banyan Systems. Vines has a minor following because of its name services.

**BBS**   Bulletin board system: a system for people to call into with their home computers and modems to exchange messages, software, or pictures. These systems usually are free to their users.

**Bridge**   A device attached to a network cable to connect two like topologies.

**Byte**   A basic unit of data storage that contains a single character.

**Cabletron**   A company that provides data communications equipment such as hubs, concentrators, bridges, and routers.

**CD-ROM**   A compact disc (CD, like those used for music) that stores computer data.

**Central Processing Unit**   (CPU): the part of a computer system that does the actual "thinking" or information processing of the computer.

**Cluster**   The smallest unit of disk data storage.

**CMOS**   Complementary metal-oxide semiconductor: a type of low-power memory that stores information about the configuration of IBM clone AT. It is operated by a battery so it is not erased when the machine is turned off. When the battery goes dead, so does the computer's ability to communicate with various components.

**Concentrator**   A device used to attach workstations and servers to a 10Base-T network.

**CONFIG.SYS**   A text file generally found in the root directory of a bootable floppy disk or hard disk on a computer running MS/PC-DOS or OS/2 that establishes the first level of the operating environment as the computer is booting up.

**Cylinder**   The area of a disk that a read/write head can access without repositioning.

**Data**   Information.

**Data Line**   A telephone line dedicated for computer use.

**Dedicated Line**   A telephone line used only for data.

**Downloading**   The transferring of programs and data from a remote computer to your computer, generally by using a modem.

**Ethernet**   A modern networking topology using RG58 or RG8, unshielded, twisted-pair, and fiber-optic cable, achieving 10 Mb/s.

**External Drive**   A data storage unit not contained in the main computer housing.

**FAT**   File allocation table: All DOS disks use FATs to keep track of which clusters are assigned to which files. Simply put, the FAT is an address book for locating files on the disk.

**Fiber Optics**   A cable made with a glass interior for transmitting light, as opposed to a copper interior for transmitting electricity; fiber-optic cables can transmit huge amounts of data.

**Floppy Disk**   A small, flat magnetic storage device that easily can be transported or stored.

**Fractional T1**   A fraction (or segment) of a T1 line.

**Hard Disk**   A device used to store large amounts of information. A hard disk maintains the information stored on it after the power is turned off.

**Hub**   A device used as a wiring center. In a network, a hub is where the cables from each workstation come together.

**Internal Drive**   A data storage unit contained in the computer housing.

**ISDN**   Integrated Services Digital Network: a new type of telephone service that uses digital technology as opposed to analog.

**Keyboard**   A device resembling a typewriter keyboard, used to enter information or control a computer.

**LAN**   Local area network.

**LAN Manager**   A network operating system produced by IBM and Microsoft. LAN Manager is not very common.

**Lantastic®**   A very popular peer-to-peer network operating system.

**Laptop Computer**   A personal computer larger than a notebook computer. These computers are not as popular as the notebooks but have been available for several years.

**Leased Line**   A telephone line leased from the telephone company for computer use. This is the same as a dedicated line.

**MAU**   Multistation access unit: these devices are required to attach workstations and servers to a Token ring network

**MHS**   Message handling system: a group of programs that allows messages to be shared between users on separate networks.

**Modem**   Modulator/demodulator: a device that converts digital signals to analog signals for transmission over the telephone system.

**Multiplexer**   A device used to share a cable between multiple devices.

**NetWare**  Networking software produced by Novell. NetWare versions 2.x, 3.x, and 4.x are server based. NetWare Lite is a peer-to-peer network operating system.

**Notebook Computer**  A personal computer the size of a notebook. These computers are gaining in popularity as their price decreases and power increases.

**Novell**  A company based in Utah that provides the industry-standard network operating system software.

**Optical Disk**  A permanent, usually removable, data storage device that uses a laser to read and write the information it contains. These devices are not subject to erasure when exposed to a magnetic field.

**Original Program**  Refers to the original disks which came with a software package.

**Packet**  A method of transferring information over amateur radio bands using computers.

**Password**  A word, phrase, or number that has some secret meaning and is used to access data on a computer or to access an online service or BBS.

**PC, XT, and AT**  Terms used to describe the level of technology in the personal computer line.

**Peer to Peer**  A method of networking that allows every computer on the network to share its resources with all other users. This method makes good use of available hardware in exchange for data security.

**Peripheral**  Any device attached to a computer.

**Printer**  A device used to produce printed computer reports and documents.

**Radio LAN**  A method allowing computers to communicate by radio frequencies, as opposed to wire or fiber-optic cable.

**RAM**  Random access memory: computer chips that provide rapid access to information. This information can be read and written. RAM memory requires power to maintain the information it contains. RAM is not used for permanent storage, and data is lost when the power is turned off.

**ROM**  Read only memory: computer chips that provide rapid access to information. This information can only be read. ROM memory does not need power to maintain the information it contains. It is primarily used for the special programs required to start a computer.

**Router**  A device attached to a network cable to connect two unlike topologies.

**Sector**  A portion of a track (an arc) on a floppy or hard disk.

**Server Based**  A method of networking that uses a single computer on the network to hold all shared programs and data.

**Software**  A collection of computer instructions designed to perform a specific task.

**T1**  A high-speed telephone line used for telephone systems or computer communications, achieving 1.544 Mb/s.

**Terminal**  A device used to allow humans to enter or to access the information stored in the computer.

**Thick-net**  Ethernet using RG8 cable; Thick-net can cover distances up to 1800 feet.

**Thin-net**  Ethernet using RG58 cable; also known as "cheaper-net" because of the cost compared to Thick-net. Thin-net can cover distances up to 600 feet.

**Token Ring**  A modern networking topology using shielded, twisted-pair, unshielded twisted-pair, or fiber-optic cable using a token passing technology, achieving either 4 or 16 Mb/s.

**Topology**  A term referring to the physical connection method used to connect computers on a network.

**Uninterruptible Power Supply**  Basically, a surge protector with a built in battery. This unit clamps excessive power from the outlet and runs the computer for a short time on its battery in case of power loss (i.e., the lights go out), which enables computer users to save their work and "power down" (turn off) the computer if the power fails.

**Unix**  A time-sharing operating system allowing powerful processors to share their power with many users. Xenix and AIX are version of Unix produced by other companies.

**Uploading**  The transferring of programs and data to a remote computer from your computer, generally by using a modem.

**Video Display Unit**  A device resembling a television screen, used to display information contained in a computer.

**Virus**  In general terms, a computer program which is introduced into a computer from the outside, either by copying files by modem from another computer or by placing a floppy disk in the computer. The virus automatically copies itself into the computer and begins overwriting your files and system, replicating itself and otherwise damaging the usability of the system.

# Index

## A

Access Data, 92
Access number, 175
A drive. 61
Alchemy, 72
AnaDisk, 45, 72, 81
Animations, 72
ANSI bombs, 57, 106
ANSI graphics, 106
Antistatic packaging, 142–143
Anti-virus software, 45, 79
Applets, 70
ARCnet, 124
Arrest warrant, suspect identification,
    112
ASCII, 44, 71, 92
ASCII Armor, 95
Attribute search, 71
Audit trail, 45, 120
Authorization code, 175
AUTOEXEC.BAT, 44, 46, 60, 62
    for PROFILE, 73

## B

Backups, 3, 5, 26, 33, 45, 66
    battery, 136, 138, 139
    equipment for making, 9, 145
    hardware, 48
    PC-Tools, 46
    tapes, 134
Banyan Vines, 130
Battery backup, 136, 138, 139
B drive, 61
Bernoulli drives, 46, 48, 134
*Boardwatch*, 103
Bookstores, 103
Boot disk, 43–44, 57–64, 66

procedure for making, 61–63
Booting, 60, 66
    defined, 59
    password, 61
    problems, 64
Bulletin board services (BBS), 3, 44, 99–114,
        123, *See also* On-line investigations
    chat sample, 109
    "elite" acronyms, 115–117
    law enforcement disclaimers, 103
    locating sites and illegal activities,
        100–105
    offline mail readers, 110–111
    passwords, 90, 91, 104
    privacy issues, 34
    site/suspect surveillance, 111–112
    sysop interactions, 103, 104
    voice verification, 109, 110

## C

Cables, 4–5, 18, 33, 34, 36, 124
    investigator supplies, 48, 142
    tagging, 32
Cabletron interface, 138
Capture files, 107, 108
Case agent, 56
Case law, 151
Case supervisor, 9
C drive (hard drive), 61
CD-ROM drives, 135
Cellular One case, 153–171
Central Point Backup, 46
Chat rooms, 99
Child molesters, 44, 188–200
Child pornography, 91, 99, 103,
        194–195
    on-line service provider records search
        warrant, 183–188

Chronological worksheet, 56, 65, 68
Circuit boards, 17, 31
CMOS, 46, 60, 63
    boot password, 61
Coding, encryption, 87–97
Collection of evidence, *See* Evidence
        collection and preservation
Common carrier, 175
Communications server, 6
Communications software, 107
    network operating systems,
        128–132
Compass, 67
Compression programs, 146
Computer crime case law, 151
Computer evidence, 14, See also
        Evidence
    legal questions, 34–35
    locating, 54
    paraphernalia, 13–14
    seizure and preservation, *See* Evidence
        collection and preservation
    stolen computer, 90–91
Computer professionals, *See* Expert
        assistance
Computer Search Warrant Program,
        43
Computer systems, for investigators,
        See Investigative tools
Com Systems, 176
Concordance (WordPerfect), 70
CONFIG.SYS, 44, 46, 60, 62, 66
    for PROFILE, 73
Copying procedure for floppy disks,
        80–81, 146, *See also* Backups
Copy machines, 20–21, 32
Corel Draw, 146
Counterfeiting, 20–21, 205–207
Counter surveillance, 112
Court procedures, 147–149
Credit, secure for on-line investigation,
        110
Credit-card fraud, 99
    residence search warrant example,
        188–191
Crime scene investigation, 51–57
    advance planning and preparation,
        51–5
    executing the warrant, 54
    plan of attack, 52–53

search teams, 52
search warrant preparation, 53–54, *See
        also* Search warrants
securing the scene, 54
seizure of evidence, *See* Evidence
        collection and preservation
team functions, 56
CSHOW, 72
Cyberphobia, 1

**D**

Database, 69
Database management systems (DBMS),
        69
Database servers, 122
dBase, 144
Debriefing, 57
Debugger, 90–91
Dedicated modems, 124
Degaussing, 67
Deleted files, 3, 77, 80
Desk top evidence, 22
Dialed number recorder (DNR), 153,
        175
Digital communications systems,
        127–129
Disk Catalog System, 79
Disk Copy Fast (DCF), 146
Disk drives, 31, 45, 61
Diskettes, 14, 16
    bootable, 43–44, 57–64, 66
        procedure for making, 61–63
    copying, 80–81, 146
    evaluating, 44–46, 71–77, 79–81
    evidence on, 26
    finding, 23–25, 67
    formatting, 61, 63–64
    high-density and low-density,
        63–64
    investigative supplies, 141–142
    labeling, 37, 67, 79
    preservation considerations, 31
    seizure procedures, 67
    storing, 37, 40, 41, 67
    unusual formats, 72, 81
Display, 146
DL files, 72
DL-VIEW, 72
DNR (dialed number recorder), 153, 175

Documentation (of investigative
     procedures)
  crime scene investigation, 56
  diskette evaluation procedures, 79
  evidence collection and preservation,
     26, 34
  on-line investigation procedures, 108
  pretrial preparation, 147
Documentation (computer/software
     manuals), 19, 32
DOS, 144
  bootable disk, 61–63
  versions, 43–44
Double Space, 44

**E**

Education, *See* Training and education
Electronic Communications Privacy Act,
     34–35
E-mail privacy protection, 34–35
Encryption, 87–97
  common use, 96
  on-line resources, 96–97
  PGP, 93–96
Entrapment, 103
Erased files, 3, 77, 80
Ethernet, 45, 46, 124–125, 138, 145
Evidence, 13–19, *See also* Evidence collection
     and preservation; specific types of
     evidence
  computer hardware, 14, 17
     legal questions, 34–35
     signs of computers, 24
  computer paraphernalia, 13–14
  evaluation of, *See* Evidence evaluation
     and analysis
  forms of, 69–70
  locating, 19–25, 54
  manuals, 19, 32
  modems, 17–18
  monitors, 22–23
  paper, 13, 26
  PCMCIA cards, 18
  on person, 23–24
  photographing, 10, 32, 66
  printers, 18
  software, 19
  storage media, 14, 16, 17, *See also*
     Diskettes; Magnetic tapes

Evidence collection and preservation, 3,
     26, 32–33
  backups, *See* Backups
  bags for, 31, 142–143
  cautions and considerations, 30–33
  documenting, 26, 34
  labels, *See* Labels and tags
  legal requirements, 33–35
  problems for untrained
     investigators/computer
     professionals, 2–5
  steps for seizing a computer, 65–67
  storage, 37–42, 142–143
  suspect access, 3, 29
  technical evidence seizure and logging
     team, 10–11
  transport, 11, 33, 67
  turning off computers, 29, 65
Evidence evaluation and analysis,
     69–77
  analysis tools, 70–77, *See also*
     Investigative tools
  outside technical assistance, 77
  procedures for floppies, 79–81, *See also*
     Diskettes
  technical evidence seizure and logging
     team, 11
Evidence storage facilities, 37–42
Expert assistance, 1, 2, 9
  evidence evaluation, 77
  importance of evidence orientations,
     2–4
  including in search warrant language, 171,
     174, 204, 210
  network investigations, 132
  technical evidence seizure and logging
     team, 11
  vendor technical support, 27
Expert witnesses, 147, 148
Extensions, file, 83–85

**F**

File extensions, 83–85
File management programs, 44–45, 71
File name search, 71
File servers, 6, 54, 121
FLI files, 72
Floor plan, 51
Floppy disks, *See* Diskettes

Forensic analysis, *See* Evidence evaluation
  and analysis
Formatting disks, 61, 63–64
  unusual formats, 72, 81
Fox and hound, 5
Fried, Andy, 46, 66, 72


## G

Garbage, 24
Gateways, 122–123
GIFs, 103, 187, 194–195
GL files, 72
Glossary, 215–219
Graphical user interface (GUI), 70
Graphics and graphic images, 70, 123
  ANSI, 106
  GIFs, 103, 187, 194–195
  tools for viewing, 72, 146
GRASPRT, 72


## H

Hackers
  acronyms, 115–117
  recognizing, 15, 28, 177
  search warrant examples
    residence search, 171–182
    voice mailbox access, 153–171
Hacking, 177
  defined, 175
Hacking, phreaking, virus, anarchy,
    carding, and terrorism
    (H/P/V/A/C/T) BBSs, 99–114,
    *See also* Bulletin board systems;
    On-line investigations
Hanna, Gord, 72
Hard copy evidence, 13, 26
Hard disk lock, 61, 63, 66
Hard Disk Sentry, 61
Hard drive (C:), 61
Hard drive management programs,
    44
Hardware, defined, 174
Heat, and computer media, 31, 37
HEX, 44, 71, 90
Hidden files, 3
High-density disk, 63–64
High Tech Crime Investigators Association,
    132

HPFS disk, 61
H/P/V/A/C/T Bulletin boards, 99–114, See
    also On-line investigations


## I

IBM ThinkPad, 136–37
Indexing program (WordPerfect),
    70–71
Integrated Services Digital Network (ISDN),
    127–128
Internet, *See also* On-line investigations
  encrypted communications, 96
  relay chat (IRC), 99
  underground BBSs, 99–114, See also
      Bulletin board systems
Interrogation skills, 10
Interview area, 56
Interview team, 10
Investigative tools, 9, 43
  advance preparation, 52
  bootable disks, 57–64
  compass for detecting electromagnetic
      fields, 67
  desktop computer systems, 133–136
  hardware, 43–46, 139–140
  miscellaneous useful items, 48–50
  portable computer systems, 136–139
  software, 43–46, 66, 70–77, 92,
      143–146
Iomega Zip drive, 134, 137
IRC, 99
ISDN, 127–128


## J

Jargon, 107, 108
Jurisdictional issues, 100, 120–121
Jury instructions, 151


## K

Keyboards, 14


## L

Labels and tags, 32, 33, 37, 39, 66
  disks, 37, 67, 79
  investigative tool kit supplies, 48
  legibility, 42

Lamers, 115
LAN, 119
Lantastic software, 45, 46, 130, 144
Laplink software, 18, 45, 66, 80, 145,
    146
Laptop or notebook computers, 18,
    136–137
Law enforcement, computer criminal
    advantages over, 1
Law enforcement disclaimers,
    103
Law enforcement tools, *See* Investigative
    tools
Legal issues, *See also* Search warrants
    case law, 151
    court procedures, 147–149
    evidence collection and preservation,
        33–34
    jurisdictional issues, 100, 120–121
    need for hardware evidence,
        34–35
    privacy protection, 34–35
LIST, 106
Local area network (LAN), 119
Log files, 108
Lotus 123, 92
Low-density disk, 63–64

## M

Macintosh systems, 46, 64
Magnetic fields, 31, 37, 67
Magnetic tapes, 14, 17, 48, 134
Mainframe computer evidence, 3–5, 26–27,
    network gateways, 122–123
Manuals, 19, 32
Mares, Danny, 46, 66, 72
Maresware, 72
MAU, 125
McAfee, 79
Microsoft Windows, 70
Microsoft Windows for Workgroups,
    131
Microsoft Windows 95, 131
Microwave technology, 126–127
Mini-applications, 70
Minicomputer evidence, 3–4, 27
Modems, 17–18, 124, 135, 175
Monitors, 14, 22–23
MOSAIC, 146

MS-DOS, 144
    making boot disk, 61–63
    versions, 43–44
Multistation access unit (MAU), 125–126
Murphy's Law of Computer Investigations,
    49

## N

NetWare, 91, 128–130
NetWare Lite, 130
Networks, 4–5, 65, 119–132
    components, 121–123
    crime scene security procedures, 54
    defined, 121
    investigative software, 46
    jurisdictional problems, 100,
        120–121
    operating systems, 128–32
    passwords, 91
    physical connections, 124–128
    technical assistance, 132
    types, 123
Norton Utilities 70, 71, 77, 80
Notebook or laptop computers, 18,
    136–137
Novell NetWare, 91, 128–130
NT Advanced Server (NTAS), 131
Number Search, 176, 177

## O

Offline mail readers, 110–111
Off-site storage, 14
On-line investigations, 99–114
    acronyms, 115–117
    BBS chat sample, 109
    cautions and warnings, 112–113
    dealing with passwords or encryption,
        96–97
    establishing probable cause, 105, *See also*
        Search warrants
    guidelines, 105–111
    locating sites and illegal activities,
        100–105
    mainstream systems, 104
    modems, 18
    offline mail readers, 110–111
    paperwork, 108
    privacy issues, 34–35

role-playing, 105, 106–111
search warrant examples
    service provider records, 183–188
    suspect's residence search,
        188–200
surveillance, 111–112
suspect identification, 107, 112
use of video, 107
voice verification, 109
Operating systems
    mini-applications, 70
    MS-DOS versions, 43–44
    network, 128–132
Operation Sundevil, 67
Oracom BBS, 90
OS/2, 144

**P**

Paper evidence, 13, 26
Passwords, 23, 24, 87–92
    BBS access, 104
    for booting, 61
    breaking or bypassing, 90–92, 146
        on-line resources, 96–97
        socially engineering, 3, 61, 89, 91,
            92
    common uses, 88
    defined, 87
    sources for, 89
PC-Tools, 3, 46, 146, 92
Pedophile, 188–200
Peer-to-peer network, 9, 45, 46, 123,
    130
PGP, 93–96
Phone numbers, 18, 109
Photocopy machines, 20–21, 32
Photographing evidence, 10, 32, 56, 66
Physical search team, 10, 52
PKZIP, 87, 92
Plastic bags, 31, 70, 123
    graphics files, 72
    sample BBS advertising, 101–103
POST, 59–60
Power on Self Test (POST), 59–60
Power PC systems, 64
Power supply, 49, 50, 136, 138, 139
Power tools, 48, 139
Preservation of evidence, *See* Evidence
    collection and preservation

Pretty Good Privacy (PGP), 93–96
Printers, 135, 138
Print servers, 121
Privacy protection, 34–35, 153
Probable cause, *See* Search warrants
Procomm Plus, 107
Prodigy case search warrants,
    183–200
Professional organizations, 132
PROFILE.BAT, 73–76
Profile disk, 46
Publicity, 1–2
Purchase orders, 48

**Q**

Qmodem Pro, 146
Quattro Pro, 92, 144
Questionnaires, 104
Quicken, 90, 92
QUICKFLI, 72
QWK, 111

**R**

RCMP Investigative Utilities, 72
Read only memory (ROM), 59–60
Remote access, 119
Reports, 56
    using WordPerfect, 71
RIP graphics, 146
Role-playing, 105, 106–111
ROM, 59
Routers, 122

**S**

Scanners, 70
SCSI devices, 134, 135, 137
Search procedures, *See* Crime scene
    investigation
Search programs, 71
Search teams, 52
Search Warrant Database program, 146
Search warrants, 53–54, 151–212
    amending, 26
    case examples
        hacker (residence search), 171–182
        hacker (voice mailbox access),
            153–171

on-line crimes (service provider
    records), 183–188
on-line crimes (suspect residence
    search), 188–200
place of business, 200–212
computer templates, 43, 154
identification of participating civilian
    experts, 171, 174, 204, 210
limitations for e-mail activities,
    35
password-protected files and, 92
suspect identification, 112
writing, 152
Search warrant team, 9–11
Security and arrest team, 10
Seizure of evidence, See Evidence
    collection and preservation
Servers, 121, 123
Shareware, 45, 143
Sketch and photo team, 10
Skip trace databases, 112
SMEAC, 52–53
Social engineering of passwords, 3, 61,
    89, 91, 92
Software
    defined, 175
    evidence, 19
    investigative tools, 43–46, 66, 70–77,
        143–146
        for finding passwords, 92
    network operating systems,
        128–132
Spreadsheets, 69
Stacker, 44
Stalking, 99, 186, 188–200
Static electricity, 31
    antistatic packaging, 141–142
Storage-enhancement programs, 44
Storage media, 14, 16, 17, See also
    Diskettes; Magnetic tapes
    preservation considerations, 31
Storage of evidence, 37–42, 142–143
Super Store, 44
Surveillance, 111–112
Suspect
    access to computer evidence, 3, 29
    identification of, 107, 112
    on-person evidence, 23–24
System operator (SYSOP), 90, 91, 103,
    104

**T**

Tapes, See Magnetic tapes
Tape servers, 122
Tax fraud, search warrant example,
    210–211
Team approach, 2, 9–11
    crime scene investigation, 56
    debriefing, 57
    search teams, 52
Technical assistance, See Expert
    assistance
Technical evidence seizure and logging
    team, 10–11
Technical terms, use in courtroom,
    148–149
Technology complexity, 5
Telecommunications fraud,
    search warrant samples,
    153–182
Telecommuting, 119
Temperature, 31, 37
10Base-T, 125
Terminal software, 107
Terminate-and-stay-resident (TSR)
    programs, 62
Testimony, 147–149
Text search, 71
Thick-net, 125
Thin-net, 125
ThinkPad, 136–137
Token Ring, 125
Tool kit, 47–48, 139–140, See also
    Investigative tools
Training and education, 2
Transport of evidence, 11, 33,
    67
Trap and trace order, 153–154
Trash, 24
TSR programs, 62
TYPE, 106
Typing styles, 107, 109

**U**

UART, 135
Underground bulletin boards,
    investigating, 99–114, See also
    On-line investigations
    acronyms, 115–117

UNERASE, 71, 77, 80
Uninterrupted power supply (UPS), 49, 50,
    139
UNIX systems, 28, 131
UPS (uninterrupted power supply), 49, 50,
    139


## V

Vehicles, 24
Vendor technical support, 27
Video, 10, 54, 72, 107
Viewdisk, 45, 72
Viruses, 60, 66
    scanning and removal, 45, 79
Voice mailbox access search warrant,
    153–171
Voice verification, 109, 110
VSHIELD, 79


## W

Warez, 99
Wide area network (WAN), 119
Windows, 70
Windows for Workgroups, 131
Windows 95, 131
WordPerfect, 144
    concordance and index features, 70–71
    passwords, 91, 146
Word processing, 69
WORM drive, 134
WPCRACK, 91, 146
Write-protect, 79


## X

XTreePro Gold, 44–45, 71, 77, 80, 90, 106,
    144